THE LOST SKILLS AND CRAFTS HANDBOOK

THE LOST SKILLS AND CRAFTS HANDBOOK

ALAN TITCHMARSH

BBC BOOKS

1

BBC Books, an imprint of Ebury Publishing
20 Vauxhall Bridge Road, London SW1V 2SA

BBC Books is part of the Penguin Random House group of companies
whose addresses can be found at global.penguinrandomhouse.com

Penguin
Random House
UK

Design copyright © Woodland Books Ltd 2021

Originally published as *The Complete Countryman* by BBC Books in 2011
This edition published in 2021

www.penguin.co.uk

A CIP catalogue record for this book is available from the British Library

ISBN 9781785947018

Printed and bound in Great Britain by Clays Ltd., Elcograf S.p.A.

The authorised representative in the EEA is Penguin Random House
Ireland, Morrison Chambers, 32 Nassau Street, Dublin DO2 YH68

Penguin Random House is committed to a sustainable future for our
business, our readers and our planet. This book is made
from Forest Stewardship Council® certified paper.

CONTENTS

CHAPTER 1

COUNTRY ARTS AND CRAFTS

PRACTICAL CRAFTS

GROW YOUR OWN WALKING STICK

Now, you might think that walking sticks are just for those who are a bit shaky on their pins. Not a bit of it. A stout walking stick makes a great companion when you're out for a country stroll, for helping you climb hills and slash aside nettles.

You might be lucky enough to find a suitable stick already growing in the countryside. Ash or hazel are the favourites for walking sticks, though you can also use sturdy stems from oak, sycamore and other trees. The most suitable sticks are to be found on trees that have been previously coppiced, which encourages them to grow long, straight, strong stems. If you can find one with a bend or knotty bit that makes a natural handle, it's a simple matter just to cut it virtually ready to use. Cut just above the 'handle' at the top, then cut the stick off a bit longer than you want, and remove any leaves or small side shoots to tidy it up. You can then trim the finished stick to exactly the right length for your height. 'Instant' sticks are most easily spotted in winter, when the leaves have fallen from the trees, but if you happen to see a suitable piece in summer it's perfectly fine to cut it then.

Otherwise you can 'train' your own stick. Search for a suitably straight young stem that's still pliable, ideally during the growing season when the stems are at their most bendable, and tie a knot in it, or tie it over at an acute angle with string, so it forms a handle in due course. Then leave it to continue growing until it's thick enough to cut and the handle 'sets' solidly – perhaps a year or two later.

If you want to start from scratch, grow an ash or hazel tree in a stretch of your own mixed country-style hedgerow or a corner of your wild garden, and coppice it (cut it down about 15cm/6in from the ground) when it's several years old to make it produce suitable shoots. Save the straightest and strongest to make into a walking stick. Again, bend the handle into shape and secure it with strong string or tie a knot in it while it's still whippy enough to bend easily, and leave it for a year or two. Then cut the stick, ideally over the winter some time between leaf fall in autumn and well before bud-burst in spring, when there's naturally as little sap as possible in the wood.

Once you have cut your walking stick, leave it to season for a while in a cool, dry shed. Then make a metal ferrule to protect the tip from wearing down through use. Use a hacksaw to cut a 2.5cm (1in) length of copper pipe of suitable diameter (available from builders' merchants) and hammer it on over the end of the stick. Whittle the end of the stick slightly if necessary, and to make it fit tightly, heat the piece of pipe to make it expand so it slips on. It will then shrink slightly as it cools, making a tighter fit.

You can leave a stick as it is, with the natural bark – sanding off any rough stem bases – or varnish it (it doesn't need 'peeling'). That'll give you a good basic country walking stick. But if you get the 'bug', you might enjoy trying a few more elaborate versions.

To make a stick with a carved handle, select a suitable strong, straight shoot growing out at an acute angle from a thicker branch. This time, don't just cut the straight shoot – cut the branch a few inches either side of the point where the thinner shoot emerges, so your stick has a lump of thicker branch attached at the handle end. Then carefully carve that to make a curved handle with a fist-grip, or carve it more to create a figured handle.

A thumb stick is a special kind of walking stick that's a little longer than usual, with a V-shaped notch at the top instead of a conventional handle.

It's designed for hikers walking over rough or hilly countryside, and as the name suggests, is used with your thumb hooked over the notch, instead of the palm of your hand grabbing a conventional knob or handle. If you want to make your own thumb stick, it's just a case of finding a suitable long, straight, strong stick with a pair of equal-sized shoots forking out from the top, and cutting it off at the top 5–7.5 cm (2 or 3in) above the place they branch out so you are left with a 'V'. The shank of the stick needs to be rather longer than for a normal walking stick; thumb sticks are usually about 1.3–1.5 metres (4 feet 6in to 5 feet) high – for maximum comfort they want to be roughly the same height as your shoulder. The idea is to give the user extra purchase over uneven or sloping ground, when a normal stick would drop down the dip and be of little use.

Shepherds' crooks are long, straight sticks with large, curving metal hooks at the end instead of handles; the hook is just the right size to catch a sheep by the hind leg. Ask a blacksmith to make you one out of metal, unless you can buy one ready-made from an artisan walking stick-maker. Pare the top of the stick roughly to fit, and heat the open end of the metal crook to make it expand so it can just be forced over the end, and as it cools and shrinks it'll make a tighter fit. Some shepherds' crooks have their hook carved from a piece of ram's horn. These can be glued onto the shaft, but they need to be really firmly secured if they are to be strong enough to use for practical purposes – many are simply decorative pieces useful for walking but less robust when it comes to catching your ewe.

MAKING A BESOM BROOM

Cut an armful of 1–1.2 metre (3–4 feet) long twigs from a birch tree in autumn, after leaf fall. Choose a tree whose canopy needs a little thinning, then bundle them up and leave them to season in a woodshed or similar place so they dry out slowly for several months. It's important that they remain flexible rather than turning brittle. Stand the bundle up on end and tap it down so the thickest ends of the twigs are all lined up, then roll the bundle round, pressing as you go, so the twigs are packed tightly together. Push a stout wooden broom handle that's been sharpened at the end, or a strong 90cm (3ft) length of home-grown hazel pole, into the bunch so that the twigs overlap the handle by 30–45cm (12–18in), and fix securely in two or three places with strong lengths of garden wire twisted tight with pliers so the twigs can't slip out. Lastly, snip the thin ends of the twigs so they are all roughly the same length to form the long, flexible 'bristles' of the brush; it should end up looking like the traditional witch's broom, standing roughly 1.2–1.3 metres (4 feet to four-feet-six) tall. Use it to whisk wormcasts off a lawn, or to sweep up leaves round the garden, but

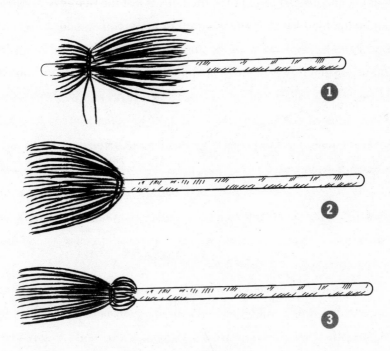

remember that it is most effective when held horizontally, almost parallel to the ground, rather than upright like a conventional broom.

> *As an alternative to birch, bundles of long heather stems can be used to make a similar sort of broom. These were once much used north of the border as indoor brooms for sweeping solid stone floors.*

BASKET WEAVING

Baskets of various shapes and sizes were once used for all those jobs that today we'd use carrier bags, cardboard boxes and plastic trays for. There were special baskets for shopping, for picking crops or carrying them to market, or to fit on the front of a bike so that tradesmen could use them to make deliveries; basketry was even used to make eel traps, bird cages and crab or lobster pots, and for a long time office-workers had woven cane 'in' and 'out' trays on their desk for stashing paperwork. Basket making was still being taught in art and craft classes when I was at school, and it was regularly used in occupational therapy to help patients recovering from long-term conditions, by encouraging mental and manual dexterity, not to mention concentration.

Today, baskets are mostly used as decorative containers for fresh fruit, eggs or dried flower arrangements, as cutlery trays inside drawers, and for smart picnic hampers, while wicker chairs are popular as conservatory furniture.

Willow is the traditional material for making baskets. Basket-makers use long, thin, straight willow wands with the outer bark peeled off; when woven together these become what's know as wickerwork. Willows were once specially cultivated for basket-making in many parts of the country where the ground is naturally boggy, but those that still exist today are found on the Somerset Levels. The species that's used for the job is the common osier, Salix viminalis, which grows very vigorously so that crops of 'withies' – the strong, straight, slim stems – can be harvested fairly often without weakening the growth of the 'stools'.

Willow for basketry is cut during the winter; traditionally the job was done using a sickle to cut a handful at a stroke. The withies were tied into bundles and taken down river on a small boat to a collecting point where groups of workers stripped the bark from each stem individually by pulling it sharply through a forked blade in the end of a long iron bar set into the ground, but nowadays it's a bit more mechanised. The willow was then stored until needed.

Before it can be turned into baskets, dry willow must first be soaked so that it regains its flexibility; domestic basket-makers dunk it in a bath of cold water overnight so that it's ready to use the following day. It then needs to be used shortly after it's been removed from the water, otherwise it starts to dry out and become hard again, especially if you work in a heated room.

HOW TO WEAVE A BASKET

To make a basket you need a flat wooden base of the right shape and size for the type of basket you plan on making. Today they are sold at hobby shops, usually made of plywood, with ready-made holes to take the 'uprights'. (The same shops sell the willow, or 'cane' as it's often called.) You'll need two grades of cane – a slightly thicker one for the uprights, and thinner cane that's used for the actual basket-weaving.

First the uprights are inserted into the holes in the wooden base; these, together with the base, will provide the structural strength of the basket's framework. The uprights are pushed through the base by several inches, then the base is turned over and the protruding lengths of cane are woven together to make a 'rim' on which the basket sits. More importantly it holds the uprights firmly in place so they can't be pulled out.

With the base and uprights in place, the work is turned right-side up and thinner 'cane' is woven between the uprights to make the sides of the basket. The first length of cane is held in place by tucking one end behind one of the upright rods, then the other end is woven round the rods from there on, bending it alternately behind, and in front of, each rod in turn. When you reach the end of the length of cane, make sure the very end is left inside the basket, where it won't show. Use a short-nosed pair of secateurs to snip the protruding end off short, so it's tidy. Start weaving with a new piece by tucking it in behind the same rod that the last piece of cane ended at, so again it is inside the basket – the join won't show on the outside of the work.

Once you've got the hang of basic weaving, you can move on to more advanced techniques. More decorative effects can be created by weaving

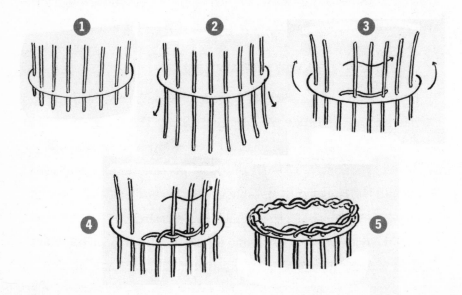

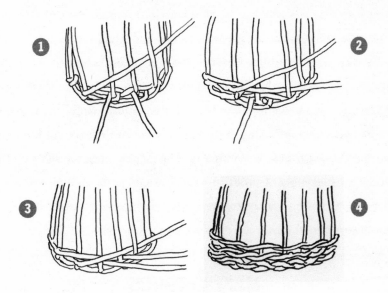

with three parallel rods all at once, or by weaving two behind and one in front of each upright rod. It's also possible to miss out sections and alternate basketry with open space where the uprights are crossed over to make a decorative row of diamond shapes, before the sides continue with more weaving.

When you've reached the top of the work, the rim of the basket needs finishing off neatly. To do this, the ends of the rods are bent over and woven to make a rigid border that stops the weaving unravelling and gives the finished basket a strong edge.

ALTERNATIVE BASKET-MAKING MATERIALS

If you fancy creating naturally coloured baskets, use the stems of coloured-stemmed dogwoods or ornamental willows, which you can grow at home especially for this job. Good varieties include: Cornus alba 'Westonbirt' (sealing-wax red stems), Salix alba vitellina 'Britzensis' (orange stems), Salix alba vitellina (golden yellow stems) and Salix daphnoides (purple stems).

Salix purpurea has variable colouring to its bark, varying from light purple to shiny green. You can use stems removed in normal pruning, but if you want any quantity, consider growing a row of plants especially – they root easily from cuttings pushed into the ground where you want them to grow, any time during the winter. Allow the young plants to establish themselves for three years before taking your first crop; from then on cut the plants down hard (to within 7.5–10cm/3 or 4 inches of the ground) every few years. This makes them produce long, straight, unbranching stems that can be harvested in much the same way as 'proper' basket willow, but without stripping the bark afterwards.

MAKING TRUGS

Trugs, or 'Sussex trugs' as they are often called, are traditional shallow 'baskets' made from thin wooden slats. Trugs are traditionally used for gathering cut flowers, vegetables, salads, fruit and other relatively fragile produce from the garden; they are also good for collecting eggs, given a handful of straw in the bottom as 'cushioning'.

The basic structure of the trug is formed from two slim ash or sweet chestnut 'wands' split in half lengthwise with a sleaving axe called a 'froe'. These are steamed to soften them so that they are pliable, then bent round a jig to create two rounded shapes; one of these, shaped into a hoop, becomes the handle of the trug and the other is shaped into a rectangle with curved corners that becomes the rim of the trug. The two are slotted together so they cross in the middle. Strips of thin, split cricket-bat willow are then nailed to one end of the rim and bent round before being nailed to the other end. (These strips are prepared in advance, steamed to shape and shaved down so they are narrower at the edges than in the middle so the pieces fit together to create a boat-shaped 'bowl'.) Wooden 'feet' are nailed to the base of smaller trugs so the finished trug stands up straight.

Stored in a dry shed, I get upwards of five or six years' use out of mine before their bottoms go, and they are wonderfully user-friendly, slung over your arm while you go about your tasks in the garden.

HURDLE-MAKING

Hurdles are one of several traditional woodland products that are still made in winter when coppice is cut. Suitable poles of various thicknesses are set aside ready to use for this job. Each hurdle is like a lightweight rustic fencing panel. There are two types of hurdles: gate hurdles and wattle hurdles, both with very different jobs.

Gate hurdles – usually made from sweet chestnut – are the original temporary sheep fencing. A gate hurdle looks a bit like a rustic five-bar farm gate made from natural poles, with a longer spiked pole at each end so it can be pushed into the ground to make it stand upright. It had all sorts of uses in the past. A gate hurdle could be forced into a weak spot in a hedge to stop the animals from wandering, but its main use was to construct temporary enclosures known as 'folds' to restrict sheep to particular areas of a field. This was commonly done when sheep were turned out onto unfenced stubble fields, or fields of turnips or kale in the autumn or winter, and at any time a shepherd needed to restrict them to a particular area of grazing instead of letting them have access to an entire pasture all at once. In country gardens, hurdles are useful as rustic boundaries for a kitchen garden or other working area, and dwarf hurdles perhaps 30–45cm (12–18in) high and 45–60cm (18–24in) long are great favourites of mine for pushing in along the edges of borders to keep flopping flower stems off the lawn, so the mower can pass alongside without chopping up the blooms.

There's a fair bit of skill in making serious sheep hurdles, but it's not too difficult to make a few small ones to use as rustic edgings for your flowerbeds at home, or to stop the dog running straight down the garden path and crashing into the veg patch beyond. Simply scale down the full-sized 'recipe'.

HOW TO MAKE A GATE HURDLE

Use a bill hook to trim a pair of strong sweet chestnut or ash posts, a little longer than waist-high, to shape. Strip off the bark and 'whittle' them so each has flat sides. Drill a row of seven evenly spaced holes about 2½cm (1 inch) in diameter up the side of each post, going right through the wood. These perforated posts will be the vertical ends of your hurdle.

Next make the rails from 'green' (i.e. unseasoned) sweet chestnut or ash – you need seven for each hurdle, about 1.2 metres (4 feet) long, from slightly slimmer lengths than you used for the upright posts. Taper the ends so they fit tightly into the holes in the posts, with 2½cm (1 inch) or so sticking out of the far side when they are in position. Slot the horizontal rails into the vertical posts and hammer a nail through the end of each rail so it can't be pulled back through the hole. Cut off the protruding ends. Then cut three more halved poles to form braces, one upright across the centre of the hurdle, and two sloping ones forming a V shape from the bottom corners to the centre top, and nail these in place to give the structure lateral strength.

To fix hurdles in place, make a pair of holes in the ground a hurdle's-length apart by hammering a spike a short depth into the ground, then pulling it out. Stand the hurdle in place with the spikes at each end resting in the holes made by the spike, then use a wooden mallet to drive the pointed ends gently down into the ground. When you have several hurdles in place in a row, you can tie the tops of the end poles together to hold them more firmly in place. The technique is exactly the same for making the smaller garden hurdles.

Wattle hurdles are like sections of basketry, made by weaving lengths of split hazel round a series of upright hazel poles to make large, oblong panels. Wattle panels were originally used in medieval house construction; the panels were set into a timber frame and plastered with a mixture of mud, chopped straw and manure, sometimes with chalk added, to form wattle-and-daub walls. Interior walls of humble cottages would often be made from plain unplastered wattle panels, to save effort, though in more upmarket establishments they were plastered and lime-washed (the original 'emulsion paint'). Wattle hurdles might also be used as temporary enclo-

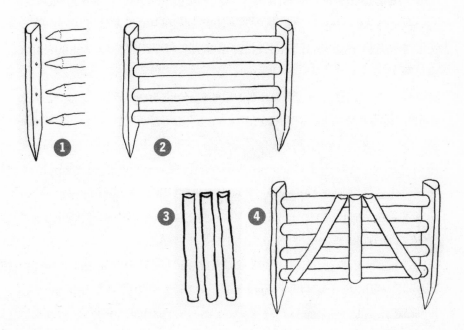

sures for sheep, perhaps to make a pen into which a sheepdog can gather a small flock of sheep if they need attention, and at lambing time to make a temporary enclosure for expectant ewes or a group of orphan lambs.

Wattle panels made from slim, but unsplit poles are often used as rustic fence panels for gardens. They make good windbreaks for exposed gardens and they're ideal for screening-off a kitchen garden, or providing temporary shelter for a young hedge while it grows up, but they have a rather limited life – usually about five years – before the wood becomes brittle and they start to break up. Spraying them with a water-based timber preservative will help to prolong their life. Hazel hurdles will last a year or two longer. Again, the real thing requires woodland craft tools and skills to make, but it's not difficult to create a small version at home for use in the garden.

HOW TO MAKE A WATTLE OR HAZEL HURDLE

The first essential is a thick, heavy log split in two down the middle and stood cut-surface up (today we'd probably use a railway sleeper), with a row of holes driven into it at regular intervals every 15–20cm (6–8in); this acts as the 'mould' or 'template'. Next you need a supply of hazel poles to form the uprights of the hurdle. The uprights need to be as tall as you want your panel to be, with points at the bottom ends. At each end of the hurdle you need a slightly thicker pole that's about 15cm (6 inches) longer than the others, with a longer point at the tip. Lastly you need a supply of split (correctly known as 'riven') hazel, or else slim, straight 'green' hazel or willow stems that are capable of bending without breaking, which will be used to make the horizontal 'weave' of the wattle.

To assemble the hurdle the uprights are stood in the holes in the 'mould', with the longer, stronger poles at each end. (These will give the finished hurdle greater stability when they're pushed into the ground.)

Then 'weave' the split hazel or slim 'wands' backwards and forwards between the uprights. At the end of a row, tap the work down so it sits tight against the top of the 'mould', then bend and twist the remaining length of hazel stem you're using so that it forms a 'hinge' that easily bends round the end-post without breaking, then use it to continue 'weaving' the next row. When you reach the end of the first piece of hazel, tuck the end of a second length into the work alongside it to hold the new piece in place, and continue weaving with that; it's exactly the same as basket-weaving (see page 6). When you reach the end of the second row, again tap the work down firmly and continue 'weaving' until you reach the top of the upright posts. (Traditional hurdle makers always left a small square hole in the weave near the centre-top of each hurdle, so the end-user could put their arm through to carry a number of wattle hurdles at the same time.) The finished wattle or hazel hurdles can be stacked until you need to use them.

POST AND RAIL FENCING

Post and rail fencing is extensively used in the countryside to fence paddocks, particularly for horses and ponies, which often injure themselves by running into barbed wire, but it's also used anywhere where barbed wire is unsuitable or unattractive. It makes a cost-effective boundary for a country garden, which doubles as a support system for blackberries, Virginia creeper or large climbing roses that may be difficult to accommodate elsewhere. ('Rambling Rector' and 'Kiftsgate' both look particularly stunning grown in this way, and they flower far better when their main stems are trained out horizontally along a fence.)

Traditional post and rail fencing consists of strong (usually oak or chestnut) posts that are usually square in cross section, with a row of two or three oval-shaped holes cut through them. The horizontal rails are usually flat-sided, or nearly so, and these have their ends chamfered to slot into the holes in the posts. The holes are usually wide enough to take the ends of two rails, which enter from each side of the post and 'wedge' each other firmly into place to form a continuous straight row running the entire length of the fence.

A more economical version is often constructed using rustic fence posts that have been split to give them one flat face, and narrower split poles as the horizontal struts, nailed together so that the flat sides of the posts and the horizontal rails are face to face to make a strong join.

Most people employ a local firm to supply and erect this type of fencing since they'll have all the right equipment for driving posts in quickly and efficiently, and the experience to do a good job. But if you decide to do it yourself, the trick is to mark out a straight line along the boundary and clear it of weeds and rubbish, then put a post in at each end of the run. Dig holes for the posts and check that each is upright (with a spirit level). Hammer rubble round the base of each post to hold it firm before returning and re-firming the soil. Then fix a taut string between the first and last fence posts, along the top, to use as a guideline for keeping the fence straight.

The posts need to be buried 50–60cm (20–24in) deep, with their centres 2.4m (8ft) apart. Start work at one end; put in a second post but don't fix it firmly in place; attach the pair of rails, or 'cross members', from it to your first post. This gives you the chance to check they run parallel and are lined up correctly with the line running between your two marker posts. When you have the first section of fence correctly aligned, put more rubble down the hole and use the end of a spare wooden post to ram it firmly down so the second fence post is fixed firmly in place. Work your way along the entire fence in the same way, putting in a loose post, connecting the poles, lining it up properly and then firming the post in place. Tubular post hammers can be used to knock in the posts (rather than a sledgehammer which will often split the ends) but it is more difficult to keep the posts vertical than it is if you dig holes and adjust them as you go.

It's quite common to find that a post and rail fence is reinforced in some way, when it's used round a field intended to house smaller livestock. Some people will fix strong wire mesh (such as 'pig netting' or 'sheep netting', which has large, strong squares about 10cm/4in wide) to post and rail fencing, which makes the resulting enclosure far more dog-proof, or suitable to hold livestock such as sheep, pigs or goats, which could push their way between the horizontal rails of plain post and rail fencing. Attach the wire to the uprights before you put the cross-members in position; this makes for additional strength. (Don't use this sort of netting if horses are kept in the paddock since they get their hooves tangled in it and it can cause injury, or at least pull off a shoe.) As belt and braces, some owners also add a single strand of electric fencing along the very top of a post and rail fence to prevent livestock such as horses or cattle leaning over the top to eat out-of-reach grass, which can damage the fence, or they'll use a single strand of electric fencing halfway up post and rail fencing with 'pig netting' or small-mesh wire netting at the base to keep smaller animals in. Check all fences regularly for repairs.

HEDGE-LAYING

A neatly laid hedge is a far more effective barrier than a normal hedge – it's the age-old way of keeping livestock in. It is a living, growing, self-renewing 'fence' made of hedging plants that have been bent over at an angle and 'woven' through a series of posts knocked into the hedge-line.

When a hedge is properly laid there are no gaps at the base or weak spots where animals can push through. As a bonus, a well-laid hedge needs a good deal less maintenance than a regular hedge since it grows far more slowly than usual. But it does take a fair bit of work to lay a hedge in the first place. It's a winter job, traditionally carried out when there's no other work to be done on the land.

Hedge-layers start with an existing hedge which has usually been a bit neglected, so it's overgrown in places and gappy in others. The only materials you need are a billhook, a sledgehammer, a supply of ash or hazel posts roughly 5cm (2in) thick and 1.8m (6ft) long and pointed at one end, and some long, slim, straight hazel or willow poles about 3m (10ft) long, a little more than finger-thick. (All of these can be cut from your own area of coppice, if you have some on your land.) It's a good idea to wear heavy leather gloves since a lot of hedges consist largely of hawthorn, which is prickly and hard on the hands; stout gloves also offer some slight protection against cutting yourself with the billhook.

The first part of the job is to clear any brambles, nettles and other rubbish from the base of the existing hedge, and then thin out the stems of the plants that form the hedge. Chop out or saw off thick old stems at ground level, leaving the younger ones that ideally are about 2.5cm (1in) thick.

Start 'laying' at one end of the hedge. Use the billhook to cut about three-quarters of the way through the first stem, leaving a bit of wood and the bark attached to it as a 'hinge' so the stem can be bent down. You'll think that it can't possibly survive, but it will! Lay it along the line of the hedge. Do the next half dozen or so stems in the same way. (There's a 'hook' at the end of the billhook blade, which is used for snagging an individual stem and pulling it towards you if you can't reach it easily.) Then use the sledgehammer to knock a row of six posts in along the hedgeline, from your original starting point, spacing them about 76cm (2ft 6in) apart. Don't hammer too hard or the posts may split. Now weave the slanting stems between the posts, leaving the bushy tops pointing into the field.

Proceed all the way along the hedge, cutting partly through the base of about half a dozen stems at a time, then banging in the next few posts and weaving the 'laid' stems in round them. When you reach the end of a run of hedging, finish off by 'weaving' three or four of the long, springy, finger-thick poles along the top of the posts, in the same way as weaving baskets, then tap the weave down firmly with a mallet and cut the tops of the posts off level. Lastly, clip the newly laid hedge tidily so the top is all the same height and the sides are an even thickness. It's a slow, hard job but a hugely satisfying one.

The following spring, forests of young side shoots will grow upwards from the slanting main stems; these will thicken up the hedge. You'll need to trim the whole hedge once a year (again, this job is usually done in winter or very early spring, when there's little farm work to be done, and well before any birds start nesting in the hedge) but it won't grow as much as a normal hedge, which means that far less trimming than usual is involved. A laid hedge can last up to twenty years before it needs doing again.

RESTORING A BADLY NEGLECTED HEDGE

When there's an old hedge which is in very poor condition with lots of gaps, it's not essential to pull it out and replant; it can be restored. Cut it down to a few inches above ground level in late winter. Strong new shoots should appear the next spring, and they'll emerge quite thickly from the old stumps. Any serious gaps can then be filled by planting new hawthorn saplings. Within three or four years you'll have a respectable fringe of strong new hedge round the field, which can then be laid quite easily since all the stems will be about the right size. While the new hedge grows there's clearly not a good enough boundary to keep livestock in the field, but the ground can be used to produce a crop such as potatoes, mangels for stock-feed, or grass to cut for hay.

DITCHING

A lot of country hedges are accompanied by a ditch, running round the outside of the field, to allow rainwater to drain away quickly from the pasture. 'Ditching' was another traditional winter job, usually done by farmhands after trimming the hedges, and it involved clearing ditches of brambles, weeds and rubbish, then shovelling out the accumulation of silt so that when snow melted in early spring or there was a spell of torrential rain, surface water ran into the ditches. Ditching was vital to prevent country lanes from flooding, and it also avoided muddy patches forming in fields where livestock would then turn the grassland to unproductive mud. The silt removed from ditches is usually quite rich in nutrients from decomposed leaves etc., so it was often spread along the foot of the hedge. It was also traditionally used on cottage gardens, particularly for top dressing veg plots. Today, ditches along country roads are usually cleared by the council, and the silt removed along with the rubbish, but farmers still do the 'hedging and ditching' round fields within their own land.

DRY STONE WALLING

Dry stone walls started life when early farmers picked up the stones that littered their land and piled them up out of the way, round the edges of the fields. The original piles made useful markers indicating ownership of the land, and when livestock was introduced it made sense to stack the stones in rows so the animals couldn't wander. Over many generations of stone-picking, walls 'grew up'. Today if you go walking in countryside where the fields are outlined with dry stone walls, such as in Yorkshire and the Lake District, it's clear from even a casual glance that a dry stone wall involves a fair degree of craftsmanship – it's much more than just a pile of loose stones.

Seen in cross section, a dry stone wall consists of two walls that lean in slightly towards the centre, which is filled with a mixture of smaller stones, rubble and soil. (This is how wildflowers and even small trees are able to grow in dry stone walls. In Cornwall the walls known as 'Cornish hedges' traditionally have a row of plants – often hardy fuchsias or valerian – growing along the top.)

The two outer walls that make up a dry stone wall are linked periodically by a wider stone that runs the full thickness of the wall, right through the centre, to 'tie' the two sides together, very much like the metal ties builders use when building houses of brick with cavity walls. At the foot of the wall are the largest stones of all, which act as 'foundations', and along the top you'll usually find a row of flattish stones stood on end, or a row of larger, flat, coping stones that cover the entire top of the wall, to make a 'capping' that helps to keep water out.

A new dry stone wall takes a long time to build, but once done it will last for centuries, with only minor repairs if perhaps a small section collapses – if it's repaired quickly it should prevent further damage where livestock or walkers push through, or weather gets in and erodes the soil centre.

HOW TO MAKE A DRY STONE WALL

First mark out the area for the base of the wall and excavate a trench, since the wall needs to rest on bedrock or very solid subsoil. (You can't build a heavy stone wall on soft soil as the weight will make the ground sink unevenly causing stones to fall out.)

To make the foundations for the wall, lay a firm base of large, flat stones. This should extend slightly wider than the base of the wall itself. Then at each end of the section of wall you are planning to build, set up a timber frame the same shape as the cross-section of the wall. Run several taut strings between the two frames to act as guides so the stonework is constructed to the right shape and size, with edges that slope at the correct angle; this helps to keep the work uniform all the way along.

Then start building the wall up, using the biggest stones at the bottom and slightly smaller stones as the wall rises. The great art of making dry stone walls lies in choosing stones that fit together fairly well. As the two outer walls rise, the centre is packed carefully with smaller stones and soil, again taking care that they all fit together to make the shape as strong and solid as possible. And as each new course of stones is added, the strings running between the timber frames are raised so the waller still has his guidelines to work to. Expert wallers do the job by eye!

When the wall reaches roughly half its eventual height, a series of large stones is placed across the centre of the wall to act as 'ties' and the work continues as usual up to the top which, due to the sloping sides, will be less than half as wide as the base of the wall. The final job is to crown the top with a row of coping stones to keep out the rain.

STILES FOR CROSSING DRY STONE WALLS

Where walkers need to cross over a dry stone wall to follow a footpath, a special type of stile is called for. The conventional step-type stile used in lowland fields is not tall enough, and even if the landowner left a gap in the wall, a normal stile wouldn't prevent the notoriously agile hill sheep

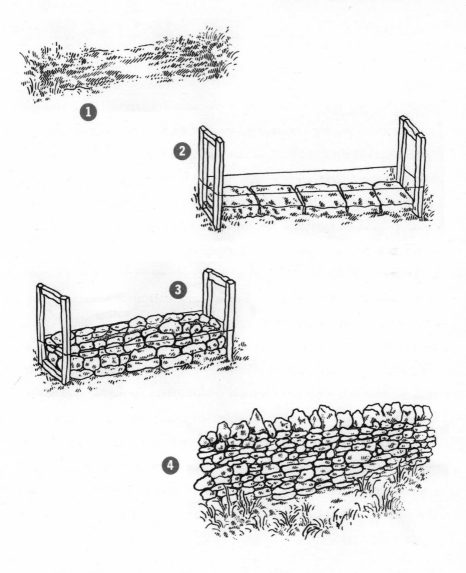

getting through. Ladder stiles are the answer; they consist of a tall set of stout timber steps (complete with handrail) that go up-and-over the full height of the wall. This type of stile is deliberately designed to be too steep for even the nimblest sheep, and they are not that easy for walkers who aren't as nimble-footed as they might be either.

MAKING WHISTLES

Whistles have been used since prehistory for attracting attention, as basic one-note musical instruments, and at celebrations or special occasions for the sheer joy of making a noise and letting off steam. Nowadays, apart from policemen, referees at football matches and school teachers on playground duty, there are relatively few serious uses for whistles. But a loud, piercing whistle is a useful piece of safety equipment for hikers and ramblers in remote places as a means of making contact with companions lost in fog, or as a means of letting search and rescue services know where casualties are in case of accidents. But whether you truly need one or not, it's great fun to make your own, from the same sort of materials that our primitive ancestors used: bone or wood.

HOW TO MAKE A WHISTLE

Choose a short piece of stick from a youngish (1–2 year old) stem of a tree or bush with hollow or pithy stems; elder is a good example. Cut your stick about 10–15cm (4–6in) long, with a leaf-joint at one end since the stems are solid at the joints. Push a thin piece of wire carefully up through the centre to remove the soft pith, but don't hollow out the whole length of the stem – leave the end with the leaf-joint untouched so the end is 'blocked'

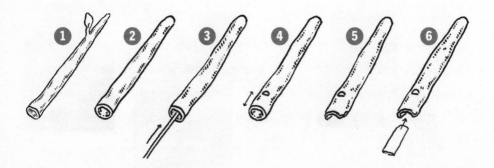

naturally. Measure an inch down from the open end of the tube, and then make a small sloping cut at 45 degrees to the stem and a straight cut at 90 degrees to the stem, so the two meet to form a small notch. Whittle the open end slightly so it makes a flat mouthpiece to blow into, and wedge a flattish sliver of wood into it so there's only a small hole to blow through; this hole needs to be in line with the notch cut in the top of the whis-tle. Primitive people used to make something very similar out of slender animal bones with a knuckle at one end and a broken-off end at the other end which they blew down, with a small hole bored carefully into the top surface to create the sound.

THATCHING

Thatch is the very oldest form of roofing used in this country; it's covered Iron Age huts, medieval hovels, farmhouses and barns, and Victorian farm workers' cottages. Over the last 150 years a lot of thatch has been replaced by cheaper or more low-maintenance roofing materials such as corrugated iron, slates or concrete tiles, but nowadays many picturesque thatched period country houses are listed buildings that have to have their existing appearance maintained using traditional building materials.

The type of material originally used to make thatch varied all round the country depending on what was available locally. In East Anglia and other boggy areas, reeds (common reed, Phragmites australis) were mostly used. In the north of Scotland and the Hebrides it was more often heather; elsewhere bracken made an economical roofing material, and in cereal-growing lowlands the straw left over from crops of oats, barley, rye or wheat was used – traditional varieties had long stems that made them suitable for the job.

Today, although Norfolk reeds give a far longer-lasting thatch (75 to 100 years), they are also expensive and in short supply, so most thatching is done with wheat straw. It's no longer possible to use left-over straw from cereal crops because modern wheat varieties have short stems, designed to prevent crops being flattened in bad weather, so instead, special varieties have to be grown deliberately for thatching. A straw thatch, however, will only last between 25 and 45 years.

Thatch makes for great-looking rustic chocolate-boxy cottages, and it provides natural insulation that keeps heat in and sound out. It's the most practical form of roofing for old cottages made of cob or wattle and daub, since they need a deeply overhanging roof to stop their earth-based building materials deteriorating and washing away in the rain, and thatch does the best job. However, it's seen as a greater fire risk than a tiled roof; owners of thatched homes tend to be nervous on bonfire night when smouldering spent rockets can shower down on them. Insurers often demand a premium for thatched roofs, and due to the risk of sparks, a policy may insist that open fires aren't used, or that wood-burning stoves meet specific requirements.

The sight of a charming, old-world cottage being re-thatched, looks the very picture of an idyllic rural scene. But there's a heck of a lot more to it than meets the eye; even today a trainee thatcher has to serve a seven-year apprenticeship.

First, the straw has to be prepared – usually by the apprentice. After the wheat is harvested, the loose stems are collected and forked into layers which are damped with water to make the stems more pliable. Then, hand-fuls of straw are pulled out individually and laid out in the same direction so that, gradually, a higgledy-piggledy heap of straw is turned into straight bundles. Six bundles at a time are gathered up into the 'mouth' of a long, forked stick; the 'mouth' is closed with a string to hold the bundles in place, and the stick is used to carry the material up the ladder onto the roof to the master thatcher.

Most thatching today consists of re-thatching a roof that's reached the end of its working life. The old rotted thatch will be stripped off, leaving a layer of sound thatch underneath to act as the base for a fresh new top layer. The thatchers work on one strip of the roof at a time, while the rest is covered with tarpaulins. With long-straw thatching, the thatcher starts at the eaves by spreading a 10cm (4in) thick layer of straight straw placed at 90 degrees to the ground. This is combed flat with a special tool known as a side rake, then fastened in place with a long hazel stick which is held down by a row of bent hazel 'hairpins' with sharp points at each end, which are hammered into the older thatch below. He then moves up the roof, laying a second row of thatch so that it overlaps the first slightly (and covers the hazel stick securing it). He keeps working in this way until he reaches the ridge of the roof, then works across the entire roof in the same way, one strip at a time.

Thatching with short straw or reeds uses slightly different methods, but all thatchers finish the roof-ridge off decoratively – often with a scalloped finish – and may include an ornamental feature such as a peacock, pheasant or squirrel somewhere on the roof as their 'signature'.

TYING KNOTS

Knots have 101 practical uses in the countryside, for anything from tying up your trousers to making your own rope-mesh hay-net for feeding a pony, and the ability to tie the right knots for particular purposes is essential for all sorts of people including farmers, fishermen and sailors, and climbers, whose lives may depend on it.

Knots are also used decoratively; they inspire jewellery designs (lover's knots and Celtic knots feature regularly in brooches, etc.) and knots are used for spacing pearls and semi-precious stones such as amber to make necklaces. A collection of tidily tied knots mounted on a board and framed is often used as a rustic display in beach-hut style summer houses in seaside gardens, in country lobbies just above the row of family Wellington boots or on boats.

The great art to tying useful knots is twofold. First you need to know which knot to use for which job, and then practise, practise, practise until you can almost do them instinctively – when you really need a knot, there won't be time to look up the instructions in a book.

THE REEF KNOT

For tying string round parcels, for tying up trousers when your belt breaks, or on a sailing boat to reef sails and for tying up sail covers.

Use with string that has two working ends; cross one end over the other and tie a simple half-knot, then cross the opposite working end over the other and make a second half-knot; pull both ends tight – the knot should lie flat and form a rough figure-of-eight shape.

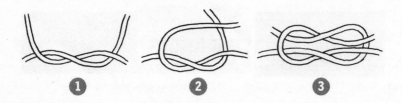

1   2   3

Remember the old rhyme, 'left over right, and right over left' and you'll always tie a reef knot and never a granny knot; a granny will slip, and a real reef knot will not.

THE BOWLINE

For making a loop at the end of a length of rope that stays securely put without slipping or tightening. Used for making a loop at the end of a mooring rope to throw over a bollard to secure a boat.

It's easier to do than it is to describe. Start with the short end of the rope pointing towards you and the long end away from you. Take hold of the rope with the fingers of both hands, spacing your hands about six inches apart, 30cm (1ft) from the end of the rope. Make a loop by crossing the rope in your right-hand fingers over the rope in your left-hand fingers. Holding the loop in position with the fingers of your left hand, take the end of the rope with your right and pass it behind the lower curve of the loop and up through the centre, then pass it round the back of the long end of the rope, and back through the loop again. Tighten the knot you've created round the neck of the loop and it'll hold firmly without slipping or turning the loop into a noose.

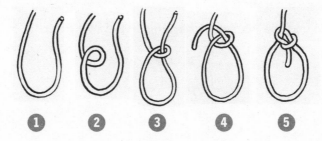

THE SHEET BEND

Used in making nets, or to join two pieces of rope together when they are of slightly different thicknesses, though it can also be used to join two ropes of the same thickness.

Make a loop in the end of one rope, then pass the tip of the second rope through it from back to front, then around behind the first rope and back under itself at the front, so you end up with two loops looped through each other. Pull it tight.

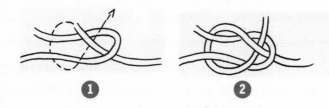

THE CLOVE HITCH

This looks like two turns of rope placed one on top of the other, and is very easy to tie. It's used in net-making, for securing fenders on a boat and for tethering a horse to a rail in a hurry, with a rope attached to its halter. The clove hitch at its best is used to secure something that pulls steadily against the knot from the same direction. Otherwise it can easily loosen and come undone, so it's not something to leave for long.

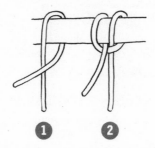

Pass the rope over and round the rail from front to back, then cross the rope over itself in front of the rail and pass the rope over the rail again, also front to back. Tuck the spare end under the diagonal crossing the centre of the knot and pull it tight from the 'long' end. To release the knot quickly, give a sharp tug on the short end; the knot immediately loosens.

THE ROUND TURN AND TWO HALF-HITCHES

Used for securing a rope to a post, ring or rail, for mooring a boat or tethering a horse.

Pass the rope twice round the post or ring, then cross the working (short) end over the other (long) end so it makes a loop and pass the working end through this. Pull it tight so it slips up to the post or ring. Make a second loop in the same way, passing the working end through again, making sure it's in the same direction as last time, and again pull it tight so the pair of tight loops slip up to the 'long' end of the rope, jamming them tight.

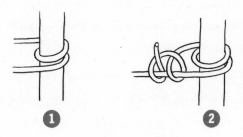

THE SHEEPSHANK

Not so much a knot as a hank! It's used to shorten a length of rope when you don't want to cut it (perhaps to take up some temporary slack), or to double up a weak section of rope to strengthen it, but it's mostly for tidying a rope up so it can be hung up without fear of tangling or uncoiling and getting itself in a terrible mess.

Gather the part of the rope to be tied up into a 'hank' so it's bunched together in a series of parallel lines with U-shaped bends at each end. Make a loop in the rope coming from the bottom of the hank and twist it 90 degrees so it crosses on itself, then slide it over the U-shaped lower end of the hank of rope. Do the same with the rope coming from the top of the hank, and slide the loop over the U-shaped upper part of the hank of rope; tighten the loops at both ends of the hank.

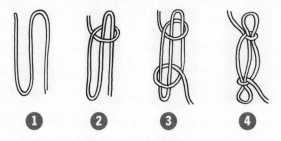

MAKING A CRICKET BAT

There are still quite a few villages with their own cricket teams, and for much of the summer, Saturday afternoons are enriched by the traditional sound of leather on willow from the village green as the local lads take on a team from a nearby village. The cricket pitch is cut especially for the occasion: in the very centre a square of grass is shaved short for the wicket, where the main action takes place, surrounded by the outfield where the grass is cut roughly to lawn-length – this is where the fielders take up their places, waiting to make catches. Larger villages and small market towns often have a cricket pavilion, with screens and scoreboards and folding seats for onlookers. There is a strong social side to village cricket; a lot of the after-match action being centred round the village pub, and the cricket club often organises dances or end-of-season suppers.

PRODUCTION OF CRICKET BATS

Cricket bats are made from a special variety of white willow, *Salix alba* var. *caerulea*. They were traditionally made by hand. Pieces of willow wood were cut roughly to size then treated with wax at both ends and left to season slowly to make sure that the finished wood wouldn't crack or warp. A piece of timber was then cut with a saw to roughly the size of a blade – the maximum length allowed is 96.5cm (38in) and the maximum width is 12cm (4.75in) – and shaped so that one side of the blade was flat and the other had a raised ridge up part of the centre. The bat was next pressure-treated to strengthen the fibres, using a pressure of 900kg (2000lb) per 6.5sq cm (1 sq in); on a small scale bats were pressed between pieces of flat iron using clamps. A splice was then cut in one end of the blade to fit the handle, which was made of cane interspersed with strips of rubber. The base of the handle was cut into a wedge shape which was fitted tightly into the splice in the blade and fixed with wood glue. A draw-knife, or planer, was then used to pare the blade to shape. It was then finished with sandpaper; a cricket bat took a great deal of sanding in several sessions over a number of weeks to produce the required fine finish. The handle would then be brushed over with glue and tightly bound with twine for strength before a grip was pulled over it, then the blade was waxed.

The eventual owner would rub linseed oil into the wood regularly to stop it drying out and splitting, and to maintain the suppleness; in time, an old bat would turn a rich yellowy-brown colour, almost as if it had been varnished.

DECORATIVE CRAFTS

All sorts of arts and crafts that, today, are undertaken for fun and to decorate the home, once had serious purposes. They would have been carried out in the evenings, after the day's 'serious' work had been done, usually around the kitchen table after supper, or in an armchair by the fire, originally by candlelight, and they'd have provided a few much-needed home comforts for people living in the countryside.

POTPOURRI

Potpourri is a natural air freshener made from dried flowers and herbs plus other fragrant ingredients which could include citrus peel, fir cones, pine needles and shavings of scented bark such as cedar. In grand old houses it used to be placed in a decorative china potpourri jar which was often shaped like a dovecote or something similar, with plenty of holes for air to percolate through, but nowadays it's usually just piled into a shallow bowl out in the open, so it looks attractive as well as smelling great.

We're told that it is out of fashion now that plug-in air fresheners and scented candles are so popular, but it still has a kind of rustic charm and it's very easy to make your own using home-grown ingredients from the flower garden. Collect and dry them during the summer as the different kinds of flowers become available, then store them to blend and put on display in the winter, which is when you really need a bit of fragrance in the home – when you keep the windows shut, a house can soon start to smell a tad stale. Potpourri is designed to bring back the fresh scents of the summer country garden.

To make potpourri, pick fresh flowers when they are just approaching their best. Ideally, pick them first thing in the morning, when the dew has dried but before the sun has heated them up too much. Scented flowers are best, but others can be added for their colour. Some flowers are dried whole, while with others it's only the petals that are used.

Roses are classic potpourri flowers; red varieties keep their colour best but they are not always the strongest scented – apart from 'Alec's Red' or 'Deep Secret' – so mix them with more fragrant kinds. Pluck the petals off individually. If you grow miniature roses, whole tiny rosebuds can be snipped from their stems and dried while they are still tightly closed – red and pink ones look best. They look so dainty that they are very pretty in a dish of their own in a bedroom.

Lavender is the other classic potpourri flower. Snip whole heads off when they've expanded fully, but before they start drying out naturally, and avoid any that have turned a tad 'soggy' if it's a damp summer. You can also dry whole stems of lavender complete with the flower heads, then cut them all the same length and tie them with ribbon like sheaves of lavender 'straw'.

The petals of pinks, calendula marigolds, delphiniums and citrus blossom are also good for making potpourri, as are whole chamomile flowers.

Fragrant herbs help to give finished potpourri 'body', so pick individual leaves of bay, myrtle, lemon verbena and rosemary needles, using only those that look perfect – avoid torn, tattered or blackened ones. You might also like to use leaves of purple sage, pineapple sage, mint (especially unusual kinds such as eau de cologne mint, which smells just as the name suggests) and many of the various scented-leaved pelargoniums, which are available in apple, citrus, spice, mint and pine fragrances; they all dry out quite attractively. Lavender leaves can also be used; they retain all the scent of the flowers and tend to keep it a little longer.

Dry the potpourri ingredients in a dark, dry, airy place that's not too hot. The airing cupboard is fine if the door is left ajar so there's some air circulation, otherwise use a corner of a spare bedroom or utility room that's well away from a window. Spread the petals and flowers out thinly, ideally only one layer deep so they dry quickly, and stir them gently every few days to help them dry evenly. 'Found' ingredients such as fir cones, pine needles and acorns should also be well dried; they'll often take a bit longer to dry thoroughly than flowers and herbs, so treat them separately. It's also worth drying out some twists of citrus peel: lemon, orange, tangerine or mandarin, or thin slices of fresh kumquat. These dry best in a baking tray left in a very cool oven for several hours; in the airing cupboard they tend to go mouldy. They keep only a faint fragrance, but they give the finished potpourri mixture more colour, texture and variety.

When completely dry, store the flowers, herbs and peels etc., in cardboard boxes lined with tissue paper in a warm, dry cupboard till you are ready to make up your potpourri. (Avoid using screw-top jars since flowers may turn musty or go mouldy in a totally sealed container.) It's essential to keep the dried flowers and herbs in the dark, as their colours soon fade when they are exposed to sunlight.

To turn the various ingredients into potpourri, lay them out on a table along with any others you have bought – perhaps whole spices such as cloves, nutmeg or cinnamon sticks or whole nuts – ready to start assembling your potpourri. But don't just tumble everything randomly together; as a general rule it looks best to 'mix and match' ingredients that team up naturally, so make separate potpourri mixtures of herbs, spices and country garden flowers. Pile them into suitable containers such as baskets or pretty china bowls to suit the place you'll be displaying them.

The big mistake most people make is to try to keep potpourri for far too long; it's at its best for the first three months or so, but after that it tends to lose its scent. You can 'freshen it up' by sprinkling a few drops of floral oil (the sort sold for aroma-therapy at chemists' shops); lavender or rose are best for the job but you might like citrus or one of the herbal varieties. You can keep 'refreshing' a bowl of potpourri for another three to six months, or as long as the petals and leaves still look fresh and colourful. But after a year the colours of potpourri fade and it starts to look very sad, so it's best binned and replaced with a fresh new season's batch.

ORRIS ROOT

Traditionally, orris was used to preserve the scent of potpourri. Orris is the root of a particular species of iris. When dried and powdered, orris root has its own perfume, rather like violets. It's not that easy to buy nowadays, but it's fairly easy to grow and make your own. Grow *Iris florentina* in a sunny part of the garden, and after a couple of years dig it up in the same way as you would to divide a bearded iris growing in your herbaceous border; remove a tuber or two, grate them finely and leave the 'shavings' in a warm place to dry, then use an old coffee grinder or a pestle and mortar to turn them to powder. Store in a dry screw-top jar and stir into potpourri as needed. In medieval homes, before people owned chests of drawers, orris dust was sprinkled between layers of linen sheets stored in chests to keep them smelling fresh instead of turning musty in winter.

DRYING FLOWERS

When you enjoy having cut flowers in the house, it's very easy to continue out-of-season by using flowers that you've dried during the summer.

Only certain kinds are suitable, but enthusiasts often grow a few rows in a special 'cutting garden' or in the veg patch, so they can be 'cropped' without making gaping holes in the best borders.

Some of the most suitable flowers for drying are annuals, including helichrysum (straw flower), statice, cornflower, larkspur and safflower, also seedheads of poppies, love-in-a-mist and decorative grasses. Quite a few perennials also dry well, particularly achillea, acanthus, santolina, liatris, echinops and eryngium. Some seedheads are also good for drying: physalis is brilliant for the rows of orange, ping-pong ball-sized 'Chinese lanterns' that hang from the stems in autumn, and ornamental grasses and honesty are fun. You can also dry heads of teasel from the wild garden; they look good lightly sprayed with white or silver to create a frosted effect, especially for Christmas decorations.

Pick flowers and seedheads for drying very slightly before they are at their best, since they'll continue to develop for a short time while they are drying. (If you pick them at their best they'll often 'go over' and fall apart when they are fully dried. This is particularly true in the case of seedheads of ornamental grasses.)

All the above can be tied up in small bunches and dried hanging upside down in an airy place out of direct sunlight; a utility room or shed is ideal. If you want to dry hydrangea heads, gypsophila, love-lies-bleeding (amaranthus), then they do best stood in empty jars to dry out right-way-up. Some arrangers stand hydrangeas in a solution of glycerine (from chemists) and water, which makes them take on fascinating tints and shades as they dry out, besides preventing them from turning too papery. And although you can dry grass seedheads and honesty upright, the very best results come from lying them flat on a clean cloth on a slatted shelf or a wire-netting framework. This is also the best way to dry any flowers that droop, bend or try to turn up to the light if you dry them any other way.

Once they are completely dry, you can arrange dried flowers, grasses and seedheads in much the same way you'd use fresh flowers in a vase – but of course without any water. If they need support, use brown flower arrangers' foam to hold them in place, not the green sort that's meant to absorb water and support fresh flowers. They can also be used for making potpourri and for crafts such as collage.

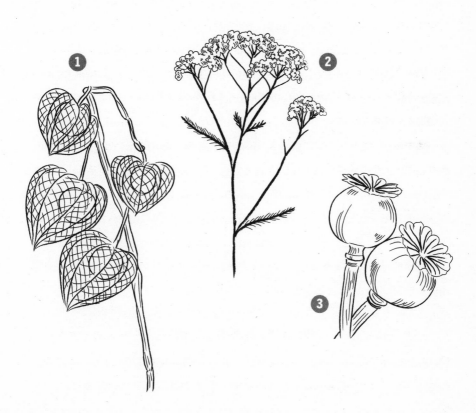

If the flowers aren't needed straight away, store them carefully in a cupboard in cardboard boxes with lids (old shoeboxes are perfect if the flowers fit inside, or in small bunches loosely wrapped in tissue paper to avoid the blooms getting dusty).

Helichrysums have heads that droop after they've dried, so they are usually snipped from their stems and used as loose flowers – perhaps added to potpourri to beef it up – or they are given 'fake' stems made from florists' wires. These have to be pushed through the flower head, then the top end is hooked over so it holds. The wire is then pulled back down so the hooked end is hidden in the bloom where it won't show. Leave the long bottom end of the wire to act as a 'stem' which can be wrapped in green tape if it's going to show and you want a more realistic-looking finish.

Delicate seedheads such as grasses tend to hang on to their seeds best if sprayed with a kind of fixative; look for suitable products in craft shops. Traditionally hairspray was used, but it needs treating with caution as it makes the finished heads very inflammable.

Dried flowers don't keep in pristine condition for as long as some people think. When they are on show in an arrangement in a room they gather dust which is difficult to dislodge – a gentle shake or a light waft with a hairdryer on a cool setting can help. They also fade when exposed to sunlight and can turn quite brittle in a warm, dry room so they crumble or break if touched. Old arrangements can look quite 'tired', so it's best to use them for no more than one year and then replace them with a freshly dried batch, and do a new batch each summer.

GROW YOUR OWN GOURDS

Ornamental gourds make great natural decorations. They grow on long, scrambling, annual vines that look good trailing over an arch or on a fence or trellis; they can also be grown in a tub on the patio, given suitable support. (Three plants grown this way up a tripod of rustic poles makes a great project for children.)

Raise your own gourd plants from seed; a packet usually contains a mixture of several different varieties. Sow two per 9cm (three-and-a-half inch) pot on a warm windowsill indoors in April, and don't plant the young plants outside until the last frost is safely past, which won't usually be until mid to late May. Grow them in rich soil or a tub of potting compost in a sheltered, sunny spot and allow the vines to climb using their tendrils. In summer it's fun to watch the baby gourds appear, swell up to roughly fist-size and change colour.

The decorative fruits start to dry out naturally on the plants in autumn. Cut them in late September or early October, before the first frost, clean the skins with a damp cloth and bring them into a warm room to finish drying slowly. A lot of people like to varnish their gourds to make them shiny, but this can make them rot faster since the skin can't 'breathe'. This won't matter if you only plan on keeping them over the winter, but a better alternative is to buff them up with a soft cloth and a spot of spray-on furniture polish.

FLOWER CONFETTI

If you're planning a country wedding in summer, real flower petals make a fashionable and 'green' alternative to paper confetti or rice. Petals are often acceptable at venues that don't allow conventional confetti or rice due to the mess left behind afterwards (but always check in advance). If you have a well-stocked garden or have a local supplier, you can use fresh flower petals, but there's always a risk that the 'juice' will stain clothes; white and very pale pastel petals are safest in this respect, but even so, dried petals are usually preferred. They are also far easier to prepare in advance and store, and can be ordered from specialist suppliers, usually flower farms who prepare their own mixtures.

CUTTING GARDENS

When you want to cut flowers in reasonable quantities to bring indoors without spoiling the look of your borders, the solution is to keep a 'cutting garden'. This can be located somewhere that's not on view from the house, and which is kept especially for cut flowers. Some people like to create a separate bed, and others will use one end of the veg patch or allotment. To be cost-effective, raise your own annuals from seed, and be sure to include some of the many bulbs, perennials, shrubs and roses that provide good cut flowers, too.

Hardy annuals: *Grow from seed sown in rows where they are to flower, from mid March to the end of April. Good kinds include calendula, Ammi majus (Queen Anne's lace), candytuft, cornflower, marigolds, larkspur and sunflowers; also several small ornamental grasses such as quaking grass.*

Sweet peas: *Hardy annuals, but usually sown in late October/early November in a cold frame or unheated greenhouse (for the earliest flowers) or February/early March under cover in small individual pots and planted out in late March or April when 5–7.5cm (2–3in) tall. To produce flowers with long, straight stems, train each plant up its own string and remove all the tendrils. You will, though, be able to pick perfectly usable flowers from plants allowed to scramble up netting or trellis, which take less work.*

Half-hardy annuals: *Grow from seed sown in a heated propagator in a greenhouse or on windowsills indoors in March. Prick the seedlings out when they are big enough to handle and don't plant them outside until after the last frost, around mid to late May – at the same time as young plants you may have bought from a nursery or garden centre. Good varieties include antirrhinum, aster, amaranthus, cosmos, eustoma, salpiglossis, phlox, stocks, zinnia and annual rudbeckia.*

Perennials: *Usually bought as reasonable-sized plants for planting in spring, but many kinds can be grown from seed, treated as either half-hardy annuals sown in February, when many kinds should flower the same year, or as hardy annuals sown outside in May/June, in which case the young plants need transplanting to flowering places in autumn; they'll start flowering the following year. Good kinds include: achillea, astilbe, astrantia, delphinium, echinacea, eryngium, rudbeckia, scabious, gypsophila, pinks and Sedum spectabile (ice plant) which some arrangers pick as flat green heads of buds instead of waiting for the pink flowers to open.*

Bulbs, corms and tubers: *Start frost-tender kinds in pots under cover and plant them outside after the last frost – dahlias are particular favourites with arrangers. Plant hardy kinds such as liatris, ornamental alliums, lilies, dutch iris and spring bulbs, including daffodils, as soon as the bulbs or roots become available in the shops, or order from bulb catalogues.*

Roses: *Any roses can be used as cut flowers, but the most popular varieties for cutting are the heavily scented red varieties such as 'Alec's Red', 'Deep Secret' and 'Fragrant Cloud'; orange-red 'Superstar' is an old favourite with fragrance and good long stems. Keen flower arrangers often like unusual* *colours; they'll often grow stripy roses such as 'Harry Wheatcroft', 'painted' roses (such as 'Sue Lawley'), green roses (such as 'Greensleeves') or caramel-brown roses (such as 'Julia Clements').*

PRESSED FLOWERS

Pressing flowers was a great hobby when I was at school – sandwiching common wildflowers between sheets of newspaper and flattening them under a rug in the front room. Garden flowers, too, are quite acceptable for pressing, and some – such as pansies – are particularly successful. They can be used to make homemade greetings cards, bookmarks and pictures. Pressing flowers is a great way to get children interested in flowers and crafts, as they can use the end result to make small gifts for grandparents. Sheets of plain or coloured card, and also blank greetings cards sold especially for this job, are available from craft shops.

You can still use the newspaper and rug – or the large-book-and-blotting paper method – but nowadays proper flower presses are available, again from craft shops. The best flowers for pressing are those with naturally fairly flat faces since they don't change shape; pansies and violas are great favourites. With more three-dimensional flowers, it pays to 'arrange' the petals nicely before applying pressure so that they press in a reasonably natural-looking position. If you want to press the sort of flowers that have a hard, chunky centre (like the yellow bit in the centre of daisies, or the green calyx at the base of a rose bloom), remove the petals carefully, press them individually and then re-assemble the flower complete with authentic stalk as you stick it onto backing paper. If in doubt as to how a particular flower will turn out, try one or two first to see what happens – you've nothing to lose.

Most flowers and leaves are completely dry after two weeks in the flower press. Arrange them carefully on your chosen card and glue them in place with a suitable craft glue.

It's not only flowers that you can press; when you want to make a posy-effect for a picture it's handy to have some pressed foliage as well – and it doesn't have to be the foliage from the flower you are pressing. You can cheat and use any leaves that press well and create a suitably decorative effect. Flat grass blades are easy to press, and ornamental varieties with red, gold or stripy leaves look stunning. Anything with striking shapes, such as horse chestnut leaves, also look good. You can press autumn leaves, too; those of Japanese maples are especially stunning and will keep most of their colour – pick them when they show superb colours but before they start to dry out naturally, and press them flat straight away before they start to curl up at the edges. Leaves that won't press well, are thick, juicy or succulent ones, so avoid cyclamen and sedums.

But if you are pressing flowers for a school botany project, or making a picture in the style of a botanical illustration, then you'll need to be strictly accurate. Aim to show an open flower, a bud, stems and foliage, and possibly even roots of common types. Lay them out attractively and identify them either with typed labels or your best handwriting. You'll have a souvenir that lasts longer than your lifetime.

HOW TO MAKE A POMANDER

A pomander was originally carried by the upper classes when they had to travel through the streets in medieval Europe, since it was thought that something nicely scented could ward off plague and pestilence. Judges at the time would take a pomander with them into their courtroom as an antidote to the 'noxious airs' rising from the jails below, and today judges still carry 'nosegays' – small bunches of flowers – on official occasions. Today pomanders make lovely, natural, fragrant Christmas decorations redolent of citrus and spice; try lining a row of them up along a mantelpiece or hall windowsill at Christmas.

For each pomander you'll need a citrus fruit (an orange was the traditional choice but you can use lime, lemon, grapefruit or tangerine), enough whole cloves to cover or decorate your citrus fruit, and a length of narrow ribbon about 30cm (12in) long.

Use a sharp-pointed cocktail stick to make a series of evenly spaced holes all over the surface of the skin of the fruit, then press a whole clove into each hole, pointed end first, leaving the knobbly end flush with the skin. You can make patterns with the cloves but for the longest-lasting pomanders, cover the entire surface of the fruit with cloves – but remember to leave a bare narrow strip all round it where the ribbon will go. (If you fancy a more heavily spiced pomander, dust the clove-studded fruit in powdered nutmeg, allspice or cinnamon immediately after pushing the cloves in; enough of the powdered spice will stick to the dampness on the skin.)

Lastly, tie the ribbon round the fruit so that it crosses over top and bottom and is held firmly, then tie the loose ends of ribbons into a bow on top of the fruit or use it to make a loop to hang it up.

CANDLE-MAKING

In bygone times, impoverished country families made their own candles using tallow from clarified beef, bacon or pork fat (often left over from the Sunday joint), with plant material as wicks – they'd use the pith from the centre of dried rushes, or the furry stems of dried mullein plants. The resulting candles were a bit smelly and smoky; they also spluttered badly, and didn't give off much light.

Wealthy households always used the far superior beeswax candles. These were made by dipping weighted wicks into melted beeswax, and as fast as each coat of wax started to set, it was dipped again to gain an extra layer, so the candles grew fatter. Artisan candle-makers would make a dozen or more candles at a time by draping a row of long wicks over a stout pole, then dangling these down into a vat of melted wax. By lifting each end of the pole up and down, pairs of candles formed. When they were cold and the wax was thoroughly set, each pair of candles was separated by cutting through the length of wick that joined them.

Now candle-making is a flourishing hobby, and craft centres and hobby shops sell kits containing everything you need. But when you have a home-grown supply of beeswax, you can do it yourself from scratch.

HOW TO MAKE A CANDLE

For your candle wicks, use good-quality cotton string. You next need a mould. Use a strong plastic tube of suitable diameter (perhaps cut the bottom half off an empty washing-up liquid bottle, for a large, fat, church-type candle). Lubricate the inside with a little vegetable oil so that the candle can slide out easily afterwards. Cut a length of string a few inches longer than the length of your mould. Drip a blob of molten beeswax into the base of the mould and press one end of the string down into it, then give it a few moments to set firmly so that it is fixed securely. Then tie the other end of the string to the middle of a short, straight piece of stick rested on the rim of the mould; wind the string round it just enough to tighten the wick until it hangs straight down the centre of the tube. Stand the mould upright on a tin plate or similar heatproof surface that can catch any spilt wax safely.

Now melt the beeswax by heating it gently inside an old, but clean, tin can standing inside a saucepan of hot water. (Don't put it directly into the pan or you'll have a dreadful job cleaning it afterwards.) When the wax has melted you can add other ingredients to colour, scent or decorate the finished candle. You can use food colouring or special dye for candles bought from a craft shop, some scented oil (the aromatherapy type, in whatever fragrance you fancy – lavender is always popular) or some pieces of dried herbs, spices, dried lavender flowers or pieces of dried petals or small fragments of mixed potpourri. Mix these in well so that they are evenly distributed. Alternatively, leave the wax completely natural with nothing added; pure beeswax will produce a pale, creamy-coloured candle.

Pour a little of the melted wax carefully into the bottom of the mould. As soon as the base starts to set, stand the mould in a container of cold water before filling the rest of the mould with melted wax. When the entire tube is firmly set and cold, cut the wick off about a centimetre (a quarter of an inch) above the top of the wax and slide the candle out of its mould. (If it sticks, plunge it briefly in hot water, or as a last resort cut the base carefully off the mould and push it out from there.) For a fancier finish, perhaps to make decorative candles for Christmas, buff the exterior of the candle gently with a piece of kitchen paper that's been moistened with a few drops of vegetable oil, then sprinkle it very sparingly with glitter or a few dried herbs or spices, but don't overdo it – a very light 'gilding' is quite enough.

ECONOMY TIP

Whether you burn homemade candles or ones you've bought from a shop, save up any drips of spilt candle wax along with your old candle stubs. When you have enough, melt them down in a tin can in a bath of hot water, using the method opposite and you can reuse them to make a new candle, which only needs a new piece of string for the wick.

PATCHWORK AND QUILTING

Originally, patchwork and quilting were two different crafts, but today they tend to be thought of as one and the same thing and are mostly used to make patchwork quilts, which act as decorative bed-spreads or can be hung on a wall just as you might hang up an expensive handmade or antique rug.

PATCHWORK

In my youth, patchwork was one of the many handicrafts children learnt at junior school. While we lads did manly things like woodwork, the girls would be doing needlecraft of various sorts, and patchwork was a regular favourite. Girls would be asked to bring small scraps of leftover material from home, and shown how to stitch them together to make tea cosies or cushion covers. They'd cut stacks of identical-sized octagonal shapes out of cardboard, then lay each one onto a piece of fabric only slightly larger. Next, they'd fold the edges of the fabric over the cardboard templates and stitch them loosely into position with long, loose stitches over the back of the shape. When they had a goodish pile of fabric-clad octagons, they'd over-sew the edges neatly together so that they formed a honeycomb-like piece of patchwork. Once they'd stitched enough together to make the shape and size required for their finished item, they'd snip the stitching that held the cardboard shapes in place, remove them from the octagons of cloth, and then sew the whole piece of patchwork onto a 'backing cloth' to make the finished article. Oh, it took ages to do but the sense of achievement was worth the slog!

Patchwork was – and is – cheap to do, yet it produces very attractive items from 'leftovers'. In days gone by thrifty housewives always saved up all their remnants of fabric and off-cuts from other jobs, so they didn't need to buy anything. Half the skill lay in choosing, from amongst the various odds and ends, pieces that would go well together in the finished work. Most people chose a mixture of patterns in several shades of one colour, so the result looked stylish rather than garish. And back in the days when country folk did patchwork to make larger items like throws, bedspreads, or even curtains out of oddments, they'd usually use squares or diamonds instead of octagonal shapes, since they were faster to sew and made better use of the material, so there was less waste. But the end result was still very homely.

QUILTING

Think of a quilted jacket and you'll see the difference between patchwork and quilting straight away. A quilt is two layers of fabric with a thicker, fluffier, insulated layer between them, held in place by decorative stitchwork.

A patchwork quilt is pretty and practical; it might consist of fabric shapes sewn on to a plain-coloured cover with a thicker, insulated layer inside, or it could be a patchwork cover that sandwiches a thicker insulated layer in between, with stitching outlining the patterns made by the patchwork.

Quilting is often done by a group of enthusiasts, and the work is usually stretched on a frame that holds the underlying fabric taut while the decorative pieces are being stitched on. A few country villages still have quilting clubs today. In the USA, handmade quilts are heirlooms passed down through country families, and the style – recreated in ready-printed fabric – is still much in use for traditional bed coverings there today.

SPINNING

Natural sheep's fleece is thick and fluffy, far removed from the woollen yarn used for knitting or weaving into fabrics. It takes a complicated process to turn the raw fleece into a useable product.

As it comes straight off the sheep, a fleece is dirty, so it's first washed well to remove grease and dirt, then allowed to dry. Next it needs to be carded. This is done a small handful at a time, and involves 'combing' the rough wool between two 'carders', which look like long-handled dog-brushes, with a mass of short, hooked wire bristles. By brushing the two repeatedly together with a blob of wool between them, the fibres are 'combed' out so that they give you a much fluffier bundle of wool that's far easier to spin. (The job was originally done using teasel heads, which are hard, fat, tubular seedheads covered with short, bristly hooks.) The carded 'fluff' is then roughly rolled by hand into a fat cylinder, ready to spin.

The earliest yarns would have been made by simply twisting and stretching the 'raw' wool by hand; it took ages. The invention of the drop spindle speeded the job up quite a bit. A drop spindle is little more than a short length of wooden pole with a hook at the top, and a heavy weight at the bottom that incorporates a reel for the finished thread to be wound round. A bundle of clean, carded wool is attached to the hook at the top and the pole is turned, which starts the device spinning. As it spins, the fibres in the wool are automatically teased out straight and twisted into a similar sort of yarn that you'd have if you bought a ball of knitting wool. As the spindle keeps turning the yarn gets steadily longer, then when the bottom of the weight reaches the ground, the yarn that's been made is wound round the reel and the spinner continues, adding more loose, fluffy wool to the original bundle at the top of the spindle. The result is a bit rustic – uneven and very obviously handmade – and it takes a long time to produce a useful quantity of useable yarn, but cottagers didn't have a lot else to do during the long winter evenings, and you could spin wool this way even in weak candlelight.

Today you can still use a drop spindle if you only have a small amount of fleece to turn into yarn, but most modern spinners use a spinning wheel. Here a bundle of raw loose wool is slowly fed from a 'storage cylinder' through a rotating 'flyer' that twists and pulls it into yarn, which is wound onto a reel, the whole thing being powered by a foot-operated treadle that turns the large wheel. Using this ingenious contraption it's possible to convert a much larger volume of fleece into yarn of a more even thickness and uniform quality, since it maintains an even tension throughout (as against the drop spindle where the tension is constantly varying). It's a satisfying craft; according to keen spinners, a spinning wheel is therapeutic to use.

Natural homespun wool can be used for knitting, both by hand or using a knitting machine, and a lot of sheep-owners like to turn their fleeces into sweaters, knitted woollen jackets, coats and cardigans, throws or shawls for members of their family or for items to sell at craft fairs. It's not just sheep fleeces that can be spun into yarn; llama and alpaca fleeces can be used (alpaca is wonderfully soft and silky), and some people will even spin the fluff clipped from their poodle, or combed from their Persian cat, to knit into highly personalised sweaters.

WEAVING

Some craftspeople like to weave yarn to make into more specialised fabrics, particularly tweed to make clothing, and for wall hangings, throws and rugs. You sometimes meet spinners and weavers at craft fairs selling a wide range of fascinating homemade items, and demonstrating how they make them.

Weaving involves criss-crossing vertical and horizontal threads tightly together to make cloth. The original method of weaving was exceptionally slow and tedious, since a row of horizontal threads tied to a wooden frame had to be separated individually and a vertical thread woven backwards and forwards between each one, then at the end of the row the vertical thread turned round the last thread and worked back along the row of vertical threads in the opposite direction.

The invention of the loom changed all that. This large weaving frame is arranged something like a tabletop, with very long threads that are unwound at one end as the work progresses, and a shuttle that passes between them adding the cross-threads, with the finished cloth being wound onto a roll at the other end. Work progresses much faster, since the long end-to-end threads (the warp) are fed through a metal plate contain-ing alternate slots and holes, so that by raising and lowering the plate the two sets of threads are automatically separated, allowing the shuttle that bears the side-to-side threads (the weft) to pass between them. The slotted plate is operated by a foot pedal, so the operator can get quite a speed up. Between every run of the shuttle, a stick-like device is used to press the last row of work down firmly against the last, so the finished cloth is dense and evenly textured. If you see a large loom in action, it has rather a Heath Robinson air about it, with beams going up and down, threads moving, and shuttle flying, with the operator working in such harmony that he or she seems to be part of the machinery. Although a loom looks easy to use, it needs a fair degree of coordination, and a lot of the skill lies in setting up the loom and preparing the warp threads just right at the outset.

KNITTING WOOL

For people who don't want the bother of turning home-produced fleeces into useable yarns and knitting wool, it's possible to send them off to a factory and get them back ready-processed. Firms advertise in small-holders' magazines.

Single-strand yarn is mostly used for weaving; for knitting, three-ply wool is used. This is made by twisting together three thin strands of yarn in the opposite direction to the natural twist of the original yarn, in much the same way as thin rope, so the two opposing twists give the finished knitting wool a springy effect – this is what gives sweaters etc., their 'bounce' and 'stretch', as against woven fabric where the yarns are stretched taut during weaving.

Used knitting wool can be recycled. Years ago it was very common for thrifty country housewives to unpick old, worn-out pullovers by hand, wash and rewind the best of the wool (making their husbands or children sit with hands held outstretched to loop it round, forming it into hanks) and then re-knit it to make something new. Even small oddments of knitting wool weren't left to go to waste: they were knitted into squares that were sewn together to make patchwork blankets or cushion covers, or used to knit useful small items such as tea cosies or kettle holders, and I can still remember the aching arms as I held the hanks of wool for my mum!

NATURAL DYES

A good many craftspeople enjoy using natural-coloured wool from the different breeds of sheep to make garments or rugs in a range of cream, white, grey, beige, brown and black shades, but when a larger range of colours are required the wool has to be dyed. (When tweed is made, for instance, the colours that form the characteristic speckled patterns are created by using different coloured warp threads, and changing the colour of wool in the shuttle so they create a contrasting effect where the different colours cross.)

Synthetic dyes allow any colour or shade to be used, but many craft enthusiasts enjoy dying their wool using natural fabric colourings they've made themselves from plants. Plants provided the original dyes used hundreds of years ago; even today, enthusiasts say that plant dyes have a character and vibrancy that you don't find in modern synthetic ones. The dye obtained from particular plants often bears little relation to the colour of the plant itself. The final colour it produces will also vary in shade according to the colour of the original wool and the mordant (the chemical added to dye to 'fix' it to the fabric) used, so it's interesting to see how each batch turns out.

Onion skins produce rich yellow, brown or orange shades. Marigold (Calendula officinalis) makes shades of yellow. Bloodroot (Sanguinaria canadensis) lives up to its name by producing reddish orange shades.

Horsetail gives light yellow and greeny yellow shades. (Any gardener will be glad to find a good use for this notorious weed!) Dyer's chamomile (Anthemis tinctoria) makes amber or khaki-ish shades, weld (Reseda luteola) produces beautiful yellow shades, and madder (Rubia tinctorum, which was cultivated by dyers from the Anglo-Saxons onwards specially for use as a dye-plant) produces orangey shades of red-brown or pink. It has to be said that there are plenty of plants that yield dyes in rather earthy shades of yellows, tans and browns, but some colours are very under-represented. Blues can be produced using indigo or woad, but they are some of the most difficult and complicated dyes to make.

To create natural dyes you need suitable plant material. The best natural plant dyes are made using fresh materials, but don't pick them from the countryside – the dyes are just as good when the plants are grown in controlled conditions in the garden. A lot of suitable plants are quite common; parsley and nettles for instance. When fresh ingredients aren't available, dried leaves, petals or roots can be used (these can be home-grown or bought from craft suppliers specially for dying) and you can freeze berries to use.

You also need a mordant. A mordant is a chemical added to the plant material which makes the colour soak into the wool better, and makes the end fabric more colour-fast, though it also contributes something to the colour itself. All sorts of strange substances have been used as mordants throughout history: vinegar, salt and wood ashes to name a few. (The weirdest by far has got to be urine, which was once collected in buckets overnight by Hebridean islanders to use for 'fixing' the colours of Harris tweed.) But the most used ones are metallic: alum (an aluminium salt), chrome, tin or iron.

The exact recipe differs for each particular plant and mordant combination, but roughly the same sort of process is followed for each. You need a large stainless steel pan, something like a large preserving pan, which is kept especially for dyeing.

The natural woollen yarn (which has already been spun) is first tied into loose hanks, then soaked in a sinkful of hot water, ammonia and soft soap for an hour, followed by another hour's soaking in a fresh sinkful of the same solution at a slightly lower temperature. This part of the treatment is to get rid of oil or grease from the wool, which prevents the dye being properly absorbed. The wool is then rinsed well and dried, then kept – still in hanks – until you're ready to dye it.

It's then pre-soaked to ensure that the wool (which is naturally rather water- resistant) is thoroughly wet right through, before being treated with the mordant and the plant dye, which has been previously prepared.

Dye plants that have tough woody stems are chopped and then soaked overnight in enough soft water to just about cover them (a lot of enthusiasts save rainwater especially for this job). Soft or softer plant material, including berries, petals and the like, can be used straight away; they only need to be covered with water. Use your stainless-steel dye pan for this or you'll ruin your saucepans.

Heat the pan of water and plant material gently, but don't quite let it boil, then simmer for several hours before letting it cool. Strain it and pour it back into the (empty) dye pan. Add the wet, mordanted wool, and bring the mixture very slowly back to simmering point; simmer gently for another hour. When it's 'done', the wool is lifted out and rinsed, first in hot water, then again in progressively cooler water and finally cold water, then the hanks of wool are hung up tidily to dry.

It's worth pointing out that natural dyes will tend to fade in sunlight, and though the effect can be charming, you may want to preserve the colours by keeping throws and clothing somewhere out of direct sunlight when you aren't actually using them, to keep the colours looking fresh and vibrant for longer.

WOODTURNING

If you visit a country fair today, you may well see a woodturner selling his work, and he'll almost certainly be a retired gent who does it as a paying hobby. This is because although ordinary people once relied on wooden bowls, plates and dishes instead of expensive china, nowadays 'turned' wood items are mainly used decoratively by folk who appreciate the beauty of the natural grain of the wood, and the skill that's gone into making these items.

Since suitable wood for turning is in rather short supply, woodturners will often keep an eye out for gardeners felling ornamental trees such as cherry, walnut, pear or apple, since those have particularly attractive grains when the wood is cut across, turned and polished. But yew, maple and elm are also suitable; they are some of the many sorts of wood that were once used for making fine furniture.

A whole tree trunk has to be sawn into suitable-sized pieces and stored for some time to season, otherwise the finished items may split or buckle out of shape after they've been inside a warm house for a while. When the timber is seasoned and ready to use, the turner fits it to a lathe, which these days is electrically operated. He then uses a series of small tools to gouge the spinning section of wood into the right shape for a plate, bowl or whatever it may be. These days, pieces of polished wooden fruit are also popular; they can be used as ornaments in their own right, but they are often piled up in a turned wooden fruit bowl. Once the piece has been shaped, inside and out, it is sandpapered, finished with beeswax polish and buffed up, again all on the lathe. Individual items take hours of work to complete fully, but there's a huge satisfaction to be had from the process for anyone who loves wood.

CANAL-BOAT PAINTING

The canal system was created in the late eighteenth and early nineteenth centuries as a means of linking places where raw materials were produced or imported with the factories that processed them and the cities that consumed them. At the time, canal barges were the only means of hauling heavy loads of goods such as cast iron, coal, sand, china clay and metal ore over long distances to fuel the growing Industrial Revolution.

Rising costs and competition meant that the men who worked on canal barges were eventually forced to move their families on board, so barges became portable homes as well as work-boats. A complete lifestyle revolved round canal boats, which came to be decorated in a characteristic folksy style, not unlike that of traditional gypsy caravans. Entire boats were covered with a cheery mixture of flowers (especially roses) and scenery (particularly churches, great houses or castles) against a coloured background divided into squares or ovals garnished with stars and scrolls. Even the metal buckets, milk cans and water jugs used on board were decorated in the same style. Some of the decoration was personalised, but much of it was done in the livery of the various companies that owned working canal boats.

The art of traditional canal boat painting persisted even when canals were superseded by railways and trunk roads, and narrowboats were reinvented as leisure craft for folk who enjoyed cruising the canals, enjoying the peace, quiet and wildlife.

HOW TO PAINT TRADITIONAL CANAL-STYLE ART

First divide up the area to be painted into a series of rectangles with narrow strips in between them; if you're painting containers, outline spouts and handles, paint the strips, spouts and handles bright red and the rectangles, black. Later paint your scenes, roses, castles, etc. – into panels in the black areas, and add white stars and scrolls anywhere there doesn't seem to be enough decoration; you can also outline some of the red stripes in white to further brighten up the effect.

Some enthusiasts prefer to use dark blue or a deep green in place of the red background colour, so feel free to use a little artistic licence.

The same style looks very good used for metal tubs and troughs on a patio, and it's especially stunning used for a herb garden outside the back door, since herbs tend to be very 'green', so their looks are improved by colourful containers.

CHAPTER 2

HOME CRAFT SKILLS

HOME-BREWING

For centuries, country people made their own beer, mead, cider and country wines at home. Well, they were free, which was what attracted me to them when my wife and I were first married! The ingredients grew on the doorstep; they were either picked from the countryside or grown in the garden, and mead (which is 'wine' made from honey) would have come from the householders' own hives. Some people still enjoy doing a little home-brewing today, to save money, avoid additives, or make good use of a surplus of garden produce – though one or two 'extras' sometimes need to be bought.

BEER

Beer is made from malted barley, which is basically whole grains of barley that have been moistened and allowed to start germinating, then dried and 'cracked'. This process alters the flavour quite considerably; it also causes the starch in the grains to turn to sugar, which feeds the yeast that makes the alcohol.

In commercial breweries that make 'real ale' today, malting, as it's known, is all done in highly controlled conditions where temperature and humidity are monitored to ensure the perfect brew. Old-fashioned ale or stout is made from malted barley alone, but to make beer, hops are added for flavouring – they give beer its bitter taste. The finished product is then sent out to the pubs in barrels, which were traditionally transported by horse-drawn dreys. On delivery, the landlord puts his beer barrels down into his cellar and lets them settle for a while before connecting them up to the pipes that deliver the beer, a glassful at a time, to the pumps on the bar. Today a few giant breweries make most of the beer that's sold, but in the past most local pubs used to brew their own 'out the back', and until fairly recently you could find a few country pubs that still did.

But before Victorian times it was very common for farm labourers to make their own beer at home. It was very weak, but since there was no piped water at the time and wells or pumps might be contaminated, beer was far healthier than water, since the water used for making it had to be boiled first, thus killing off any 'bugs'. Beer also provided lots of calories and B vitamins, which bolstered an otherwise poor diet, since many farmhands lived on little more than bread and beer. (William Cobbett, the nineteenth-century agriculturalist, pamphleteer and traditionalist, despaired of the rise of tea for the way it deprived farmhands of their beer and replaced it with a nutritionally empty drink, besides ranting about the waste of time occupied in tea-making by their wives who, he thought, had better things to do. Such as brewing beer?)

KEEP IT CLEAN

All the equipment you use for any sort of home-brewing should first be thoroughly cleaned and then sterilised (buy suitable products from homebrew shops) to ensure unwanted bacteria don't find their way in by accident. They'll ruin your brew.

HOW TO MAKE BEER

Today most people wanting to brew their own beer buy a kit and just follow the instructions, though real enthusiasts will buy the ingredients separately from homebrew shops and do it themselves from scratch. There are various recipes but all follow similar steps.

Soak plain barley grains (as harvested from the field or sold specially for brewing, not pearl barley used for cookery) in warm water for four days, then drain and spread out the plumped-up grains thinly on a clean surface. Keep them at a temperature of between 18°C and 29°C (65°F and 85°F) for roughly ten days, spraying occasionally with tepid water and turning them regularly. By now the grains should have grown very short shoots, so 'kill' these by putting them in a cold oven and heating it up to 50°C (120°F). Check regularly, and when the barley is dry and brittle (test it between your teeth) turn the temperature up a little – by no more than another 10°C (20°F), for a quarter of an hour. It should now have a roasted, malted smell. Then 'crack' it; use a rolling pin or a heavy duty blender. Aim to just break the grains up a bit, you don't want them turning to powder.

Tip 12½ kilos (27½ pounds) of the malt, as it's now called, into a large clean plastic bin (a brand-new swing bin or plastic dustbin is ideal – you'll need to insert a plastic bung with a tap a few inches from the bottom). Into this, mix 23 litres (5 gallons) of water that's been boiled and left to cool down to 66°C (150°F), so it makes a 'mash' – this looks something like old-fashioned pig swill. Cover it with a clean cloth and leave it overnight to settle.

The next morning open the tap and allow the wort (as the liquid that runs off is called) to drain out of the bottom of the bin into a large sauce-pan or jam-making pan. As you do this, drizzle boiling water from a kettle over the mash that's still in the bin to 'rinse' the grains; you'll need to collect 23 litres (5 gallons) of wort altogether. Then put the saucepan onto the stove and add 225 grams (8 ounces) hops tied up in a muslin bag or cotton pillowcase, plus a little sugar if you want to make a stronger beer.

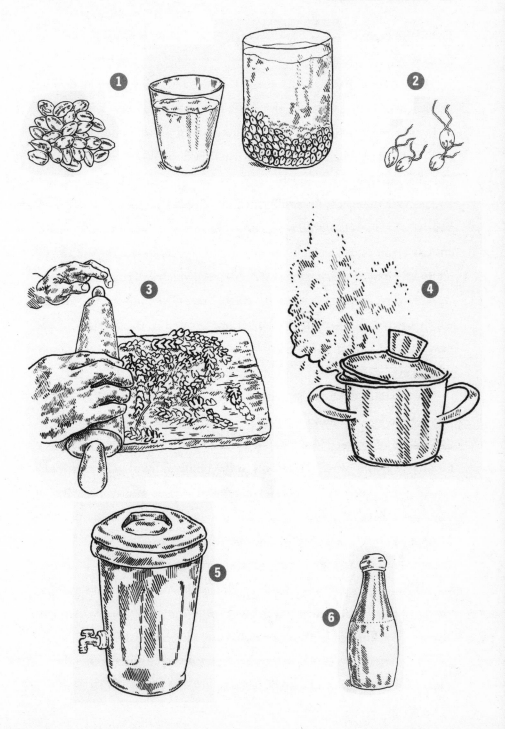

Boil for an hour. Cool the brew as quickly as possible, perhaps by standing the container in a bath of cold water, till it reaches 16°C (60°F).

While it cools, prepare your yeast. Take out a jugful of wort, and cool it separately until it reaches roughly body temperature, then stir in a sachet of brewer's yeast and stand it somewhere warm (in the airing cupboard, or by the Aga perhaps) so the yeast can develop. When the rest of the wort has reached 16°C (60°F), add the jug of yeasty 'starter', stir well and transfer the whole lot to a fermentation vessel. (Homebrew shops sell large plastic buckets with lids especially for this job, but a brand new and entirely clean plastic dustbin is fine.) Cover it with a cloth, or put the lid on, to keep out flies, since they carry bacteria which will ruin your brew.

After three days a thick, foamy, yeasty crust develops over the surface, which needs to be skimmed off. This can be used as the 'starter' for the next batch of beer if you are going into production seriously, or it can be used as live brewer's yeast for making bread.

A week later the beer is ready to be siphoned off into a clean barrel, which produces traditional flat beer. Avoid stirring up the sediment in the bottom of the container, and leave the barrel to settle in a cool place for at least two to three days so it's in the best condition before you start drinking it – don't try to keep it too long or it goes past its best. If you want gassy beer, use thick bottles capable of withstanding the pressure without exploding, and get the beer bottled as early as possible while it's still fermenting a tad. Don't use normal screw-top bottles that soft drinks are sold in, buy proper beer bottles with clip-down flip-tops (the sort that are like old-fashioned ginger beer bottles) and reuse them for subsequent batches. The finished beer can be tasted any time onwards.

A lot of work? Yes, but if you're feeling creative and enterprising there's a lot of satisfaction – and a lot of decent pints – in it!

CIDER

When you're used to commercial bottled or draft cider, you're in for a shock when you experience the homemade kind – it's more like scrumpy: cloudy, flat and not at all sweet, but it's the real thing and a great way to use up surplus apples. You can use whatever apples you have (a mixture of cooking and eating apples – and even a few crab apples – is best), though in cider orchards, traditional cider-apples are grown, which are small, sour, and often grotesquely misshapen. The important thing is that the apples should be really ripe; it doesn't matter if there are a few bruised, bird-pecked or maggoty ones in with them. It also does no harm at all if, after being picked, the apples hang around for a few weeks before you start turning them into cider – if anything, it helps them develop more sweetness.

Perry is the same sort of thing, only made with pears; again you can use whatever you have but perry orchards use perry pears, which are very hard – you wouldn't want to try eating them.

HOW TO MAKE CIDER

First turn your fruit into juice. To do this you need a fruit press; some gardening groups or wine circles own one that they hire or lend out to members, otherwise it's probably best for several friends or neighbours to club together and share one as it's a fairly expensive bit of kit you only need for a day or two every year. It looks like a large bucket with handles at the top and a 'lid' which you screw down to exert pressure on the fruit inside to squash it flat, and the juice comes out of a chute in the base.

Roughly chop the fruit so it's a bit broken up, otherwise it's almost impossible to squash. As a rough guide, expect to get 4½ litres of juice from 5½ kilos of apples (a gallon from 12lb). The dryish pulp that's left behind after pressing was traditionally fed to the pigs; this and letting the animals forage for windfall fruit under trees in the orchard resulted in sweet, tasty pork. If you don't keep pigs, then hens and other livestock will enjoy it – otherwise put it on the compost heap.

There's no need to add anything else to your freshly squeezed apple juice; no sugar or yeast is required, because the fruit comes complete with all that's necessary. (You can certainly leave out the traditional dead rat, which was once thought essential for 'real' farmhouse scrumpy.) Pour the juice into a large clean container or some buckets covered with several layers of muslin or other cloths. For the first few days fermentation is fast and furious, then, when it's calmed down, perhaps a week later, pour the liquid into a clean wooden cask or a few well-sterilised glass demijohns (the containers that are normally used for making homemade wine) and fit fermentation traps to them. Keep the containers at a steady temperature and out of direct sun, and when the fermentation has stopped you know all the sugar has been turned to alcohol, and the cider is ready for tasting. Since the yeast is still alive, the brew will usually still be naturally slightly fizzy.

Cider will keep for a while, but like beer, the character of it will change slowly the longer you leave it. However, it's the simplest form of homebrew you can have, and the best one to 'cut your teeth' on, assuming you have a good supply of free apples. If you don't grow your own fruit, look out for people offering surplus fruit for free at the side of the road, or check out farmshops who sometimes sell off second-best, bruised or damaged fruit very cheaply.

MAKING APPLE JUICE

If you don't want the bother of making cider, simply extract the juice from sweet eating apples and use it fresh, just as it is, as pure apple juice. You can use a fruit press to do the job, but if you only have small quantities to do, it's easier to use an electric juice extractor. This works by grating the fruit finely and then centrifuging it to remove the juice, which is dispensed into a separate container from the pulp. Juice extractors are available from most electrical stores for about the same price as a coffee-maker.

Any juice you can't use straight away can be frozen for another time. Pour the juice into polythene containers with sealable lids and pack them into the freezer; frozen fruit juice keeps for six months to a year, and as it defrosts it's ready-chilled.

Don't expect home-grown apple juice to be just like the apple juice you buy in cartons at the shops. Home-pressed apple juice looks a tad cloudy, but that's as it should be – it hasn't been pasteurised or pressure-filtered or treated in any way. It's also a slightly different colour; freshly pressed apple juice quickly turns a slightly amber shade due to oxidisation, because it doesn't contain preservatives. This doesn't spoil the quality, but if you want to keep the original colour, stir the juice of half a lemon or half a level teaspoonful of vitamin C powder to each pint of freshly squeezed juice. This also gives a slight 'bite' to the flavour, which makes very sweet apples more tangy.

MAKING VINEGAR

Almost any beer, cider or wine will turn itself into vinegar naturally if it's left uncovered during the brewing stage so that fruit flies (also known as vinegar flies) can get in. They tend to fall in and drown, which doesn't look too attractive, but at least the presence of bodies warns you what's happened. If you aren't too squeamish, you could simply strain the bodies out and bottle the liquid when it's finished fermenting, rather than let it go to waste.

But any batch of homebrew cider or wine can be deliberately turned into vinegar; it's a good way to use up a batch that's 'gone sour', perhaps because equipment wasn't properly sterilised, or bacteria has found a way in somehow or, if you prefer, you can make vinegar from perfectly good red or white wine, or cider.

Soak some clean birch twigs in good-quality 'bought' vinegar for a few hours. Then drain them off and pack them loosely into a funnel, which is stood in the neck of a cleaned and sterilised bottle. Pour ready-made red or white wine, cider (or sherry, for a particularly posh vinegar) or a batch of homebrew cider or wine that's 'gone sour', slowly through the funnel so that it runs all over the vinegar-soaked twigs, and picks up the vinegar bacteria from them en route. Cap the bottle securely. It should very soon start to taste acidic, like a bought vinegar, but you can test it by pouring a little over a slice of cucumber (just enough to cover it) and leaving it out in the kitchen for a couple of days. If it goes mouldy your vinegar isn't acid enough, so it won't keep for long (maybe only for a week or two in the fridge), though if it tastes okay it may well be fine to use over the next week or two in salad dressings.

COUNTRY WINES

Rural people have been making country wines for a long time, using all sorts of locally sourced ingredients instead of grapes: wayside flowers (cowslip, dandelion or elderflower), berries from the hedgerows (elderberry, blackberry), or fruit from the garden (gooseberries, etc), and also more unlikely ingredients such as wallflowers, oak leaves, pumpkins or pea pods. It has to be said, some country wines prove to be rather an acquired taste (pea pod in particular). Results can be rather variable and usually improve significantly with practice – and with keeping. Many a novice has abandoned several bottles of country wine at the back of the shed when their first taste proved a bit 'iffy', only to find years later that the stuff had matured very well – this is particularly true of elderberry, which really needs to be 'laid down' for several years before you drink it.

I can't advocate picking wildflowers to make wine, but surplus garden fruit and any bought cheaply at a farm shop are all good wine-making ingredients, plus dandelions from your lawn (just don't pick them if they have been doused in weedkiller or other chemicals). Rosehips make a particularly good wine, which isn't over-sweet (a common fault with many country wines). One of the great successes, when you can pick the flowers from your own garden or nearby hedgerows, is elderflower champagne (or, as we should probably call it nowadays, sparkling elderflower wine, which doesn't have quite the same ring).

Although home winemaking has taken a big dip in popularity over the last twenty years, you can still find specialist home-brewing supply shops that sell the equipment needed. It doesn't take much to get started. But if you aren't using winemaking 'kits', you need to find a good book for advice on how to brew your own because there isn't one stand-ard formula you can apply to every fruit, flower, berry (or pea pod) to produce good wine.

OTHER TRADITIONAL COUNTRY DRINKS

Wine isn't the only way of converting surplus fruit or hedgerow crops into drinks. You can use elderflowers to make a country cordial which is very tasty and entirely non-alcoholic. When I was a lad, a lot of families brewed their own ginger beer and kept what they called a 'ginger beer plant', which wasn't horticultural at all, but rather a yeast culture that was kept going and used in batches.

Now that fruit growing is the latest gardening craze, all sorts of people are looking for novel ways to use surplus crops – one of which is to make your own liqueurs. Sloe gin is an old country favourite that's enjoying a comeback and is easily made using either sloes (the fruit of the blackthorn bush), or their close relatives bullaces, or damsons. The same basic technique of immersing fruits in spirits can be used to make plum brandy, or mulberry, quince, cranberry or raspberry vodka, and so on. It's a great way of using smallish quantities or unusual fruit to make something a bit special.

HOW TO MAKE ELDERFLOWER CHAMPAGNE

Start as if you were making elderflower wine. Take a one-pint jug and loosely fill it almost to the top with fully open fresh elderflowers, snipped from their stalks. Weigh them – this volume should give you 75 grams (3 ounces); if not, pick a few more.

Place the flowers in a large polythene bucket (the sort sold especially for winemaking, which can withstand heat) or a large heavy-based saucepan. Boil 4½ litres (1 gallon) of water, then pour it over the flowers and add 1.5 kilograms (3½ pounds) white sugar, 250 grams (½ pounds) chopped raisins – old ones left over from Christmas are fine for this job – and the juice of three lemons.

Leave the mixture to cool, and when the temp-erature drops to 21°C (70°F) – which is when you can comfortably stick a finger into it – add wine yeast, one teaspoonful of grape tannin and some yeast nutrient (buy this from any good winemaking supply shop). Cover the container with a lid or a thick, clean cloth and set aside in a warmish place.

After a week or so, when vigorous fermentation takes place, funnel the liquid into a clean, sterilised demijohn and fit it with an air-lock (fermentation trap). Stand it in a warmish place where the temp-erature stays fairly even. When the liquid clears, siphon it into a second demijohn, leaving the sediment behind. You'll need to do this a couple more times over the next 2–3 months until the wine is ready to bottle.

Now, you could wait until it's completely stopped fermenting, and no more sediment sinks to the bottom, then simply bottle it up as elderflower wine. But to turn it into champagne, you need to catch it while it's still forming a little light sediment (showing that the yeast is slightly active) and siphon it off into thick bottles designed to withstand the pressure that builds up inside.

(You could save up used champagne bottles to re-use, but be aware that these are very tricky to secure – you need to wire the tops of the corks down to stop them being blown out by the pressure inside. Alternatively, use strong, thick, flip-top bottles, of the sort that are sold for making beer or ginger beer. Larger versions with clear glass are available for a variety of uses in homebrew shops.)

Store the bottles on their sides in a wine rack for the next six months. The results are not terribly predictable, but that's part of the fun. The contents of some bottles will be flat like normal wine, whilst it's not unknown for the odd bottle in a batch to explode if the contents start fermenting too vigorously again – so be warned and keep them out of harm's way.

HOW TO MAKE ELDERFLOWER CORDIAL

Pick seven large heads of elderflowers, shake them to remove any bugs and 'bits', and put them in a large bowl.

Use a potato peeler to remove the rind from one small lemon in thin strips (after scrubbing it first); add this to the elderflower heads, then thinly slice the peeled lemon and add that to the bowl of flowers too.

In a saucepan, heat up half a kilo (one pound) of white granulated sugar with ⅓ litre (⅔ pint) of water, and when the sugar has dissolved, set it aside to cool.

Once cool, pour the syrup over the flowers and fruit, and stir well to coat them in the liquid. Some recipes call for 20 g rams (¾ ounce) citric acid to be stirred in at this stage; it acts as a slight preservative but for my taste it makes the mixture too acidic. If you prefer to leave it out, add more lemon juice instead, to taste. Cover the bowl securely with a large plate or several thicknesses of clean cotton cloth and put the bowl in a cool place for 24 hours, then strain and pour it into a clean, sterilised bottle. The cordial is ready to use straight away; dilute the 'neat' cordial with water to taste.

Elderflower cordial keeps in the fridge for several weeks. It can also be frozen in small portions in an ice-cube tray, and then a couple of the still-frozen cubes can be dropped straight into a glass of chilled sparkling water to make a brilliant instant summer drink.

HOW TO MAKE MEAD

Mead is one of our oldest country wines. It is honey wine, which was traditionally made by cottagers who kept their own bees. Some eighteenth-century authors advised adding herbs and/or spices to turn basic mead into a more invigorating tonic drink.

Today mead is sometimes found for sale at country shows and food fairs, though it's not very popular – people are usually worried that it's going to be terribly sweet. It's rather extravagant to make if you have to buy the honey, but beekeepers still make their own to enjoy during the winter.

Add four pounds of honey to a gallon of water in a large saucepan or jam-making pan, bring it to the boil, and when it cools down, stir in the juice of a lemon and an orange, add a teaspoonful each of yeast, yeast nutrient and pectin enzyme, then funnel the lot into a clean demijohn and fit an air lock. Wait until it stops bubbling, showing that fermentation has stopped and all the sugar from the honey has been converted to alcohol, so the wine won't be too sweet. Then bottle it, and 'lay it down' for at least a year – it improves with keeping.

HOW TO MAKE SLOE OR DAMSON GIN

Pick 1.5 kilos (3 pounds) of sloes, bullaces or damsons, prick them thoroughly all over or put them in the freezer for a few days so the cells break down enough to let the juice leak out. You'll also need 1 ½ kilos (3 pounds) of white granulated sugar.

Take a large glass screw-top jar (an old-fashioned sweet jar is about the right size) and fill it with alternate layers of fruit and sugar until you have filled it right up to just below the top, then top it up to the rim with gin. (It takes roughly a litre/1 ¾ pints; there's no need to buy a fancy kind, supermarket own-label is fine.)

Screw the lid on the jar and stand it in a cool, dark place for 3–4 months, turning it gently every day (but don't shake it) until all the sugar dissolves, then strain off the gin into a clean screw-top bottle.

Drink the gin 'neat' as a liqueur, or add a shot to sparkling wine or homemade elderflower champagne for a fresh-tasting cocktail. Meanwhile, the 'spent' fruit left behind in the jar can be used to make delicious and faintly alcoholic pies or crumbles. For me, damson gin is the best since it is not quite so 'dry' as that made from sloes.

HOW TO MAKE ROSEHIP WINE

This is a good way to make use of the large, plentiful hips of Rosa rugosa if you grow the plant as a hedge in your garden, but it's also very good made with wild rosehips picked from the countryside – just avoid places close to busy roads because of the traffic fumes and dust.

Pick the rosehips after the first frost if possible, or else store them in the freezer until you're ready to use them – this helps break the cells down so the juice is released more easily, though it's not absolutely essential. You'll need 1 kilo (2 pounds) of hips to make 4½ litres (1 gallon) of wine.

Put the rosehips through a coarse mincer, or crush them up a bit in a bucket using a piece of wood, then place them in the bottom of a large brewing bucket. Add 1½ kilos (3 pounds) of white sugar, then pour 4½ litres (1 gallon) of boiling water over the top and stir well. When it's cooled enough to comfortably stick a finger in, add a teaspoonful each of yeast, yeast nutrient and pectin enzyme (all available from winemaker suppliers).

Put the lid on the bucket or cover the top with a thick clean cloth and keep it in a warm place, stirring once or twice a day, until the vigorous fermentation calms down, then strain it into a demijohn.

Three months later, siphon it into a clean demijohn, leaving the sediment behind in the bottom of the old one, and repeat this process again after a further three months. Bottle and cork.

PRESERVES

The traditional way of preserving sudden gluts of summer fruit was by turning it into jam or jelly. Then in midwinter, when Seville oranges (the rather ugly-looking, bitter-tasting sort) came into season, country housewives would also make marmalade. Although home preserving reached its peak during the last war and immediately afterwards, when all sorts of luxury foods were in short supply, it is making a comeback today, now that so many gardeners are growing fruit again.

Since all fruits are different, you can't simply use a standard formula for everything; there are thousands of different recipes. All sorts of fruits and berries can be used to make traditional jams or jellies to use on toast, bread and butter or scones, or as ingredients for desserts, but some of the sharper-tasting berries, such as cranberries, make jellies that are traditionally used as accompaniments to meat, poultry or game. And if you only have small quantities of several different fruits, it's quite okay to blend them to make a mixed fruit jam.

Jam-making is quite scientific; the sugar acts as a preservative, and the pectin plus natural acids present in the fruit 'set' the jam or jelly when it has been boiled long enough. Fruit that's naturally low in pectin (such as strawberries and blackberries) needs to have pectin added. You can buy it in bottles at supermarkets and specialist cook shops, or buy special jam-making sugar which has already had pectin added. Otherwise the recipe needs to include some apples or redcurrants which are naturally rich in pectin, and if the fruit is not very acidic (again, strawberries spring to mind), the recipe may also call for lemon juice.

To make jam you need a preserving pan (which is a large, squat, metal bucket with a large handle and a lip for pouring), a jam-maker's thermometer and a wooden spoon with a very long handle so that you can stir without risk of boiling jam splashing up onto your hand. Prepare a supply of clean jam jars, which can be secondhand but must be well washed and sterilised just before you need them. (The best way to do this is to heat them slowly in the oven or a large saucepan of water for 20 minutes to kill any germs. The jars need to be hot when you put the molten jam in them, otherwise the glass would crack.) You'll then need some jam-pot covers with elastic bands to hold them in place, also a supply of the waxed paper discs that sit on top of the jam before the cover goes on, and perhaps some stick-on labels on which to hand write in order to identify the finished jars. The basic technique for making jam is to boil the fruit with just the right amount of sugar (usually ½kg/1lb of fruit to ½kg/1lb of sugar), stirring all the time so that the bottom of the pan doesn't burn, and regularly removing the scum that comes to the top. A jam thermometer gives a good indication as to when the right temperature has been reached, and this needs to be maintained until the mixture reaches the point when the jam will 'set'. The traditional test is to drop a spoonful of boiling jam onto a cold plate then push it gently with your finger; if the jam forms a surface-skin that wrinkles, it will set when it's put into jars. (If jam is put into its jars before it's been boiled long enough, it won't set, so it always stays soft and runny. It still tastes nice, and makes a good sauce to pour over ice cream, or to use in cooking, it just isn't proper jam.) Nowadays microwave ovens have revolutionised the art of jam-making, as all sorts of jam can be 'thrown together' in minutes and kept in the fridge. But traditionalists still prefer doing it the 'old way'.

Jelly is like jam, but without any bits of fruit in it. It is made by cooking the fruit in water, then the mixture is tipped into a jelly bag (a large reusable bag made from very fine plastic mesh) which is suspended from a special frame – or sometimes hung from a hook in the ceiling – so the juice drips down into a pan while the solid fruit, skins and pips are kept out. It's important not to be tempted to squeeze the bag to force more juice out because this makes the juice cloudy, which means murky jelly later. (Mum hung her crab apple jelly bag at the bottom of the cellar steps and woe-betide us if we touched it!) The juice is then measured and the right amount of sugar added (usually 1¾ litres/a pint of juice to ½kg/1lb of sugar), then it's boiled until the correct temperature is reached, and the setting point is achieved as for jam. Some fruits are traditionally made into jelly rather than jam; redcurrants in particular, since the small pips are irritating when they get stuck between your teeth. Apple jelly is the basis of traditional mint jelly, eaten with lamb – only here the fruit is cooked in a mixture of water and white vinegar instead of plain water. The same recipe can be adapted to use with other herbs such as thyme, rosemary or sage or a mixture of your favourites.

A conserve is something different again; correctly speaking it's a thick, sweet fruit syrup rather like a jelly that's not quite set properly, with whole pieces of fruit suspended in it – it's very rich and unctuous. Conserves are traditionally eaten on scones with clotted cream, or used as tart fillings, though they are also brilliant spooned over ice cream. Raspberries and strawberries are the fruits most often used in this way, but if you grow something special, such as mulberries or Japanese wineberries, it's worth using the same recipe for those – but using only the most perfect fruit.

Marmalade is often thought of as 'orange jam' – at least, by people who aren't British. The original marmalade was quince marmalade, but it was nothing like the spread for breakfast toast that we know today. It was thick and chewy, more like fruit-flavoured rubber, which was sliced up and eaten as sweets for special occasions, rather like us having a box

of chocs today. Quince marmalade arrived in this country when Edward
I was king (1272–1307), all because his Spanish wife, Eleanor of Castile,
missed her traditional taste of home. Quince trees were brought over
and grown especially for the job in the grounds of the Tower of London,
which was a royal residence at the time. Orange marmalade as we know it
today is thought to have come about as a result of another royal marriage.
Catherine of Aragon, Henry VIII's first wife, missed the oranges from
her native Spain and since fresh oranges didn't last long enough to reach
Britain in good condition (due to the lengthy overland and sea journey
involved), they were preserved specially for her benefit – and marmalade
was invented. It's basically orange jelly with 'bits' of coarsely chopped or
thinly sliced cooked orange peel added. You can also make lime marmalade, or indeed use any citrus fruit you fancy.

HOW TO MAKE MARMALADE

Take 900 grams (2 pounds) of seville oranges and one lemon; remove the
peel thinly, making sure you don't take any of the bitter white pith with it
(use a potato peeler). Slice the pieces of peel into thin strips, then cut the
fruits in half and squeeze them to remove as much juice as possible.

Put 1.9 litres (4 pints) of water, plus the juice and peel of all the fruit,
into a preserving pan. Tie the pith and pips up in a piece of clean white
cotton cloth and drop that into the pan too. Bring the mixture almost to
the boil then let it simmer for two hours without a lid.

At the end of that time the peel should feel soft if stabbed with the tip
of a knife. (If you like a darker, stronger flavoured 'Oxford'-type marmalade, keep boiling the mixture for longer, until it's as dark as you want, but
don't let it burn.) Then lift the parcel of pips and pith out of the liquid and
stir in 1¾ kilos (4 pounds) of sugar. Heat gently and stir well.

Once the sugar has completely dissolved, skim off any scum that's formed on the surface, bring the mixture to the boil, and continue to boil rapidly (still stirring and removing any scum) for about fifteen minutes. Test to see if it 'sets' in the same way as jam (see page 78).

When the marmalade is ready, leave it standing – off the heat – for about fifteen minutes, and stir it well before putting it in clean, sterilised pots so that the shreds of peel are mixed evenly. Pot, cover and label it the same way as for jam.

HOW TO MAKE ROSE PETAL JAM

This is a real luxury of the sort that can't be bought in shops; it was once a great favourite with Victorian ladies and it's very do-able when you grow your own roses. Dark red, strongly scented roses are the favourites for this job.

Pick the roses when they are just fully open, ideally early in the morning before they dry out too much in the sun. Pull the petals from the heads, then use scissors to remove the white bit at the base of each petal, as it tastes bitter. You'll need 225 grams (8 ounces) of petals, which looks like quite a lot.

Put the petals in a bowl and sprinkle them with the same weight of caster sugar, then cover the bowl (cling film is ideal) and leave for eight hours so the scent of the roses flavours the sugar.

Put 1.2 litres (2 pints) of water and the juice of two lemons in a large saucepan, then add 225 grams (8 ounces) of sugar and heat the liquid gently so the sugar dissolves slowly. Stir in the rose petals and all the sugar that's with them, and simmer gently on a low heat for twenty minutes.

Turn up the heat and bring the mixture to the boil, then let it boil vigorously until it thickens, which takes about five minutes, stirring constantly to stop it sticking to the pan. When cool enough, pot the mixture into small, clean, sterilised jars. A pot of rose petal jam with a pretty label makes a very attractive gift, and with any luck the recipient will appreciate all the trouble you took!

HOW TO MAKE STRAWBERRY CONSERVE

To make a conserve you need fairly small, fully ripe fruit that's all the same size and is perfect in both shape and condition. The strawberries then need the green hulls pulled out along with the plug that goes down into the centre of the fruit.

Use 450 grams (1 pound) of fruit to the same quantity of sugar. Place alternate layers of strawberries and sugar in a bowl, cover with a clean cloth and leave for 24 hours, so the sugar draws a lot of the juice out of the fruit.

Put the lot into a large saucepan and bring it slowly to the boil, then boil rapidly for five minutes, stirring all the time so the jam doesn't stick to the bottom of the pan. Return the jam to the bowl and leave it in a cool place for another 24 hours.

Return the cooled jam to the saucepan, heat slowly to boiling point then boil rapidly for ten minutes, again stirring all the time. This time, leave the mixture to cool slightly then pot it up into clean, sterilised jars the same way as for jam.

You can use the same technique for making conserves from other berries, such as blackberries and loganberries, but this is an especially good way to use up surplus raspberries.

There is simply nothing to compare with home-made strawberry conserve and clotted cream spread on a warm, freshly baked scone. Heaven!

HOW TO MAKE CRAB APPLE JELLY

The traditional favourite crab apple variety for this job is 'John Downie', whose large, red-flushed, flask-shaped fruits produce the most delicious aromatic pink jelly, but any crab apples can be used; use all one variety, or a mixture.

Halve 900 grams (2 pounds) of washed, ripe crab apples, then bring them to the boil in 1.2 litres (2 pints) of water in a large saucepan or preserving pan and simmer gently until all the fruit is tender (but don't be tempted to mash them, or the juice, and later the jelly, will become cloudy).

Tip the cooked fruity goo into a jelly bag and leave it to drip over a bowl for several hours to collect the juice. Strain the collected juice to remove any bits.

Measure the strained juice and weigh out 450 grams (1 pound) of sugar for each 600ml (1 pint) of juice. Put the juice and sugar back in the pan and heat gently until the sugar dissolves. Raise the heat and boil the liquid until a blob of the syrupy mixture 'jells' when dropped onto a chilled plate.

Allow the jelly to cool slightly, then pour it into sterilised jars and cover it in the same way as for jam.

This jelly is brilliant on bread and butter or on toast, though a spoonful also goes well with pork or cold turkey.

HOW TO MAKE LEMON CURD

Lemon curd is a great country favourite that's not often made at home today. It is traditionally used as an alternative to jam on bread or toast, or as a filling for a Victoria sponge cake, or in lemon curd tarts. But unlike jam, lemon curd does not keep for long – only a month – so it's a good idea to make small quantities and store it in a cool place, and once a jar has been opened, keep it in the fridge.

Put the grated rind and juice of two large lemons into a heatproof bowl with 225 grams (8 ounces) of caster sugar, 100 grams (4 ounces) of butter, and three beaten egg yolks.

Stand the bowl in a saucepan of hot water kept over a low heat so that it barely simmers, and stir constantly.

As the sugar dissolves, the egg yolks will gradually thicken the mixture. When it's thick enough to coat the back of a spoon and all the sugar has dissolved completely, strain the mixture through a sieve and pot it up into small jars in the same way as jam.

HOW TO MAKE MINT JELLY

Roughly chop 1.3 kilos (2½ pounds) of cooking apples (don't bother peeling or coring them, but cut out any bruises or bad bits).

Put them into a large saucepan or preserving pan with 600ml (1 pint) of water and a few sprigs of mint (spearmint or apple mint are best – or try eau de cologne mint for an unusual, fragrant twist). Bring to the boil, then reduce the heat and leave to simmer for 45 minutes, stirring regularly so the mixture doesn't stick to the bottom of the pan. Add 600ml (1 pint) of distilled white vinegar and bring back to the boil for five minutes.

Tip the mixture into a jelly bag set over a bowl and leave to drip overnight. Measure the juice you've collected and put it back in the preserving pan with 450 grams (1 pound) of sugar to every 600ml (1 pint) of juice.

Heat it slowly, stirring all the time to help the sugar dissolve, until it reaches boiling point, then boil it rapidly for 10 minutes. Test a spoonful using the cold plate method to see if it's ready to set, then skim the scum off the top with a slotted spoon and stir in four tablespoons of fresh chopped mint.

If you like your mint jelly to be green all the way through, the same as the 'bought' version, add three or four drops of green food colour, then cool and put in sterilised jars.

PICKLING

Before it was possible to bottle, can or freeze surplus summer crops, they were often preserved by pickling. Country people have traditionally pickled all sorts of vegetables in vinegar, as a means of storing them to use in winter. Pickled onions, pickled red cabbage, pickled beetroot and pickled gherkins (which are special varieties of miniature cucumbers) are old favourites. In the West Country it was traditional to pickle apples. But anyone whose garden yielded a surplus of assorted vegetables would often make picca-lilli to preserve them in a distinctive bright yellow spicy-mustard-flavoured sauce, and at the end of the summer a glut of unripe tomatoes would be turned into chutney. Well, it was just another way of making sure that crops didn't go to waste, especially after all the hard work of growing them.

The principle of pickling is that the acidity of the vinegar kills off bacteria. Any vinegar can be used. Malt vinegar is the cheapest and often sold at farm shops in autumn alongside nets of shallots or small pickling onions at the end of the summer, but it has rather a harsh, astringent taste for some people's liking. Distilled vinegar, which is clear, has less of the strong vinegary taste, and doesn't 'colour' the finished pickles. But enthusiasts often prefer the finer flavour of white wine vinegar; if you make homemade wine, you could make your own wine vinegar (see page 69).

Most pickle-makers like to flavour the vinegar they'll use for pickling with spices; make spiced vinegar a month or so before making pickle so the flavour has time to intensify. Simply add the whole spices (a cinnamon stick, 6 cloves, 6 peppercorns, a bay leaf and a teaspoonful each of mustard seeds and allspice berries to a 1.2 litre (2 pint) container of vinegar) and leave for 4–8 weeks, then strain the spices out before proceeding with your favourite pickle recipe.

To make pickles you'll need a large saucepan with a tight-fitting lid and a supply of clean screw-top jam jars that need to be sterilised in the same way as you do when making jam (see page 78). Country people always used to do their pickling in an outhouse down the garden, but when you can't, it's a good idea to shut yourself in the kitchen with a window or the back door open when you have a pickling session. Boiling vinegar is a never-to-be-forgotten smell that will percolate the whole house and linger, given half a chance.

HOW TO MAKE QUICK PICKLED CUCUMBERS

This is a good way to use up a sudden glut of cucumbers during the summer; the result is very much like gherkins.

Peel a couple of cucumbers and cut them into 'fingers' 7.5 cm (3 inches) long or else make long, slanting slices about 5 mm (¼ inch) thick.

Pour 600 ml (1 pint) of spiced vinegar into a large saucepan and bring to the boil; cider vinegar is a good one to use for this job. You might like to add a teaspoonful of sugar to make a slightly more sweet-and-sour flavour, and/or add a sprig or two of fresh dill.

Drop the cucumber pieces into the pan, making sure they are all completely covered. (If they don't all fit, use the same pickling liquid to make two or three batches, one after another.)

Bring the vinegar back to the boil and boil gently for 4–5 minutes, until the cucumber turns slightly 'glassy' looking, then remove with a slotted spoon and do a second batch (if you have more cucumber pieces left).

Pack the cucumbers tightly into a large wide-necked jar (the sort that 'bought' gherkins come in is ideal) that's been sterilised in hot water then, while the jar is still hot, top it up with the hot spiced vinegar, screw the lid on and leave to cool. When cold, keep the finished pickles in the fridge and use within two weeks.

HOW TO MAKE PICCALILLI

Cut up a mixture of vegetables into uniform bite-sized pieces; you can use cauliflower, cucumbers or gherkins, onions, white cabbage, marrows, celery, broad, runner or French beans, peppers or green tomatoes; you'll need 1.5 kilos (3 pounds) in total. (Make double the quantity if you have enough veg.)

Make up a brine solution by dissolving 225 grams (8 ounces) of cooking salt in 1.9 litres (4 pints) of water; put this in a large jar or bucket and put the prepared vegetable pieces into it, pressing them down well. Put a plate with a weight on top to keep them immersed, and leave them overnight to soak.

The next morning, rinse the veg in fresh water and leave them to drain. Meanwhile mix one and a half teaspoons of ground turmeric with two teaspoonfuls of dry English mustard powder, two teaspoonfuls of ground ginger, and 150 grams (5 ounces) of white sugar; stir this into 850 ml (1½ pints) of distilled vinegar and add the prepared vegetables; bring to the boil and allow to simmer for 20 minutes.

Use a slotted spoon to transfer the veg to clean, sterilised, hot jars, then stir 25 grams (1 ounces) of cornflower into a teaspoonful of cold vinegar and stir this into the hot vinegar mix remaining in the pan. Stir it while you bring it back to the boil for a few minutes; this will thicken it slightly.

Let it cool slightly before pouring it over the veg in the jars, filling them up to the rim. Screw the lids on straight away; store in a cool place (a pantry is perfect) and let it stand for at least six weeks before starting to use the pickle, so the vegetables can absorb the spicy flavours – they should still remain slightly crunchy.

HOW TO MAKE GREEN TOMATO CHUTNEY

Chop around a kilo (2 pounds) green tomatoes, ½ kilo (1 pound) of cooking apples and ¼ kilo (8 ounces) of onions into small pieces, then add ¼ kilo (8 ounces) sultanas (whole or minced, or a mixture of each). Put them in a large saucepan with 300ml (½ pint) of spiced vinegar. Tie up 15 grams (½ ounce) of whole, mixed pickling spices in a piece of muslin or clean white cotton cloth, and throw that into the mixture. Bring slowly to the boil, then add ½ kilo (1 pound) of brown sugar and another 300ml (½ pint) of vinegar. Boil gently until the mixture is thick enough to leave a depression when you run your wooden spoon through it. Remove the pickle parcel, then ladle the chutney into hot, sterilised jars and screw the tops on while hot.

DAIRY WORK

It's really very easy to make cream, soft cheese, yoghurt and ice-cream, and if you're prepared for a bit more time, effort and equipment, you can even make butter and hard cheeses. If you don't have access to surplus milk, you can always use cartons of milk bought from a supermarket.

The big secret when working with dairy produce is to keep all the utensils sterile and pay great attention to detail; a small error in temperature is enough to allow the wrong kind of bacteria to thrive while the right one doesn't. But with patience and a bit of practice, you can achieve very good results. There are also various electrical gadgets that take away a lot of the hard graft and guesswork.

CREAM, BUTTER AND ICE CREAM

Cream is the fat-rich part of the milk which floats to the surface. If you had bottles of gold-top Channel-island milk delivered to your doorstep, years ago, you'll remember the cream forming a layer at the top of the bottle – where it was often collared by bluetits who pecked through the foil lid to pinch it. Dairymaids of the past did much the same thing on a larger scale. To collect cream they poured whole milk into a wide shallow bowl and left it to stand in a cool place – the dairy. The cream rose to the top and was then skimmed off with a special spoon with holes in it to retain the cream but let the milk drain through. Today you could do it the same way or else use a mechanical separator, which works by centrifugal force; devices of this sort are sold by smallholders' supply shops, and they'll extract almost twice as much cream from a given volume of milk as you could by hand.

The cream collected from the top of the milk can be used just as it is. Double cream is the thickest and has the highest fat content; this floats to the very top of the bowl. Single cream is thinner in consistency as it contains rather less fat, so it's usually the second layer to be skimmed off. Clotted cream is cream that's had a special culture added to thicken it (available from smallholders' suppliers). What's left behind after all the cream has been skimmed off is skimmed milk or semi-skimmed milk, again depending on the percentage of fat it contains. In the past this was usually fed to the pigs, but today there's a big demand for it with health- and diet-conscious folk.

If you have enough cream you can use it for making butter and ice cream, but it takes a lot of milk to do so, since even the richest full-fat milk only contains about 5 per cent cream, by volume.

Commercially, butter is made by adding a lactic acid culture to cream, but at home you can simply save up cream that's been separated from the milk over several days, keep it at room temperature, and add each new batch to it every day. By then the original cream will be quite 'ripe' due to the natural bacteria that develop, which helps give butter its distinctive flavour. Wait for 12 hours after adding your last lot of cream, before churning it to make butter. You could use a genuine antique butter churn, though it normally needs quite a large quantity of cream to operate properly; smaller hand-operated versions that look like a glass jar with a paddle inside are available from smallholders' supply shops. Otherwise you could use a food mixer with the blades set to a fairly low speed, since all that's necessary is to agitate the cream fairly vigorously and continuously.

When you start churning, nothing happens for a while, then suddenly the fat in the cream 'clumps together' forming yellowy globules floating in buttermilk. At this point drain off the buttermilk, leaving the blobs of butter behind, then put some cold water into the churn, and churn the lot again. This washes all the milk out of the butter, which stops it tasting sour or turning rancid. Keep replacing the dirty water with clean cold water and churn again until the water stays completely clear. Then tip your lump of butter onto a clean board, sprinkle it lightly with a little salt and use traditional-type wooden butter pats (which look rather like small wooden paddles) to mix the butter up. The idea is to make sure the salt is distributed evenly throughout and to squeeze out any remaining water. After working it for a while, bash it into a rectangle and wrap it in waxed paper – the saltier the butter, the longer it keeps – but if you don't want over-salty butter, or you aren't sure you've pressed all the water out, then play safe and store it in the freezer, where it keeps in perfect condition for a year or more.

MILK FOR MAKING DAIRY PRODUCE

Cream is the starting point for producing butter. Traditionally, anyone wanting to make butter would keep a breed of cow that was well known for producing milk with a high fat content, (ideally Jersey or Guernsey), since this naturally produces a lot more cream, though any cows' milk will produce some cream.

Goats' milk can't be used for making cream or butter, however, because the globules of fat it contains are too small and too evenly distributed to separate out in the same way as happens with cows' milk. It can be used to make other dairy products such as soft cheese and yoghurt instead.

HOW TO MAKE YOGHURT

If you're using home-grown milk, start by boiling it for a few minutes to kill off any unwanted bacteria. Use a thermometer to follow progress as it cools; at between 25°C and 35°C (77 and 95°F) stir in a 'starter'. You might be able to buy a freeze-dried culture of yoghurt bacillus, but the easiest way is to use 2–3 teaspoonfuls of live, natural (i.e. plain, unflavoured) yoghurt. (Live yoghurt is sometimes available from health food shops.)

The mixture then needs to be kept at a steady temperature for several hours, until the milk has thickened and turned to a creamy constituency. (The exact timing is a tad variable, depending on whether you want a thinner, milder tasting yoghurt or a thicker, stronger one, and how warm you keep it. About 21–25°C/70–77°F is ideal.) There are various ways to keep the cultured milk at the right temperature. Some people leave it in a bowl covered with a close-fitting lid in the airing cupboard, or you might prefer to use an electric yoghurt maker, which consists of several pots that sit inside a covered, temperature-regulated container. But one of the simplest ways is to use a wide-necked stainless steel thermos flask; fill the interior with boiling water and leave for five minutes to kill germs etc, then tip the water out and after a minute or so (while it's still warm), pour in enough of the cultured milk mixture to fill it up to just below the top. If you do this early in the evening you'll have yoghurt ready for breakfast next morning.

Once you have a batch of your own live yoghurt, it will keep for several days in a bowl in the fridge – mix it with fresh or stewed fruit to taste, or use plain yoghurt as the basis for dishes such as tandoori chicken, or raita and tzatziki (grated cucumber in yoghurt, eaten with curries or Greek food).

But before you do anything else with a fresh batch, take several spoonfuls from it to use for starting your next batch. Don't, whatever you do, try to use fruit-flavoured yoghurt (or indeed any yoghurt containing any other flavourings) as a 'starter', as whatever you've used will introduce unwanted bacteria or mould, which will ruin the yoghurt.

BUTTERMILK

Buttermilk has a very characteristic flavour; it is basically skimmed milk (since all the fat has been taken out in the form of butter), but with a richer, more buttery flavour due to the lactic acid it contains. Some people like to drink buttermilk, but it's brilliant for making scones and can also be used in other forms of baking. Traditionally any surplus buttermilk was fed to pigs or poultry.

HOW TO MAKE REAL ICE CREAM

Ice cream is something we take very much for granted today, and until quite recently no one would ever have thought of making their own. But nowadays electric ice cream makers have revolutionised the process – just follow the directions and the device simultaneously freezes and churns the ingredients to produce perfect ice cream effortlessly. What's more, you can incorporate your own home-grown fruit, or experiment with ideas of your own. (Most machines also make sorbets, too.)

The ice cream we buy in the shops today is mostly water ice, but anyone who has their own Channel Island house-cow and a well-stocked henhouse can experience real ice cream, the way Mrs Beeton made it. (Just don't count the calories!)

Boil 600ml (1 pint) of cream and 300ml (½ pint) of full-fat milk with half a vanilla pod for a few minutes, then stir this into a bowl containing the yolks of four eggs that have been beaten with 100 grams (4 ounces) caster sugar.

Tip the lot back into the saucepan and heat it very gently over a low heat until it thickens. Strain, add a few drops of vanilla extract if needed to intensify the flavour, then pour into a freezerproof container and freeze.

Remove from the freezer several times to stir the layer of frozen crystals that form round the inside of the container into the unfrozen mixture in the centre, until it is all even.

CHEESE MAKING

Soft cheese, also known as curd cheese, is by far the easiest and fastest sort of cheese to make, and the one that's most practical for people to make at home. It doesn't keep for very long, so aim to use it within a few days. You can use either cows' or goats' milk for this.

Hard cheeses take a lot more time, equipment and skill to 'get right'; most smallholders stick to cream cheese and yoghurt and leave the more technical stuff to specialist cheese-makers (who, it has to be said, need to comply with a lot of hygiene standards and legislation if they want to sell their produce). It takes about 4.5 litres (1 gallon) of whole milk (i.e. milk that includes the cream) to make 450g (1lb) of cheese, but if you are interested, this is how it's done.

First the milk is curdled by adding rennet (an enzyme extracted from the stomach of a calf, though vegetarian rennet is also available). Most cheese-makers will also add a starter of lactic acid bacteria (from cheese-making supply firms, or a culture obtained from a fellow cheese-maker). When the milk sets firmly, it's cut into 2cm (¾in) squares and the whole lot is warmed very slowly to 38°C (100°F) and stirred, before being left to ripen slightly. The acidity is tested regularly, and at just the right stage the mixture is strained to separate the curds from the whey. The curds are then broken up into pieces the size of walnuts, and salt is added at 25g (1oz) salt to every 1¾kg (4lbs) of curd.

Next comes the cheese mould. This is a cylinder of metal or wood which looks something like an old-fashioned cake tin with a removable base, but deeper. This is lined with cheesecloth, leaving the surplus fabric hanging over the outside of the container, and packed full of pieces of curd. When it is full to the top, the overhanging edges of cheesecloth are folded back over the top and pressure is applied. Regular cheesemakers use a proper cheese press, but if you're having a go at home it's possible to put a plate the right size to fit inside the top and stand half a dozen bricks on top. Six hours later, the weights are removed, then the cheese is taken out and unwrapped. The cheesecloth is rinsed out in clean water, then the cheese is turned upside down, rewrapped, and replaced in its mould. More pressure is applied this time, up to a hundredweight (112lbs). After two days the cheese is turned again and the pressure increased to half a ton (if using a cheese press) or as much as you can balance on top. After another two days, the cheese is removed, wrapped with strips of clean cotton held in place by a flour-and-water paste (which will eventually form the rind), and sat on a slatted shelf in a well-ventilated cheese room (at home, a pantry is ideal) at a temperature of 13–16°C (55–60°F) to dry and mature.

Cheeses are turned upside down every day for a week, and after that twice a week, while they mature. If the outside starts to turn mouldy, it is brushed clean. After two weeks, whole cheeses are sometimes brushed all over with melted wax to help them 'keep' more reliably. Professional cheese-makers have their own recipes for producing a range of blue-veined cheeses, Cheddar-like cheeses and such like.

HOW TO MAKE CURD CHEESE

First you need to turn the milk sour; in warm weather it'll often do this all on its own, due to bacteria present in the air, but to help things along add a spoonful or two of live natural yoghurt.

Leave the milk in a warm place (the airing cupboard or the cupboard that encloses the central-heating boiler is ideal); it will take between one and four days to thicken – the exact time will vary according to the warmth and other conditions.

When the milk has set semi-firm (wobble the container slightly to see how it's doing, it should behave a bit like a jelly), pour the whole lot into a large sieve lined with a couple of thicknesses of muslin, cheesecloth or clean cotton fabric that's previously been sterilised by boiling for a few minutes, and stand the whole thing over a bowl to catch the drips. If you're only doing a small quantity, stand it in the fridge to 'stop' the cheese ripening any more while it drips, otherwise keep it in a cool place – this would traditionally have been done in the dairy.

The clear liquid that runs through the cloth is whey; feed it to pigs or hens as it doesn't have much other use. The milk solids left behind in the cloth are basic curd cheese.

When it is thoroughly drained, which takes a good 12–24 hours, add chopped fresh herbs, garlic or ground black pepper (or any combination of your favourites to taste) to make a herby soft cheese, or simply leave it plain.

Curd cheese doesn't keep for long, so aim to use it within 2–3 days. It's good on toast or in sandwiches (especially with cucumber and Marmite, or smoked salmon), but it makes brilliant homemade cheesecake.

If you are feeling flush or you have a neighbour with a house cow, follow the same recipe but use double cream instead of milk – this makes cream cheese, as against the more economical and everyday curd cheese.

DIY HOT-SMOKING
OF MEAT OR FISH

Cold smoking, which produces smoked salmon, requires precise temperature control, so it's best left to a commercial smokery. Keen trout or salmon fishermen will often know of one that they can take their own catches to, to be smoked professionally and then returned to them. Hot smoking, however, is something you can do at home without too much trouble.

Take a large, deep, heavy frying pan, saucepan or wok and line the base with several layers of tin foil. Mix a couple of teaspoons of brown sugar with a couple of handfuls of rice and place this in the bottom of the pan, then sprinkle a couple of teaspoons of dry tea leaves (ideally Earl Grey) over the top – these are what will create the smoke, which will be pleasantly flavoured and nicely scented. Wedge a wooden rack or several criss-crossed wooden chopsticks in place an inch or so above the tea, rice and sugar mixture.

Choose the food to be smoked (it's usually sections of salmon fillet, or whole chicken or duck breast, but you can try other meat or fish) and sprinkle it fairly generously with salt for half an hour before you start to smoke it. Before putting it into the pan, brush off as much of the salt as you can but don't wash the food. Place it on the rack, and if smoking several pieces, space them an inch apart so the smoke can circulate. Place the lid on the pan – it needs to be a fairly close fit so the smoke stays inside – and stand it on a fairly high heat (use a hob indoors, or else a barbecue, or put it over the chimney of a chiminea in the garden) for 20 minutes. By then

it'll be cooked, with a nice smoky flavour. For a more economical version or simply to create a different flavour, use oak sawdust or hickory chippings to smoke the food over.

If you don't want the bother, or you like to do a lot of food-smoking, various ready-to-use smokers are available from kitchen shops. There are self-contained electric models also ones that look like large metal trays with lids, heated by methylated spirit burners or tea-lights underneath, which use oak or hickory sawdust to generate the smoke.

HOW TO SWEEP A CHIMNEY

In Charles Dickens's day, large country houses were heated entirely by open fires and huge interconnecting chimneys which had to be swept by small boys climbing up inside them. Cottagers meanwhile swept their own chimneys by tying a bundle of holly stems to a stone, climbing up on the roof, and dropping it down the chimney, where it found its way into the hearth below, producing clouds of soot which drifted all over the room.

Since then, most people who still had open fires employed a chimney sweep to come round with his own set of dust sheets, rods and brushes to sweep their flues annually, every autumn. But you can save the fee by doing it yourself, and it's not half as difficult – or as messy – as you'd think.

You need a set of rods and a traditional-type circular, flat flue brush; DIY centres sell them with several different heads for rodding drains as well. If you have a wood-burning stove you'll need a special head for sweeping inside the flue-liner; this is bullet-shaped and only about 10–15cm (4–6 inches) wide.

Spread a dustsheet all round the hearth as a precaution and hang one from the mantelpiece – draping it over the opening to prevent it flying into the room. Fit the brush head to the first rod and push it up into the chimney, underneath the overhanging dust sheet. Screw the next rod in place and keep pushing, using a slightly up and down motion so the sides of the chimney are scoured thoroughly as you go. You also need to twist the rods slightly in the direction that tightens them up as you push. (This is important because if you twist the wrong way or even if you don't twist at all, it's just possible that a rod or the brush head will get unscrewed and end up stuck up the chimney, where it takes a lot of shifting.)

Continue adding more rods and pushing the kit up the chimney; when you get to the last two or three rods in your bundle send an assistant outside to look at the top of the chimney to see when the brush pokes out. It won't matter too much if you push the brush out of the top of a chimney that's open to the air, but if you have a cap on top to stop birds or rain getting in, you can easily knock it off, and you need a long ladder and a head for heights to replace it. There's always a risk that a dislodged chimney-cap will fall through the conservatory roof or dislodge several roof tiles on its way down.

Once the brush is visible at the top, start pulling the whole assembly back down again, still using the same twisting motion that tightens up rather than unscrews the rods. If you do it fairly slowly you won't bring a huge rush of soot down into the hearth all at once, it'll descend as a gentle trickle. Unscrew each rod in turn until the last length with the brush on top has been safely returned, then have a good clean up and vacuum, leaving the fire good to go for another year.

HERBAL SECRETS

Herbs contain an enormous number of natural substances that the plant uses for its own protection from sun, insects, disease or predators, some of which, it turns out, also have medicinal uses when applied to humans. The medicinal properties of certain plants must originally have been discovered largely by trial and error and observation, and these discoveries were passed on down the generations by monks – the doctors of their day – and 'wise old women' in villages.

In some cases ancient herbal medicine has given us modern drugs that were used until synthetic replacements or improved modern drugs became available; for example, digitalis obtained from foxgloves was used for a long time to treat heart conditions.

But the big problem with using herbs medicinally is that the active constituents present in plants can vary from season to season, or with different growing conditions, so – unlike modern pills – it is difficult to predict accurately and precisely how much of the active ingredient you are taking.

Today, using herbs for serious medicinal purposes is best left to properly trained herbal practitioners, who usually have conventional medical training as well. However, herbs are increasingly being used at home in herbal teas, homemade toiletries and face creams, etc., (which are often believed by enthusiasts to be every bit as effective and considerably cheaper than over-packaged high-street brands) as well as for treating minor ailments and as basic first aid. A well-stocked herb garden can provide ingredients for a wide range of purposes.

One of the most useful 'herbs' for first-aid is a succulent, Aloe vera, sometimes known as the burn plant. It's a typical aloe, making a symmetrical, upright rosette of thick, fleshy leaves. It's ideal for growing in a pot on a sunny windowsill indoors, though it can be kept outside on the patio in summer. The leaves contain a thick, sticky gel which is easily squeezed out if you cut a whole, or part of, a leaf off, slice it in half lengthwise, and press it flat against a wooden chopping board with the flat of a knife. The gel can be applied 'neat' to burns, scalds, sunburn or cuts, where it forms a protective seal as well as encouraging the area to heal. The gel can also be added to homemade hand creams, etc. Houseleek (Sempervivum) leaves can be used in much the same way; they are a far older burn and scald remedy that was readily available to early cottagers as the plants often grew wild on their roofs and in nooks and crannies of rough stone walls, where rosettes had been scattered by birds.

For anyone wanting to cut down on salt in cooking, dried dill seeds, freshly finely ground and used in small quantities, makes a good substitute without raising the blood pressure.

Herbs were also once used as a tonic, supplying valuable vitamins and/or minerals. Hardy annual herbs such as chervil, parsley, sorrel and common orache (Atriplex hortensis) are naturally high in vitamin C. They were often used as spring salads by medieval cottagers for the tonic effect they produced; this was badly needed at the end of a long winter when people had lived for months on a diet of dried or otherwise preserved food which was always low in vitamin C, as they'd often be suffering from scurvy-like symptoms by then. Dandelion contains a good supply of other vitamins and minerals as well as vitamin C – the young leaves make a good salad ingredient, especially if the whole plant is blanched under a bucket for a few days before picking. Nettles, too, are rich in both vitamins and minerals; young leaves can be made into nettle tea, cooked like spinach, or made into soup. (Make a potato and onion soup using chicken stock and add a handful of chopped young nettle tops per serving when cooking, then put the mixture through a blender.)

Warts were traditionally removed by smearing them with the sap from pot marigold (Calendula officinalis) or houseleek and leaving the 'gel' to dry. Results took a while and several applications were usually recommended.

For flatulence, caraway seeds were chewed before meals; today caraway is often recommended for cooking with cabbage since the slightly aniseedy flavour goes well with it and quells any tendency to windiness. Other herbs

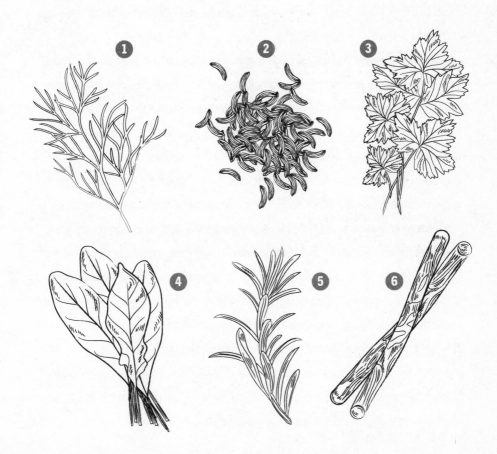

share the same reputation: dill leaves and seeds, coriander (fresh leaves or ground seeds, which are used as a traditional curry spice), also lovage seeds. But if you want to give them a try, save seeds from your own plants or use seeds bought for culinary purposes – don't use packeted seeds intended for growing since they've often been treated with fungicides.

For hiccups, try dill tea. Dill is one of the major ingredients of gripe water, which is traditionally given to babies with 'colic'.

Various oral disorders respond to herbal remedies. Treat bad breath by chewing whole dry dill seeds, or use rosemary tea as a mouthwash. To neutralise the smell of strong food, particularly garlic, on the breath, chew fresh parsley. For mouth ulcers and sore gums, use wild strawberry leaf tea (Fragaria vesca) as a mouthwash.

To help you sleep, try borage tea made by pouring a cup of boiling water over three teaspoonfuls of chopped fresh borage leaves; add a slice of lemon or a few drops of lemon juice and honey to taste. Or fill a small pillow case with dried hop flowers to make a hop pillow; inhaling the scent is meant to help you nod off. Dried lavender heads have the same reputation; you can use them in a pillow or just have a big bowl of freshly dried flower heads in your bedroom. They make the place smell nice, anyway.

For colds and sore throats, chew a stick of natural dried liquorice root; this was once sold loose from glass jars in old-fashioned sweet shops for children to eat on their way to school (it also turned our tongues an attractive shade of yellow!). Alternatively, sit with a towel over your head above a saucepan of freshly boiled water containing juniper berries, and breathe in the steam for a few minutes. Two other good old-fashioned cold remedies are sage tea and homemade onion soup – both of which are also good for laryngitis – or make an even more potent brew by mixing the two together. Warm thyme tea, used for gargling, is good for sore throats.

For catarrh and blocked sinuses, add horseradish or chilli to a dish to make your eyes and nose run.

To improve the memory, use rosemary (for remembrance, as Shakespeare so wisely observed), or take lemon balm as a herbal tea.

For insect bites and stings, rub the affected area with sap from a bruised houseleek leaf, or use pennyroyal leaves. Rub crushed leaves of summer savory on bee stings. For a natural insect repellent, rub pennyroyal or basil leaves onto bare skin.

HERBAL TEAS

Herbal teas are caffeine-free alternatives to everyday tea or coffee, which often have added health benefits. Regular favourites for frequent drinking are chamomile, mint, fennel or nettle. Use freshly chopped herbs whenever possible; if using dried herbs, halve the amount.

Chamomile tea: *Grow Roman chamomile (Chamaemelum nobile) or its double form 'Flore Pleno', which is a more compact and rather prettier plant. Add a heaped teaspoonful of fresh flowers (stems removed) to a cup of boiling water; infuse for 3–5 minutes then strain and add a slice of lemon and honey to taste.*

Mint tea: *Use spearmint (Mentha spicata) for a pleasant everyday drinking tea, as against black peppermint (Mentha x piperata), which is an indigestion remedy. Pour a cup of boiling water over a heaped teaspoon of roughly chopped fresh leaves and infuse for 3–5 minutes until it's a comfortable temperature to drink. Add honey or sugar if you prefer your tea* *sweet. (The mint tea you are given in North Africa is made by adding a lot of fresh mint to normal tea leaves and leaving the lot to brew; it's traditionally drunk strong with a lot of sugar. Some herb firms supply a special variety of mint especially for this use, otherwise use spearmint or peppermint.)*

Fennel tea: *Use plump, pale green, dry fennel seeds for the best brew. Pour a cup of boiling water over a heaped teaspoonful of dried seeds and leave till it's a comfortable temperature for drinking – put a lid on the mug to keep the liquid hot for longer, which extracts more of the flavour. Strain, and add a slice of lemon and a little honey if you like; it's nice on its own unless you have a very sweet tooth.*

Nettle tea: *Use freshly picked nettle tops; chop fairly finely and pour a cupful of boiling water over a heaped teaspoonful, then leave to stand till it's the right temperature to drink; strain first. It doesn't need honey or lemon as, surprisingly, it's very pleasant on its own – it tastes rather like newly mown grass smells, if you know what I mean.*

DANDELION COFFEE

In wartime, when imported coffee was almost unavailable, people made their own dandelion coffee substitute. It still has a small following today as a natural, do-it-yourself, healthy, caffeine-free hot beverage that's low in calories. Dandelion roots are rich in minerals, as they reach down deep into the soil, so it's also quite good nutritionally.

Choose strong, healthy plants growing in part of the garden where there's no risk they'll have been contaminated by chemicals, especially weedkillers. (Although dandelions grow in the lawn, they are regularly beheaded so the roots are unable to grow as big and strong as dandelions left to grow in open ground.) Ideally cultivate a short row in the veg patch especially for the job. (Save seeds from dandelion 'clocks' during the summer, or use cultivated dandelion seed, which is also sometimes available from specialist herb-seed or wildflower-seed firms.)

Dig up the plants in autumn, when the roots are at maximum size. Trim off the longest, thickest roots to use; wash them well and steam them for a few minutes until the white sap stops leaking out of the cut surfaces. (Don't boil them, or the goodness will leak out.)

Cut them into 1cm (½ inch) long pieces, spread them out thinly on baking trays, and keep them in a warm place to dry until they snap cleanly without bending. Then put them in the oven and roast them at 200°C/400°F. I'd suggest doing a few at a time while you gain experience, since the colour and flavour of the finished dandelion coffee will vary according to how lightly or deeply you roast the roots. They'll turn pale yellow when lightly roasted, and a darker, almost coffee-colour when they are more heavily roasted.

Let them cool completely when you take them out of the oven, so all the steam has dispersed, before storing the whole roots in airtight jars to preserve their flavour.

When you want to make your 'coffee', grind a few roots especially. Use an electric coffee grinder or the spice mill attachment on a food processor. Add boiling water and milk or honey, if required; you'll soon find the right strength to suit your personal taste.

HOW TO MAKE TRADITIONAL LAVENDER-SCENTED
BEESWAX FURNITURE CREAM

Use a large saucepan of hot water with a big, clean, tin can standing inside as a make-shift double-saucepan; in this melt 100 grams (4 ounces) of beeswax in 600 ml (1 pint) of turpentine (this must be real turpentine, the sort artists use for thinning oil paints, and not the turps substitute used for cleaning decorators' paintbrushes). Turpentine is very inflammable so this job needs doing carefully.

You'll also need another saucepan; in this, bring 300ml (½ pint) of water to the boil and then stir in 16½ grams (⅔ ounce) of soft soap. Leave both panfuls to cool down, then stir the liquid soap-water into the beeswax and turpentine mixture a little at a time, mixing it well as you go, just like making mayonnaise. It should take on a thick, creamy consistency.

As soon as you've mixed the two liquids together, add a few drops of lavender oil, or use rosemary or a mixed herb oil if you prefer a slightly different fragrance. Pour it into a suitable container (maybe an old polish tin you've saved) to cool, when it should semi-set.

(Note: you can make your own lavender or herb oil by filling a small jar loosely with fresh lavender flowers, rosemary or mixed fresh herb leaves, and covering it with olive oil – leave it on a sunny windowsill for at least two weeks for oil to take on the fragrance of the plant material. Strain the oil before using.)

HERBAL INSECT REPELLENTS

FLY REPELLENTS

Grow pennyroyal (Mentha pulegium) or your favourite culinary mint close to the back door of the house and also near dustbins or other areas at risk from flies. A bunch of mint in a jar in the kitchen, or a pot of sweet basil – the small leaved one – also helps. Greek oregano (Oreganum vulgare) deters flies and mosquitoes.

ANT REPELLENTS

Rub fresh pennyroyal leaves over doorsteps or round the edge of a path or patio; ants hate the strong minty scent and won't cross the line. The task needs repeating regularly.

MOTH DETERRENTS

Make up sachets of equal quantities of dried southernwood or worm-wood, lavender flowers and spearmint to hang in the wardrobe. Instead of real lavender, you can use cotton lavender (Santolina incana), for a slightly different scent.

Otherwise (even though you can't grow the ingredients), hang up sachets impregnated with patchouli, the essential oil of an oriental plant called Pogostemon cablin, which was originally used by silk traders to prevent moths damaging their cargo on its long journey to Europe.

MAKING SOAP

Soap is made by boiling animal fats or vegetable oils with a strong alkali. The original source of alkali was lye, extracted from wood ashes, but later caustic soda was used, and nowadays this element is normally sodium hydroxide.

Making soap from scratch isn't something many people (other than a few real hobbyists) do at home, but you can 'customise' bought soap very easily. Grate a whole bar of unscented soap (or if you are feeling thrifty and it's for your own use, save up the equivalent amount of scraps of almost-used bars that you'd otherwise have thrown out, after letting them dry out till they are completely hard).

Weigh the soap flakes and to every 125 grams (4½ ounces) of flakes (the weight of an average bar of soap) you need to add 200ml (8 fluid ounces) of water. Put the soapflakes and water in a bowl and warm slowly over a pan of hot water until the soap melts. Then stir in two tablespoonfuls of almond or olive oil and ten to fifteen drops of your favourite essential oil to perfume the soap, and mix thoroughly.

Flower scents such as rose or lavender are always popular, but you could try citrus scents or herbs such as rosemary; a huge range of oils is available in chemists and health food shops. If you want a prettier soap, stir in a few dried dark red rose petals or some dried calendula marigold petals at this point.

Pour the mixture into something that will act as a mould, or make a block of soap in a loaf tin and when it's set hard cut it into suitably sized slices.

'Homemade' soap makes good artisan-style gifts, wrapped in brown paper and tied with raffia, or floral paper and ribbon. A real fag? Yes, but it's good to know just what goes into a bar of soap!

DIY HERBAL TOILETRIES

SKIN LOTIONS

An infusion of fresh chervil in water makes a lotion that cleanses and tones the skin, and is said to discourage wrinkles. (An infusion is basically a strong herb 'tea' made by pouring a cup of boiling water over a handful of whatever herbs and or flowers you want to use, then leaving it to stand for 10 minutes and straining it when cool.) Make fresh every day and store in the fridge up to 24 hours – it doesn't keep.

Marigold flowers infused in water make a lotion that's traditionally used to clear the skin by reducing enlarged pores and healing spots. The healing properties of marigolds make the flowers popular for using in hand creams.

To fade freckles or to keep a pale complexion fair, use fresh strawberry juice, made by mashing and straining ripe fresh fruit , and apply 'neat' or mix with finely ground oatmeal to make a face pack. For more instant use you can also apply a cut strawberry straight to your face; it's also comforting for mild sunburn.

HAND AND BODY CREAM

Melt some beeswax (it won't matter if there's still a little honey attached) and slowly beat in about five times the volume of olive oil or almond oil, over a low heat. Make an infusion of marigold flowers, lavender heads and/or herbs such as rosemary, sage or thyme.

Whisk a few drops of the herbal infusion at a time into the wax/oil mixture; allow it to cool. The mixture should be soft but not runny; add more oil or herb infusion as needed. Store in a screw-top jar and use within a couple of months; it keeps best in the fridge.

BATH ADDITIVES

For a soothing, relaxing, fragrant herbal bath, use a few fresh leaves of culinary bay (Laurus nobilis), rosemary, sage, scented-leaved geraniums, eau de cologne mint, horsetail, lemon balm, lemon-scented verbena, lavender flower heads, or blend a mixture to suit yourself.

The herbs can be thrown straight into the hot water. but when you don't want to share your bath with a lot of floating 'bits', put the herbs in the centre of a square of muslin or cotton and tie the corners together to make a bag. Hang it under the hot tap when you run the bath.

Alternatively, make a strong 'tea' from a mixture of herbs such as thyme, sage and rosemary (all of which have antiseptic properties as well as a fresh, clean fragrance) and pour a couple of teaspoonfuls into the hot water just before you step in.

DEODORANT

Lovage acts as a natural deodorant. It can be taken internally (eaten as a culinary herb it tastes like celery and can be used in soups or stews or as a leafy green vegetable).

Lovage can also be added to bathwater, on its own or with other herbs, to make a deodorising herbal bath. For smelly feet, place a few lovage leaves in the bottom of shoes such as trainers.

HAIR PRODUCTS

Make your own natural shampoo from soapwort (*Saponaria officinalis*). Simmer two handfuls of chopped, fresh soapwort stems in 750ml (1¼ pints) of water in an old saucepan for 20 minutes, strain when cool and use as needed. (The same soapwort liquid can also be used for hand-washing delicate woollen and silk fabrics.)

Chamomile flowers (bottom right) make a pleasantly scented herbal rinse for enhancing blonde hair; it's like making chamomile tea but on a larger scale. Pour 1 litre (1¾ pints) of boiling water over a handful of fresh chamomile flowers and leave it to 'brew' for half an hour. When it's cooled, strain and use. For dark hair, use a similar infusion of rosemary as the final rinse after shampooing.

Nettle 'tea' makes a good conditioning hair rinse that's said to treat dandruff. Bring a bunch of nettle tops (15 centimetres/6 inches long and as big as you can hold in one gloved hand) to the boil in 60ml (1 pint) of water and simmer for 20 minutes. Store unused rinse in a bottle in the fridge, but use it within a few days.

Herbal tea made from horsestail (*Equisetum arvense*) makes a good hair conditioner for strengthening weak or brittle hair, and it's also a good nail-strengthening treatment due, it's thought, to the silica and other minerals that this deep-rooted plant collects and stores in its stems. Bruise eight fresh stalks of horsetail and cover with 600ml (1 pint) of boiling water to infuse. When cool, strain the liquid.

To use as a hair rinse, wash your hair as usual then apply as much horsetail tea as it holds without dripping everywhere, put a shower cap on and leave for ten minutes before rinsing it off with plain water.

To use as a nail treatment, sit for 20 minutes with your fingertips resting in a bowl of comfortably warm horsetail tea. You'll need to do it fairly regularly to really reap the benefit.

CHAPTER 3

KITCHEN GARDENING

You don't need green fingers to have a successful kitchen garden; the secret is a sheltered situation, good, fertile soil, and attention to detail. Edible crops make more demands than any other plants, so to get a decent crop it is important to limit yourself to what you can grow well in the time and space available. The mistake most novices make is to take on far more than they can manage. The tastiest, most tender crops are those that have had an easy life, so they grow quickly and steadily; any checks in growth can make them run to seed or become tough and tasteless.

Soil preparation is really important; more so for vegetable growing than for any other kind of gardening. Edible crops take an awful lot out of the ground (water, major nutrients and trace elements) because you are constantly removing what you grow and eating it, so it's vital to put plenty of goodness back. Fertiliser is only part of the story; a kitchen garden needs regular inputs of organic matter; this keeps the soil soft and 'fluffy' so roots can penetrate easily, and it keeps the soil aerated and well drained, besides housing a thriving community of beneficial soil bacteria. The goal of soil improvement is to create good growing conditions where hard-working crops can get on with the job.

Start preparing the soil in autumn and continue over the winter whenever the weather allows, so that the ground is ready for planting come spring. If you're starting a new kitchen garden plot from scratch, clear the ground completely of turf or perennial weeds first; don't dig them in as they always re-grow. (Annual weeds can be turned in if they are not bearing seeds, otherwise pull them out, too.) Improve the soil of an existing plot a little at a time, as the ground becomes vacant when winter crops are cleared. Spread a barrowload of well-rotted organic matter per square yard, and dig it in to evenly incorporate it. You can use garden compost, manure, spent mushroom compost – whatever you can get hold of in quantity, cheaply and locally.

Once the groundwork has been properly done, kitchen gardening is all about timing and keeping up to date with routine work. It's vital to do key operations such as sowing and planting on time – you can find full details and instructions for individual varieties on the backs of the seed packets. And keep on top of regular weeding, watering, feeding, and pest and disease control; it's the only way to produce perfect crops that everyone wants to eat. Standards need to be high; now that everyone is used to the perfect crops bought from shops and supermarkets, people tend to be squeamish about the odd slug, insect or suspicious hole in things they are going to eat.

MAKING A COMPOST HEAP

A productive kitchen garden needs regular supplies of well-rotted organic matter to improve the soil and then maintain the fertility, but it's easily produced for free by recycling your own garden waste and suitable kitchen scraps via a compost heap.

Use lawn mowings, soft hedge clippings, weeds, fallen autumn leaves, old bedding plants pulled out at the end of the season, crop remains from the veg patch, veg trimmings, fruit peel and used teabags from the kitchen. You can also use plain white paper (such as kitchen paper that you've used for mopping up spills) and discarded cotton or woollen fabrics, including old clothes.

Don't use synthetic fabrics or printed paper, woody plant remains (since they take several years to rot down), weeds that have run to seed, roots of perennial weeds, or diseased plant material (since you'll spread the infection all round the garden when you use the compost). Avoid meat scraps and tasty morsels such as bread or cooked food as they'll attract rodents.

Make a compost container to keep a freestanding heap tidy; knock four 1.2–1.5 metres (4–5 feet) posts into the ground, forming a square that's at least 90cm (3 feet) by 90cm (3 feet) – anything smaller won't heat up enough. Nail planks or wire netting all round to enclose it and stop compost material falling out; make sure the front can be easily removed to extract the finished compost in due course. Fork the soil over at the base to loosen it and improve drainage.

Start adding suitable compost ingredients; mix them together, if possible, to avoid concentrations of materials such as lawn mowings, and for every 15cm (6 inch) deep layer, sprinkle on a little soil or fresh animal manure to stop green waste drying out and act as a 'compost starter' by adding beneficial bacteria that help the other ingredients rot down.

Spread new compost ingredients out so the top of the heap stays fairly flat, and firm each new layer down as much as you can. If the new compost ingredients are dry, damp them with the hose to help the rotting process begin.

When you've filled the container to the very top, cap it with a 15cm (6 inch) layer of soil and if possible cover the whole heap with an old tarpaulin or sheet to keep the warmth and moisture in and stop the outer layer drying out in the sun or growing weeds.

After three months (summer) or six months (winter), fork the contents out and re-stack it so that the dry or uncomposted material from round the edge of the original heap goes to the bottom and centre of the new

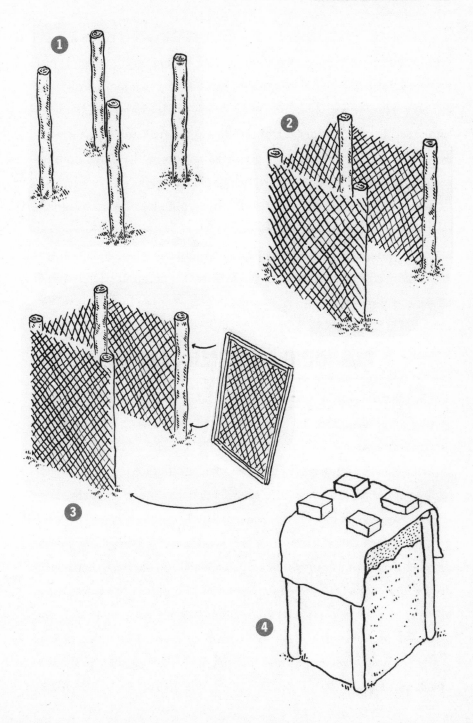

heap, while the most crumbly well-rotted material goes over the top and sides. After another three or six months, depending on the time of year, the whole heap will be full of ready-to-use compost that looks brown and crumbly, with few visibly identifiable ingredients. If you're in a hurry for some useable compost, cheat and take the well-rotted stuff to use straight away, then pile fresh compost ingredients on top of the older, unrotted material, dampen, cover and start the ball rolling again.

If you only have small quantities of garden rubbish to dispose of, instead of a compost heap use a compost bin with solid sides. It composts green materials faster since it holds the heat and moisture better, and because it works more efficiently you don't need to 'turn' the compost – it rots evenly all the way through.

PLANNING A KITCHEN GARDEN

The traditional way to plan a kitchen garden was for ease of management. I'd still recommend it today for anyone with a large kitchen garden or an allotment.

Long-term crops that occupied the same ground for many years were kept quite separate from things that needed replanting annually. Fruit trees were grown in grass in an orchard, which traditionally had livestock grazing underneath to manure the trees and keep the grass short without mowing. Soft fruit was grown in a fruit cage to keep out birds, herbs were grown in a geometric-shaped herb garden with paths for easy access in all weathers, since evergreen kinds might be needed year-round, and asparagus was grown in a bed of its own so it could be given its own yearly cultivation regime without the tall, leafy 'fern' getting in the way of other crops.

Short-term crops that came and went within a year were grown in the veg patch. This was divided into three or four rectangular plots, each used for a particular type of crop that needed the same soil preparation, to make the best use of resources and avoid carry-over or pests or disease peculiar to that type of crop. Each year the crops would be grown in a new patch – a technique known as 'crop rotation'.

Crop rotation is still considered good gardening practice, though we've tended to adapt the original rotation scheme to take account of the sort of crops people want to grow today.

Now that gardens are so much smaller, newer and more intensive means of growing crops are more practical for most people. Deep beds or raised beds allow crops to be grown at closer spacing than usual (about two-thirds the traditional spacing) so you can produce more from a limited space, and there's less work involved because the rows of vegetables soon meet in the middle and cover the ground completely, so they smother out weeds.

If space is very limited, you can restrict yourself to a small salad bed, which still yields useful crops as they are so fast-growing. Even when a tiny plot makes it difficult to practise traditional crop rotation, it still pays to avoid growing the same crop in the same patch of ground in successive years, so simply move crops round every year so you don't grow the same thing in the same patch of ground two years running.

The alternative for small gardens is to grow suitable crops on the patio in growing bags or containers filled with potting compost and simply rotate the soil instead; start each season off with new growing bags or compost, and recycle the used stuff by digging it into the garden as mulch. The most suitable crops for growing in containers include salads and annual herbs, courgettes, climbing beans, early potatoes and outdoor tomatoes, though in a particularly warm sheltered spot (and given a good summer) it's also worth trying a few heat-loving peppers, chillies and aubergines.

GROWING HERBS

Herbs were traditionally grown in a separate garden of their own. This was usually laid out in a geometrical shape, with brick or gravel paths providing easy year-round access to a big concentration of useful medicinal, household and culinary plants. Today the most popular culinary herbs are often grown in tubs on the patio, or as borders round a kitchen garden, to make the best use of limited space. They fall roughly into two camps when it comes to cultivation.

Mediterranean herbs are mainly aromatic, evergreen shrubby perennials; the most popular are rosemary, sage, bay, oregano and thyme, but you can also add lavender. These need plenty of sun, warmth and shelter with well-drained soil, and they are good for patio containers, courtyards and sunny corners. Traditional wisdom always advised not to overfeed them, as fertiliser was thought to encourage strong lush growth that was lacking in the vital oils that give these herbs their flavour and fragrance, but in practice they do need feeding little-and-often, especially when grown in containers.

Traditional British herbs such as tarragon, mint, chives, marjoram, parsley, chervil, sorrel and borage are happiest in more normal garden conditions. They like rich, moisture-retaining soil and a situation with plenty of light and sun for part of the day, but not strong, scorching midday sun.

Some of the herbs in this group are perennials that die down each winter, including mint, chives and tarragon. These can be planted in spring or summer. Dig up and divide them every few years, and move mint to a new patch of ground every two years as it is so 'greedy' it quickly exhausts the ground. Planting it in a sunken bottomless bucket will restrict its rampant spread. Others are either annuals or are treated as such for convenience; they include marjoram, chervil, parsley, sorrel and borage. With these, you'll need to sow a new batch each spring, or buy pot-grown plants from a garden centre. All of the traditional British herbs need to be watered in dry summers to keep them fresh and leafy, and when grown in containers they also need regular liquid feeding.

Nowadays several more unusual or exotic herbs are also proving popular, and these are best treated individually. Leaf coriander is an annual, grown in the same way as parsley, in pots on a kitchen windowsill indoors, or outside in patio tubs or a herb garden in summer. Scented-leaved pelargoniums need growing in the same way as normal zonal pelargoniums – in pots, which can be put outside in summer but need bringing inside for winter since they aren't frost-hardy. A huge range of varieties is available from specialist nurseries, with scents that range from pine to peppermint, citrus, apple, and rose – they are brilliant as natural air fresheners, can be used in potpourri, in the bath, and a few are good for baking in cakes. Basil (which now includes various exotic forms such as lemon basil, purple-leaved basil, etc.) is a tad delicate and does best in pots on a kitchen windowsill. If you do grow it outside, choose a sheltered patio tub during a fine summer. Genovese basil and the large lettuce-leaved basil are the two recommended for making pesto sauce.

PROTECTING CROPS WITHOUT CHEMICALS

Even gardeners who don't think of themselves as 'organic' generally prefer to avoid using chemicals on crops they are going to eat, so instead of spraying, use a combination of organic techniques to protect crops from pests and diseases.

Wherever possible, choose veg varieties that have been bred to resist disease and certain pests (these are identified in seed catalogues and on seed packets).

Use organic remedies such as copper strips round a raised bed or saucers of beer instead of slug pellets, and cover veg crops with fine, insect-proof netting to protect them from sun, wind and unwanted visitors.

Avoid spreading chemicals all round the garden; then all sorts of beneficial insects will start to build up in numbers – they will patrol your crops and help themselves to aphids, small caterpillars or soil pests.

BENEFICIAL INSECTS

Ladybirds: *Both adults and larvae feed voraciously on aphids all summer; adults are easily recognised but learn to identify the larvae, which look like tiny, charcoal-grey dragons.*

Lacewings: *Pale green insects with large, translucent, gossamer-like wings usually folded over the top of the body (it must be difficult to get them packed back again, which is probably why they don't often take off); they're aphid-eaters, mostly seen in late summer.*

Hoverflies: *Both adults and larvae are large consumers of aphids; adults are also attracted by nectar-rich flowers such as old-fashioned annuals, so grow a row or two in with veg to encourage them to your plot.*

Spiders: *Several kinds live in gardens; wolf spiders sunbathe on leaves with two pairs of forelegs extended out in front of the body and chase insect* *prey; garden spiders make the large webs you see sparkling with dew early on autumn mornings, which trap flying prey, and tiny money spiders are invaluable hunters of aphids.*

Black beetles: *Several kinds live in gardens and feed on small soil pests such as cabbage root fly, young vine weevil larvae, slugs eggs, etc., so they are invaluable; use old-fashioned tarred felt collars around brassica stems to encourage friendly beetles to stay where you want them to work and to prevent cabbage root flies laying their eggs.*

Earwigs: *Disliked by exhibitors of dahlias and chrysanthemums since they'll nip holes in petals, but very useful for clearing up greenfly.*

Wasps: *More valuable to gardens than you might think, since in late spring and for much of summer they remove masses of small green caterpillars and aphids to take back to their nests to feed their own larvae; it's not till late summer, when worker wasps stop being fed sticky secretions back at the nest, that they turn elsewhere in search of sticky soft drinks, fruit and sweet food, earning themselves a bad name.*

Centipedes: *Rather flattened and chestnut-coloured (as against the largely vegetarian, i.e. plant-damaging, millipede, which is black and tubular); feeds on numerous small soil pests and their larvae, tiny slugs and slugs eggs, also vine weevil larvae.*

CROP ROTATION

This is a modified form of the traditional four-course rotation, designed to suit the sort of crops modern gardeners want to grow.

Divide the patch into four plots, treat each one to its own special cultural routine and move the crops on to the next plot the following year.

PLOT 1: GREEDY CROPS

Soil preparation: *Well-rotted organic matter plus general fertiliser.*

Crops: *Follow early potatoes with outdoor tomatoes, courgettes, pumpkins. Sow salads in any gaps.*

Routine care: *After planting, weed once or twice (earth up potatoes as the young shoots emerge) until crops cover the ground, then the dense foliage will smother out annual weeds. Add more general feed and a scattering of chicken manure pellets before planting summer crops (tomatoes, courgettes, etc.) and use high-potash liquid tomato feed for tomatoes (also courgettes and pumpkins for best results).*

Benefit: *The dense potato foliage creates heavy shade that smothers out germinating weed seeds, which is why potatoes are well known for 'cleaning' the ground, leaving it relatively weed-free for the next crop.*

PLOT 2: PEAS AND BEANS

Soil preparation: *Well-rotted organic matter plus general fertiliser.*

Crop: *Peas, mangetouts, sugar or snap peas, runner beans, broad beans, French beans, beans for drying for winter use.*

Routine care: *Put up a framework of rustic poles or canes for beans to grow up, and use netting or twiggy pea sticks to support peas. Make several sowings over the season to keep yourself continuously supplied; sow early varieties in pots under cover and transplant, then sow later batches directly into shallow drills where you want them to crop, and for a late crop to be picked in autumn, sow early varieties of peas and dwarf French beans in July, or sow in early August and cover the crops with cloches in autumn. After pea and bean plants have finished cropping, cut the plants down leaving the roots in the ground. Use any*

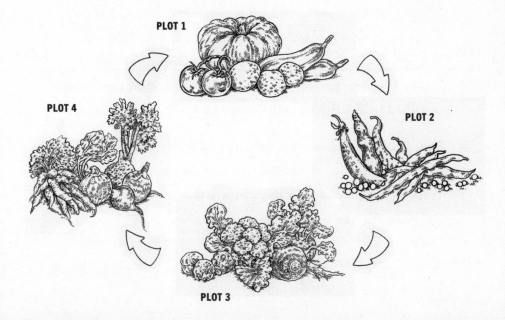

PLOT 1

PLOT 4

PLOT 2

PLOT 3

Benefit: *Peas and beans feed the next crop; the plants 'fix' nitrogen from the air via bacteria living in nodules on their roots which break down, releasing it into the soil.*

PLOT 3: BRASSICAS

Soil preparation: *Lime (but no organic matter – the two antagonise each other so must always be applied separately; lime also 'locks up' fertiliser to some extent so it's a waste of money to use it with lime).*

Crop: *Any members of the cabbage family, including Brussels sprouts, calabrese, sprouting broccoli, swedes and kohl rabi (which, though a root crop, belongs to the brassica tribe).*

Routine care: *Sow seeds in an especially well-prepared seedbed in March, April, May according to variety (see instructions on the back of the seed packet) then thin out seedlings to an inch apart and after another few weeks when they've become strong young plants, transplant them to their cropping positions at the correct spacing. The exception is swedes, which need sowing in May, then thinning – don't transplant.*

Benefit: *Brassica plants use up the nitrogen left in the ground by the legumes grown last year, and the lime helps avoid club root disease, besides keeping the pH of the soil at the right level for growing vegetables, when it's used once in four years.*

PLOT 4: ROOT CROPS

Soil preparation: *General fertiliser only, no organic matter.*

Root crops: *Carrots, onions, onion sets, shallots, beetroot, parsnips, celeriac, leeks, spring onions. For large exhibition onions, keen exhibitors use lots of manure, too.*

Routine care: *Sow in April; transplant leeks for best results, but sow other root crops (except celeriac) where you want them to grow as they don't transplant well. For late crops, sow early carrot varieties and baby beetroot in July. Sow overwintering spring onions in September, for picking next spring. Sow celeriac in March/April indoors, prick out seedlings into small pots and plant outside in mid-May.*

Benefit: *By following brassicas that don't have organic matter added to the soil and which take a lot of nitrogen out of the ground, conditions are made ideal for sowing root crops which tend to grow 'fanged' or deformed, if there's too much nitrogen or fresh organic matter in the ground.*

GROWING CUT FLOWERS IN THE VEG PATCH

Cottagers from Victorian times onwards often grew a few rows of flowers for cutting in their veg patch to sell at the garden gate to make 'pin money'. Today the veg patch is a good place to grow sweet peas or other annual flowers when you don't want to risk ruining flower borders that are 'on show' from the house.

Prepare the soil well; work in lots of well-rotted organic matter, and shortly before sowing or planting, rake in a dressing of general fertiliser such as blood, fish and bone meal.

Sow hardy annuals in rows where they are to grow, and thin the seedlings out to a few inches apart when they are big enough to handle. Good kinds include calendula marigolds, larkspur and cornflower.

Sweet peas, although hardy annuals, have large seeds often stolen by mice or pigeons when sown straight into the garden, so they are usually sown in pots in a cold frame in November (for the earliest flowers) or March/April for later summer blooms.

Half-hardy annuals need to be sown in March or April on warm windowsills indoors; prick the seedlings out into trays when they are big enough to handle and grow them on at 10–15°C (50–60°F) until planting time, after the last frost, from mid-May onwards. Good kinds for cutting include statice, cosmos, stocks and zinnia.

Dahlias are very good cut flowers but are not frost-hardy; plant dormant tubers in late April or early May, or plant rooted cuttings from mid to late May – they'll form tubers by the autumn. Dig the tubers up in autumn after the first frost blackens the foliage; cut the stems down to about 10cm (4 inches) above the tops of the tubers. After drying off thoroughly, store the tubers in nets or stacking trays in a frost-free shed for the winter, before replanting them again the following year.

GROW YOUR OWN LIQUID FEEDS

LIQUID COMFREY

Grow Russian comfrey, and in summer, when growth is at its maximum, cut the stems and press them down tightly into a plastic dustbin or similar large watertight container, packing it to the top, then add water to the rim. Put the lid on and leave for at least four to six weeks. When the leaves have turned black and are well decomposed, remove the decaying plant material and use the liquid (be warned – it looks dirty and smells foul) diluted to about one-part to six or eight of water, as a high-potash feed for tomatoes, courgettes and pumpkins.

LIQUID NETTLES

Follow the same method only using freshly cut nettles. This makes a high-nitrogen feed that's good for leafy veg and salads. Dilute it in the same way.

MANURE 'TEA'

Fill a hessian sack or an old plastic, mesh-net onion bag from the green-grocer's with well-rotted manure, and place in a dustbin, then fill to the brim with water. After six weeks, lift out the sack and dilute the liquid manure in the same way as for liquid comfrey. This is a useful general-purpose liquid feed for 'greedy' plants all round the garden, especially rhubarb, brassicas, courgettes and pumpkins, but it's also good in the flower garden for roses and clematis.

Note: It's not a good idea to use any of these on plants growing in pots or other containers, since you can't be sure of the dilution rate in the way that you can when using bottled feeds and following the instructions.

GROWING FRUIT

Fruit trees (apples, pears, plums, cherries) are traditionally grown as large standard trees, with a trunk topped by branches that radiate out all round forming a crown, but increasingly they are being grown on dwarfing rootstocks to keep them compact and trained into more space-saving forms to suit smaller modern gardens.

Apples and pears are often grown as single cordons; these are merely straight trunks about 1.8–2.4m (6–8ft) long with short twiggy 'spurs' growing out along their length that bear the fruit. Cordons can be upright or inclined – grown at an angle of 45 degrees to the ground, which allows you to grow a longer trunk and yet still be able to pick its entire length without a ladder. Spaced 45 cm (18in) apart and supported by posts and two rows of horizontal wires, a row of cordon trees makes a very pretty and productive 'fruiting hedge'.

Horizontal cordons are also available; known as step-over trees, they are ideal for edging a path or a border. Espalier-trained trees look like an upright trunk with two or three tiers of horizontal 'arms' growing out from each side of it to make a flat tree, which can be grown against a south-facing wall or fence. This is the best way to grow the fussier varieties of pears, which need more warmth to develop fully and ripen reliably in our climate, but one or two espalier-trained fruit trees supported by a row of posts and horizontal wires makes a productive and decorative way to screen off a veg patch from the ornamental part of the garden. You may occasionally find cordon-trained plums or cherries in the catalogues of specialist fruit nurseries, but they aren't often seen in garden centres. It's more usual to grow these fruits as fans against a south-facing wall. (The sour-cooking 'Morello' cherry is one of the few fruits that thrives on a north-facing wall.)

More exotic, and unusual, fruit trees are also being cultivated thanks to the newfound interest in kitchen-gardening; nowadays people are trying nectarines, peaches and apricots, which are especially successful grown as fan-trained specimens against a south-facing wall. (Apricots are the most reliable of the three when you don't have a sheltered garden; in the south of England they'll even produce ripe fruit when grown as freestanding trees as long as you choose a warm, sunny, sheltered spot.) Where space is really short, go for genetically dwarf versions sold as 'patio peaches' or 'patio nectarines'. These are ultra-compact and extremely slow-growing miniature trees, ideal for growing throughout their lives in large pots or tubs, yet they bear full-sized fruit.

If you are buying fruit trees by post from specialist nurseries which issue annual catalogues, they are usually sent out with bare roots (to save postage and production costs) and despatched in winter. They need planting straight away, but if that's not possible, 'heel them in' temporarily to keep the roots moist until you have time to plant them properly. Pot-grown fruit trees are available all year round from garden centres and some nurseries; though the choice is far more limited, you can plant them at any time of year – even when they are in flower and fruit – but they'll need to be kept well watered for all of their first summer.

Since trees will stay put for many years, it pays to prepare the ground very well before planting. Dig a hole about twice the size of the pot, or three times the size of the root system of a bare-root tree. Work a good bucketful of well-rotted compost or manure into the bottom and mix in a handful of blood, fish and bone meal. Knock a strong stake into one side of the hole to support the trunk after the tree has been planted. It will need to protrude from the ground as far as the lowest branch of the tree. If you're planting a bare-root tree, spread the roots out well in the bottom of the hole and use a mixture of topsoil and well-rotted compost to fill the hole, firming the soil gently with your foot as you go.

If planting from a pot, gently bang the container down to loosen the plant and lift it out. If the rootball is packed solid with tightly coiled roots, carefully ease a few of the larger ones loose from the mass so they can spread out into the surrounding soil once they've been planted instead of staying stuck in their rootball. (If this happens, the tree doesn't 'take off'.) Use improved topsoil to fill the gap between the rootball and the sides of the planting hole, and again firm down gently. After planting, secure the tree to the stake using two proprietary tree ties – one 15cm (6in) above the ground and the other about 2½cm (1in) from the top of the stake.

Since most fruit trees are grown on dwarfing rootstocks, they must be staked for life. For the first year after planting, keep fruit trees well watered any time the ground starts to dry out, and don't expect much – or indeed any – crop in the first year. It usually takes two or three years for fruit trees to get into their stride. Check the ties regularly to be sure they aren't constricting the trunk.

Soft fruit, which includes strawberries, fruit bushes such as gooseberries and blackcurrants, and cane fruit such as raspberries and blackberries, are sold in pots at nurseries and garden centres all year round, or in winter as bare-root plants by mail order from the catalogues of specialist firms. It's usual to plant soft fruit in rows inside a fruit cage, or else at one end of the veg patch.

Prepare the soil as you would for a vegetable garden, by digging in plenty of well-rotted manure or garden compost over the whole area, and raking in general- purpose fertiliser, then plant straight into the chosen positions. No staking is needed, but cane fruit (blackberries, raspberries, etc) need a row of posts with two or three strong horizontal wires stretched between them for support. (The exception is autumn-fruiting raspberries, which don't need supporting because they don't grow as tall as the usual summer fruiters.)

Strawberries are normally planted in beds of their own, or grown in large tubs on a patio, since they are relatively compact but also need replacing every four years, as old plants aren't very productive. (Save a few of the strongest runners each summer to replace an entire row and save the cost of buying new plants.) Rhubarb is usually grown in a bed of its own – or more often an odd corner somewhere in the garden – for convenience. It enjoys rich but well-drained soil.

STRAWBERRIES

Strawberry plants have a useful working life of roughly four years, after which they need replacing. It's easy to raise your own replacements by pegging down a few strong, healthy 'runners' produced by older plants in summer into small pots of potting compost sunk into the ground around them. Do this is in August and you'll have sturdy young plants to plant out the following spring. Dig up and dispose of old plants, and refresh the soil with well-rotted organic matter and some general fertiliser such as blood, fish and bone before replanting. Don't propagate diseased or unhealthy-looking strawberry plants – if they don't look good, buy new runners or pot-grown young plants to start a fresh row. Virus-infected plants (identifiable by their distorted or yellow-mottled leaves) will produce fewer fruits.

HEDGE VEG

Victorian farm labourers started selling their surplus veg, eggs and honey at the garden gate to raise 'pin money' to buy things they couldn't grow or make for themselves, and in time they began growing cut flowers such as dahlias especially to raise a little extra spending money. When I was a lad the tradition of garden gate sales was still going strong; when you drove through a small village or past a lone farm out in the country, there'd always be a homemade stall that looked as if it had been knocked together from old bits of second-hand timber bearing an array of home-grown produce with a handwritten price list and an honesty box for the money. Maybe it's a sign of the times but you don't see so many garden gate sales in mainland Britain today, but the tradition still continues at a cracking pace over in the Channel Islands, where they're known as 'hedge veg'.

AFTERCARE OF FRUIT

After planting and staking, water new fruit trees and bushes in well and give them a good mulch to seal in the moisture. Each year in spring, top up the mulch with a fresh 2½–5cm (1–2in) layer of well-rotted organic matter after applying a generous sprinkling of general-purpose fertiliser.

Water newly planted fruit during dry spells, and if there's a long, dry summer, even after the plants are well established, be prepared to water soft fruit bushes, fruit canes and trained fruit trees on dwarfing rootstocks while they are carrying a crop, or the fruit may be shed prematurely before it has had a chance to ripen.

Fruit trees, bushes and canes need regular pruning. Each type of fruit and all the various trained forms have their own particular set of pruning requirements (look them up in an illustrated pruning guide, or keep the instructions on the back of the label that comes with the plants when you buy them). Pruning will either need doing in summer, straight after the fruit has all been picked, or in midwinter.

Summer pruning is mostly done for cordon fruit and espaliers – each 'arm' is treated like an individual cordon. To prune these, cut this year's shoots back to a couple of buds from their base, or two leaves beyond a developing fruit. Summer-fruiting raspberries, also blackberries and their relatives, are all pruned by cutting back the stems that carried this year's crop shortly after you've picked the last of it, then the young unfruited canes are tied in to the supports ready for fruiting next year. (Autumn-fruiting raspberries are treated differently; all the stems are cut down to just a couple of inches above ground level in February each year.)

Winter pruning is used for standard fruit trees. With these, simply thin out branches that rub, cross or are overcrowded, and remove what horticultural students know of as 'the three Ds': dead, diseased or damaged wood. It's much the same for freestanding soft fruit bushes, except the aim in pruning these is to remove older stems that have carried a crop or two, leaving younger stems that will crop well in future.

Stone fruit (peaches, nectarines, apricots, plums and cherries) shouldn't be pruned in winter as they are at risk from silver leaf disease, so it's advisable to buy well-shaped trees with regularly spaced branches in the first place and then leave them alone (if you simply must cut something out, do it in early summer). If the tree is grown as a fan, rub out unwanted shoots while they are fat buds and you can do so without making an open wound where airborne infection can enter.

HEDGEROW FRUIT

Old cottagers traditionally grew several suitable species of fruit in the mixed hedge round their garden, where they provided a useful crop without making any work or taking up space. Good fruit for growing this way include sloes, bullaces, damsons and greengages, crab apples, brambles, elderberries and even rosehips, all of which had several culinary uses from jams and jellies, puddings and pies, to country wines.

Apart from damsons and greengages, most hedgerow fruit would not have been deliberately planted; plants usually grew naturally from seeds dropped by birds. Crab apples usually grew up from pips in discarded apple cores (these days you often see apple trees in the countryside where they've grown from cores thrown out of windows of passing cars).

Today, a deliberately planted mixed country hedge containing fruit and berries makes a good wildlife resource, even if you don't harvest the fruit to use yourself.

GROW YOUR OWN FIREWOOD

Most country gardens will generate a small amount of waste wood that's suitable for burning on an open heath or in a wood-burning stove. Fruit trees need regular pruning, and even ornamental trees sometimes need crown lifting (removing lower branches to make it easier to mow and walk underneath) or crown thinning (thinning out the main branches to reduce shade). And once in a while a whole tree needs taking down when it grows too big, or you need to make room for other things. Don't waste them by putting them on a bonfire.

Instead cut them into suitable lengths to fit comfortably into your hearth or the interior of your wood-burning stove, then stack them to 'season' so they become fit to use as fuel. (Use only hardwoods; conifer trees produce a lot of tarry materials that build up quickly inside the chimney.)

It's not only thick branches and whole trunks that are worth saving. Small twigs, such as those shed regularly underneath birches, make good kindling for lighting the fire, and dry fruit and vine prunings are also excellent for starting barbecues. They are all so much more pleasant-smelling and eco-friendly than petro-chemical firelighters.

But when there's space to plant a few trees especially, or you have a small patch of woodland, then it's very feasible to grow and harvest your own crop of firewood. Unless you have several acres, you won't be self-sufficient in central heating, but every little helps – and there are all sorts of other uses for woodland by-products, such as bean poles (usually hazel), posts (such as sweet chestnut) and peasticks (birch and hazel). You can even earmark a particularly handsome stump or 'character' log to bring indoors on Christmas Eve as a Yule log.

GOOD LOGS TO GROW AT HOME, FOR BURNING IN GRATES AND WOOD-BURNING STOVES

Ash: *One of the best logs for burning, and unusual in that it can be burnt 'green', without the need to season it first. The logs have light brown bark with green striation.*

Hazel: *Not a classic log, and probably not one you'd buy from a log merchant, but good for growing at home since the fast-growing tree takes kindly to being coppiced, which produces a regular supply of slim logs of an ideal size for wood-burning stoves (leave them to season for a year first), also long straight poles suitable for using as bean poles. The twiggy smaller stems and tops of longer poles make good pea sticks. Once established, hazel can be cut every 10–15 years (more often if being harvested smaller for bean poles, etc).*

Birch: *Good-looking logs that burn fairly quickly but can be burnt when only partly seasoned, often ready six months after cutting. Trees take roughly 25 years to reach harvestable size, but many of those planted in gardens are cut down when they grow too big, so this puts them to good use.*

Apple and pear: *Not planted specifically for producing logs, but when you have to cut down an old tree it yields good-quality logs for burning, which yield fragrant smoke. Season for at least one year first.*

Hawthorn: *Good to burn when you have to remove a tree from a hedgerow, the narrow trunks are easy to cut up and produce small but solid logs. Season for a year.*

SEASONING LOGS

Both home-grown wood and any logs that you buy need to be 'seasoned' before they are fit to burn. This is because freshly cut wood contains a good deal of sap and resins that prevent the wood burning well or yielding maximum heat, but they also cause deposits that build up inside the chimney where they can eventually create a fire risk and can block the narrow steel chimney liner used with wood-burning stoves.

Stack logs after they've been cut to a suitable length for your fireplace or stove. Slim branches can simply be cut to length, but whole trunks and thick branches need to be split, which helps them burn more readily.

Choose an airy, open place that's reasonably well sheltered from rain – some people stack logs against a wall, or they'll build a wooden structure that has a roof with open or slatted sides backing onto a wall or outbuilding. Make sure log stacks are well supported at each end, as logs shift slightly as they dry out and a stack can collapse, especially if it's nudged by passing garden machinery or people.

It's a good idea to stack wood that'll be ready to use fairly soon, such as ash or birch, separately from logs of beech or oak, which need to be left much longer. Most logs need to stand for a year; beech and oak need two years to season since their wood is so dense.

You can tell when logs are properly seasoned since they crack, producing a pattern like spokes radiating out from the centre, and they also feel far lighter than freshly cut logs. If you prefer a more scientific approach, you can test logs by pressing a commercial damp meter (the sort surveyors use on walls or woodwork) up against them; on properly seasoned wood it should register 'low', or below 30 per cent moisture.

BUYING LOGS

Oak and beech logs are the best value for money as the wood is very dense, so they burn longer and more slowly than other kinds, yet they put out more heat. However, they take two years to season properly, so you need plenty of storage space to stack them.

Birch and ash are good for starting a fire in the first place as they burn fast, and they can be burnt from as little as six months old. A lot of people buy nothing but birch or ash as they are easily available and don't need to be stored for long before they are fit to use, so less storage space is needed.

Even if you buy logs described as 'well seasoned', you may still need to stack them for a while before they dry out enough – it's advisable to order logs in spring or early summer to use the following winter.

When buying logs, find out in advance what size they are. For a wood-burning stove you'll need shorter logs than most people could accept for burning in an open hearth; it's worth specifying that you want them for a stove when ordering.

Longer and thicker logs take longer to burn once they've got going, and they're capable of keeping an open fire going overnight. Really huge slabs of tree trunk are only suitable for burning in a large inglenook.

In the past, ready-cut firewood was sold by the cord, which was 128 cubic feet. (Imagine a solid stack measuring 1 ½ x 1 ½ x 1 ½ metres high (5 x 5 x 5 feet) – that's just a little short of a cord.) Today logs are mostly sold by the trailer or truck-load, meaning the back of a pick-up truck. Since the size is by no means standard, it's worth having a look at a delivery first; word of mouth is the best way of finding a good supplier.

For small-scale users, plastic sacks filled with cut logs are sold in garage forecourts, garden centres and at country general stores.

If you want to economise, you may sometimes be able to buy whole logs and cut and split them yourself for rather less than the price of ready-cut logs. You may also be able to make agreements with farmers, other gardeners, or parish councils, etc., to obtain fallen tree branches or remove dead trees (with suitable insurance), doing the job of clearance for free in return for the timber. However, you can't just help yourself.

Burning waste timber, including old pallets, old fencing slats and the like, is false economy since, like conifer wood, the chemicals they contain can tar-up your chimney and cause blockages that are expensive to rectify, besides stinking out your neighbourhood when you burn them.

GARDENING WITH NATIVE TREES AND SHRUBS

When you want to encourage wildlife to visit, native species provide food such as fruit, seeds and berries, while their foliage and bark harbour insects which are food for birds and other creatures. Some truly wild species also have closely related ornamental versions that are good for wildlife, and some purely decorative garden trees and shrubs look at home in wild surroundings and are worthwhile wildlife resources. However you play it, a few trees and shrubs are of great value; besides food they provide birds with perching, roosting and nesting places, out of the way of predators.

Don't worry about giving trees or shrubs the 'right' spacing (after all, self-sown plants don't follow 'rules'), just pack a lot into a small space. Grow three trees in the space of one, with a large shrub underneath and climbers up it – it looks more natural anyway.

BIODIVERSITY

This is the big ecological buzzword these days. Basically all it means is a wide range of different species of plants, flowers, insects etc., that directly or indirectly support the larger creatures higher up the food chain. Biodiversity is a good thing to build into a wildlife garden as it makes the area part of a larger life-support system that's good for individual species but also – loosely – the health of the whole planet.

STAG BEETLES

If you live in certain parts of the country (mainly London and the South East), then your wild garden may house a very rare creature: the stag beetle.

It's quite unmistakable: a big black beetle (it's the biggest in Britain), over 2.5cm (1 inch) long. The male has a pair of fearsome nippers sticking out at the front, which he uses for fighting with other male stag beetles, which push and shove rather like real rutting stags, rather than nipping as such. The female has a body the same size but without the nippers.

Adult stag beetles only live for a month – you might spot a few flying around on warm evenings any time between June and August – but they don't eat during that time, as their main purpose in life is to find a mate, breed, and then die.

Stag beetles are attracted to dead wood, which they use as a crèche to lay their eggs in; the larvae then feed on the rotting wood for three years before emerging as the next generation of adults. This being the case, you are most likely to find stag beetles in heavily wooded gardens or in a garden within a wooded area, especially if it's a bit neglected. Unfortunately, modern forestry and woodland management tends to remove fallen trees so there's little or no rotting wood for these and other beetles to feed on, which is probably the main reason for the decline in their numbers. A loggery, however, provides just the right conditions.

COPPICING WITH CARE

Coppicing or even hard cutting-back is not a technique to use for most decorative garden trees and shrubs. It can often kill them. If you cut grafted trees or shrubs down hard you'll eliminate the named variety and leave only the rootstock behind, which grows strongly but isn't half so decorative. Hard cutting-back also 'forces' trees and shrubs to go vegetative and they'll usually stop flowering for several years afterwards. It's not a technique to use in your decorative garden to make big shrubs fit a small space – it often proves the truth in the old saying 'growth follows the knife'.

HOW TO COPPICE A TREE

The idea of coppicing is to cut down a growing tree to a stump, which then regenerates producing several long, straight shoots instead of a single trunk. The process can be repeated regularly every seven to fifteen years, and continued almost indefinitely. It does the trees no harm at all, in fact quite the reverse; coppiced trees are some of the oldest still alive today.

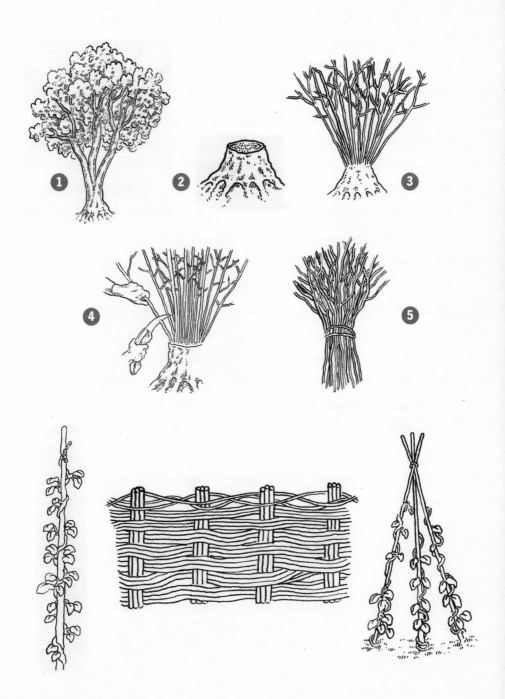

Coppicing was originally carried out to produce long, straight poles used in medieval house construction (thick poles were used as supporting uprights and roof timbers, and thinner stems were used for the wattle-and-daub wall panels). Coppiced stems also provided fencing and firewood; the thin trimmings were trussed into sheaf-like bundles called faggots that fuelled medieval bakers' ovens.

Coppicing is done in winter, between leaf fall in autumn and bud burst in spring, when the trees are bare and dormant. An established tree with a single trunk first has to be cut down to a stump 15–30cm (6–12 inches) above ground level, and then in the following years several strong shoots grow up from the stump. When they are thick enough for the job they are needed for, after 7–15 years, these poles are ready for harvesting, which again is done in winter.

Use a pruning saw to cut off all the stems to within a few inches of the 'stool' (as the stump is now known). Stack the poles and leave them to season for the winter, then trim the thicker pieces to length to use all round the garden as rustic fencing, for beanpoles (2.2 metres/7 feet is ideal) or for staking perennials and dahlias (1½ metres/5 feet). When you are trimming poles, save the twiggy tops to use as pea sticks (which need to be 1½–2 metres/5–6 feet long). Tie them in bundles with string for easy handling and prop them up against a shed wall to dry out; they usually last a couple of seasons before turning brittle.

The shortest bits, well dried out and stored in plastic sacks, make good kindling for starting barbecues, open fires and wood-burning stoves.

HOW TO MAKE A MOTH TRAP

A moth trap is the best way to find out what is flying round your garden after dark. You can buy a professional moth trap from entomological suppliers (they sometimes advertise in wildlife magazines, especially the quarterly publication sent out to members of Butterfly Conservation), but they have rather hefty price tags. Set it up outdoors on a fine evening (it needs plugging into a mains socket) and leave it on all night, then come back early in the morning before the sun gets up and 'cooks' the occupants. Tip the night's 'haul' out into large glass jars and identify them as quickly as possible, then let them go into a cool, shady bit of shrubbery where they can quickly hide themselves away for the day.

If you are good with your hands you might be able to make your own copy of a bought moth trap; it's basically a box with a special type of

very bright light suspended over the top that attracts moths, which then flutter down a chute into a chamber filled with bits of torn-up egg boxes into which the moths crawl away and hide. The whole thing needs to be protected from dew and rain since the light is electrical. Otherwise, make do with a Heath Robinson version, which is quite good enough to get you started. Moths are attracted to any outdoor electric light such as porch or patio lights; some of the stronger solar lights also attract them, or you can use a powerful torch (some extremely powerful rechargeable torches are available nowadays) with a piece of soft white cotton fabric draped over the lens. Set out a large white cloth on a table or a box, 30 centimetres (1 foot) or so under the light, and scatter torn up egg boxes over the surface of the fabric. Moths will come close to the light then drop down to the white cloth and crawl into the bits of egg box. Don't handle the moths themselves or you'll damage the delicate coating on their wings; pick up the bit of egg box they are clinging to and put them carefully into a wide-necked jar while you identify them – do so as quickly as possible, then release them straight away.

HOW TO ATTRACT BIRDS

Birds are attracted to gardens that provide them with food and water, but they'll linger longest where they feel secure, so you'll see far more birds in a garden that provides them with plenty of cover, too.

Birds are nervous creatures, and they like to withdraw to fairly mature trees and shrubs, a hedge or a climber-clad wall, where they can perch in safety between bouts of feeding. The mistake a lot of people make is to hang bird feeders or stand a bird table in the places that give the best view from the house; when they're right out in the open birds don't feel safe so they don't stay long. They'll spend more time at feeders that are closest to a safe, leafy retreat so they can hide at the first hint of a threat. Try to find a spot that fulfils their needs and gives you a good view, too.

When it comes to drinking and bathing, a wide, shallow bowl of water placed on the ground encourages birds to extend their visit, but best of all is a wildlife pond. You'll often see flocks of birds drinking and splashing about in the shallows at the same time, since there's safety in numbers. Sparrows also like to dust-bath, so it pays to have a patch of soft, fine, dry soil or silver sand under shrubs especially for them.

It helps keep their feathers in good condition, it's great fun to watch and it might just encourage these twenty-first century rarities to take up residence with you. A huge dome of a bay tree outside our back door support a two-dozen-strong colony of house sparrows (when they are not nesting under our eaves) and so the area has now become known as 'Tower Hamlets'!

Another good way to attract more birds, and a wider range of species, is to increase the amount of wild food that a garden provides over as much of the year as possible. This can easily be done by growing a good variety of plants that yield edible fruit, berries or seeds, or those that house insects such as small caterpillars and greenfly during the spring, when birds such as blackbirds and bluetits are bringing up chicks.

PLANTS TO ATTRACT BIRDS

You can feed nuts and seeds all the year round in feeders, but it's helpful if you can rely on nature, too, by planting natural food sources.

Crab apples: *Small-fruited varieties are best as they are most easily swallowed; 'Golden Hornet' is a favourite in autumn with blackbirds,* *thrushes and redwings, who pull them straight off the trees. Some varieties drop and are pecked and eaten off the ground once they've softened slightly.*

Windfall apples: *Whole eating and cooking apples are readily pecked on the ground by blackbirds, thrushes, redwings and fieldfares.*

Amelanchier: *Small garden tree producing small red fruits in midsummer, which blackbirds in particular just love.*

Sunflower: *Leave the dead flower heads so that seeds can form, then in late summer and autumn various finches will take them straight from the plants.*

Redcurrants: *Blackbirds pinch them off the plants in summer to feed to parties of fledglings they've brought round to teach how to feed themselves; it's worth growing a few bushes especially for them in a wildlife corner to watch the fun.*

Elder, rowan, cotoneaster, pyracantha, myrtle, hawthorn and **wild ivy:** *All of these treats are enjoyed by blackbirds in a changing sequence through autumn and winter. It is especially worthwhile including some of the later-ripening berries (ivy in particular) in case of a hard winter. In a very bad winter, gardens with good crops of late berries sometimes attract waxwings visiting temporarily from Scandinavia.*

Teazel: *Dramatic architecturally-shaped wild garden flower whose spiky seedheads attract goldfinches.*

Thistle: *Wild and cultivated thistles and their relatives (which include several perennial garden flowers, also artichokes), attract goldfinches to feed acrobatically from the seedheads.*

GARDEN VISITORS

Hedgehogs: *Popular prickly creatures that roll into a ball when threatened and come out mainly at night to feed on worms, slugs, caterpillars, woodlice and beetles, though they'll also eat dead birds and other carrion. They mate (rather noisily) in April, bear young in early summer and feed heavily in autumn to put on weight to see them through winter hibernation. They'll hole up in leaf piles under hedges or sheds, etc., from late October or November until March / April, but in a mild winter may emerge briefly to hunt for food. If you want to feed them (and it's worth doing so just before, and after, hibernation, and if they come out in winter), special dried or tinned hedgehog food is available from pet shops and wildlife centres, or put out whole peanuts of the sort used to feed birds (not the salted sort), or tinned cat food – but not fishy flavours, only meat. And don't give them bread and milk; they can't digest it and it upsets their stomachs.*

Foxes: *Thrive in a huge range of environments due to their ability to eat an assortment of things from mice, voles and rabbits to road-kill and dead birds. They also forage from dustbins and take food put out on lawns for birds; in autumn they'll eat fruit such as blackberries and windfall apples. Coastal foxes will patrol the beach at night in search of dead seagulls and anything else edible that's been washed up. They live in family groups and raise their cubs in a den, which might be a hole in a bank or hedge-bottom, or a hollow under a large tree stump, old shed or other outbuilding. In winter you'll often hear foxes yelping and making unearthly screams as part of their courtship; the cubs are born in early spring and you may see parents out hunting by day for a while when they have cubs to feed.*

Grass snakes: *Potentially our largest snake, up to 1.2m (4ft) long, olive green to brown (sometimes marked with darker bars) with a conspicuous yellow or off-white 'collar' round the neck. It feeds mainly on frogs, so it's usually found in grassy places near a pond, and may be seen swimming. Grass snakes often bask in the sun on fine days, or rest in damp shady places such as under an upturned boat, or large flat piece of wood. Adult females lay eggs in June in piles of rotting vegetation including compost heaps, which provide the warmth to hatch them; the young emerge in late August/early September. Grass snakes hibernate in crevices and holes from October to April.*

Slow worms: *Technically they are legless lizards rather than snakes; like lizards, they can shed their tail to escape from a predator; it eventually regrows. Slow worms have glossy bronze skin and live in wild, grassy places, often burrowing into piles of rotting vegetation (including the compost heap), feeding mainly on slugs. They mate in spring then lay eggs, from which* *the young slowworms emerge in August or September. They hibernate from October to March.*

Shrew: *Very active, small, carnivorous rodents with long, pointed, 'bottle-shaped' noses and short tails. They have to eat every few hours so they hunt day and night for worms, slugs, snails, woodlice and insects. Shrews are extremely territorial, emitting high-pitched shrieks to deter rivals; in wild gardens you'll hear them more often than see them. The young are born in April, but predators rarely take them as they taste foul; the big exception is owls, which don't seem to mind.*

Wood mice: *Also known as long-tailed field mice, these are probably the most common British mammal, but are not often seen as they're nocturnal. A wood mouse has a sandy brown back and white undersides, with very large ears, a long tail and long back legs which it uses to leap along the ground kangaroo-like when it's in a hurry. It has up to four litters of young each year, from March onwards, which it rears in a chamber inside a network of underground burrows. It feeds mainly on seeds, insects, grubs, fruit and berries, but will also bite open snail shells to eat the occupants. It is preyed on by owls, foxes and domestic cats.*

Bank voles: *The other common rodent inhabitant of a wild garden; often seen by day – look for the chunky shape, small ears, short tail, short nose and short legs with chestnut coat (slightly grey on the underside); it scurries along instead of leaping like a wood mouse. Bears four or five litters of young each year, between early spring and autumn. Feeds on hazelnuts, berries, seeds, fruit, fungi and some greenery. It is preyed on by owls, kestrels, foxes and cats.*

Moles: *Chunky, hamster-sized animals with black, velvety coats that don't lie flat in one direction like those of dogs and cats, allowing the creatures to move backwards or forwards with equal ease in tight tunnels. Moles have tiny eyes, a bare snout and large, spade-like front feet it uses for tunnelling. They are rarely seen as they live underground the majority of the time, but most people are familiar with the molehills that they push up in grassland and lawns to get rid of soil generated when they are tunnelling into a new area. (Though these make moles unpopular with lawn-lovers, molehills aren't a problem in a wild garden.) Moles feed mainly on earthworms, which they 'harvest' from the walls of special 'feeding tunnels' that are patrolled regularly; these are quite separate from the tunnels used for rearing their young; they have one litter per year, born in April or May. The only natural predators of moles are owls, since they taste too unpleasant for other potential predators.*

Grey squirrels: *Aerial athletes that leap from tree to tree or scamper across short grass. They build dreys which look rather like scruffy crows' nests (except that dreys are close to the trunk, not usually out on branches), high up in large trees for rearing their young in spring. They feed on young shoots and tree bark, bulbs, flowers, and in autumn are often seen burying nuts and acorns to act as winter reserves – grey squirrels do not hibernate. Alas, these aliens have seen off our native 10 Red squirrel in most parts of the UK – its strongholds are few and far between now, but they can be spotted on the Isle of Wight, Brownsea Island in Poole Harbour, and in parts of Scotland, Cornwall and Lancashire.*

CHAPTER 4

LIVING OFF THE LAND

....

Can you live off the land? It's the dream of a good few folk who head into smallholding or crofting. The secret of a successful smallholding is hard work and attention to detail. Livestock needs looking after 24/7: there's a lot of manure to shovel, worming and ear-tagging to do, matings and births to supervise, unexplained deaths to investigate and animals to send off to slaughter. Livestock is also a tie; it's not easy to find someone to take over for a few weeks if you want to take holidays or even go away for a few days. If you're prepared for the reality, running a smallholding is very rewarding.

But, however self-sufficient you are, there's always the odd bill that can only be paid with real money – council tax, utility bills, petrol or diesel for vehicles, vet's bills, livestock feed, seeds and fertilisers, plus any food or household goods you can't make or grow – quite apart from mod-cons and holidays that the family won't want to do without.

You can certainly make some income from sales of honey, eggs, fruit, veg, salads or herbs, at the garden gate or to local shops or hotels, particularly where the proprietors are very clued up and have a name for sourcing local fresh/organic produce, which is increasingly in demand these days. But however high the quality, many shops and restaurants need regular supplies all year round and may not be interested in irregular or purely seasonal purchases. Farmers' markets can be another good outlet for produce, as can organisations that run 'box schemes' where a selection of seasonal fresh fruit and veg is delivered regularly to participating householders.

If you raise livestock and/or poultry, you'll be able to sell surplus young stock to other breeders or as pets, and any meat you can't use or put in the freezer yourself can usually, by prior arrangement with the slaughter-house, be sold or used to offset the cost of slaughter and butchery.

Most smallholders and crofters, however, need alternative sources of income; there are several that fit in nicely with a country lifestyle, but developing any kind of income stream usually needs extra investment to get it off the ground.

Running a B&B is a favourite choice for sociable people who enjoy looking after guests, and a well laid out smallholding, especially one stocked with rare breeds of livestock or pretty poultry, is an extra 'draw'. To do B&B takes a large house, with space to provide a guest breakfast room. You'll need to bring guest bedrooms up to scratch – these days a bedroom with a TV and an en-suite bathroom is almost essential, as well as a high standard of decoration and furnishing, and a lot of guests prefer self-contained accommodation in an annexe that has its own front door so they can come and go as they please. You'll need to publicise yourself by paying for space in B&B guides and/or advertising in magazines, and be inspected to ensure that you comply with fire regulations and other legislation. The overnight rate you can charge will vary with your location and the rating you achieve with the tourist board, which is based on the facilities and standard of accommodation you offer.

If you have a talent for country arts and crafts and want to sell your wares to the public, one of the best ways to do so is by taking stands at countryside shows. You'll need to take plenty of stock along (which means having a lot of storage space at home), plus a stand with whatever leaflets, posters or point-of-sale material you have, and a suitable vehicle for deliv-ering off-road. You'll need to plan your sales strategy and book stand-space at shows well in advance – often a year ahead. Alternatively, you might sell direct to the public from local craft shops – who will want to take a commission on every sale they make on your behalf – or from a dedicated studio/workshop at home.

It's also possible to turn your specialist hobbies or interests into money-making opportunities by teaching. All sorts of organisations need specialist speakers and tutors, from adult education centres and local groups to craft centres who hold short courses, though for some it's essential to have a formal qualification. If you start doing talks or teaching, it's also worth taking some training in public speaking to learn how to project your voice and organise your material, to give a professional presentation that comes across well.

Another option is to open your smallholding to the public, either for individual special 'days' (such as 'Farm Sunday') or for more regular visits from schools or local groups. (There's currently a stewardship scheme called Educational Access, which is run by the Countryside Stewardship and Environmental Stewardship Schemes – see the Defra website.) Opening to the public involves a lot of red tape, especially regarding hygiene and extra insurance. If you're organising special days for the general public you'll be competing with other tourist attractions so you'll need to lay on more than just a guided walk-round to make a success of it – perhaps cream teas, plant sales, displays or demonstrations, and you'll need to rent portable loos and provide adequate car parking, signposts, and leaflets to assist visitors, besides arranging publicity for the event.

But one of the newest sources of additional income is from power generation. Without making a big investment yourself, it's possible to obtain rent from hosting a wind turbine or solar power plant on your land.

REDUCING OVERHEADS

There's a lot you can do to cut down overheads by using solar panels to heat your water, or generating electricity from photo-voltaic cells or wind turbines. By harvesting rainwater from roofs of the house and outbuildings to use for non-drinking purposes, such as flushing loos or washing down yards and watering crops, you can save a lot of money when you're on metered water.

MANURE COLLECTING

If you keep a lot of livestock on a relatively small area of land, instead of waiting for dung beetles to bury the manure that's deposited, go round every few days with a rubber trug and collect it up to put on the compost heap in your veg patch. The grass recovers faster, and your compost will rot down quicker given the free 'starter'.

POULTRY

....

CHICKENS

You can keep chickens in even a small garden; just make sure they've got a safe hut to sleep and lay their eggs in, and a space to run and scratch around in, and they'll reward you with delicious fresh eggs. Anyone with a large lawn can keep two to six birds in a portable ark which is moved daily. I've had great success with those neat plastic 'Eglu' runs, which are easy to maintain and to move. For a larger number of hens, you'll need a freestanding henhouse fitted with perches and nest boxes.

Perches should be placed as high up as possible, at waist level or above. Nest boxes should be the shape and size of an orange box, and fixed a handy hen's leap above ground level (which means roughly knee-high); they should be partly filled with bedding such as straw or wood shavings, which needs replacing once or twice a week. Since the eggs must be collected daily, it's best to buy the type of henhouse that has nest boxes built into the sides with hinged 'lids' that can be opened from outside; it makes the job quicker and easier, and you won't be disturbing the hens.

A henhouse also needs a securely fenced run around the outside. If the run is large enough it can be grassed over, but hens will soon scratch up the grass in a small run and reduce it to mud, so it's best surfaced with wood shavings or straw.

Hens need to be shut in at night. Henhouses usually feature a 'pop-hole', which is a hen-sized hole fitted with a sliding 'door' that can be secured in the open position by day and then lowered at night. Hens lay almost all of their eggs before about 10 am, so keeping them in until then makes certain the eggs are laid in nest boxes and not outside in the run, where they get dirty. If you have to leave for work early, then you'll need to open the pop-hole before you go and trust to luck that you can find them! Eggs laid outside may not be very fresh by the time they are discovered – they'll also attract egg thieves such as magpies and crows.

Hens need three regular inputs: water, food and grit. Clean water should be available at all times, and the best way to make sure it's kept clean is by using a proper drinker with its own built-in 'reservoir', which is topped up every day or two.

Hens will happily eat grain – usually whole wheat, though the addition of kibbled (broken-up) or flaked (flattened) maize makes for eggs with deeper yellow yolks, and chickens fed a fair percentage of maize produce better-flavoured flesh with a rather golden colour. (This is what the supermarkets and butchers mean by corn-fed chickens.) This is all my chickens are given, plus whatever they can get from scratching around under the damson trees in their grassy run. For maximum egg yields, many people feed layers' mash or layers' pellets, either alone or mixed with a little wheat and/or maize.

Although it looks rustic to throw feed onto the ground for chickens, it is wasteful (and, given hens' toilet habits, rather unhygienic), so the feed is best tipped out into a hopper first thing each morning where the birds can help themselves any time. If possible, keep the hopper under cover to prevent feed being taken by sparrows or ruined by rain.

Hens also need flint grit, which helps them grind up hard grains so they are digested properly, and oystershell grit, which provides the calcium that ensures their eggs have strong shells. Both types of grit should be available to the birds at all times. Even when they can run around outside, they won't find enough naturally. Hens also need to be able to peck at greenery, both for their health and because it improves the quality of their eggs or meat, so if they don't have access to a grassy run or veg patch, hang up a bunch of greens for them. Give them logs or branches to jump around on; the exercise does them good, and it's fun to watch.

A henhouse needs cleaning out regularly so it doesn't smell and to prevent pests or disease; it also means the hens' feet stay fairly clean so they don't tread muck into their nest boxes and dirty the eggs. Even so, do replace the straw in the nest boxes every week. Both this and dirty straw or wood shavings from the floor of the henhouse can be added to a compost heap; fresh hen manure is high in nitrogen so it makes a good activator that helps a heap rot down quickly – don't dig it straight into the ground, as it is so 'strong' it can scorch plants.

FOXES AND RATS

Once a fox has entered the run it will like as not kill all the birds, even if it does not take any of them. Sometimes the sight of one is enough to frighten the birds, which creates stress and puts them off laying. If there are foxes in the area (and there are foxes in almost every area), then you have two options. First is to fence the run to a height of 1.8m (6ft) and put wire netting across the top of it as well – foxes can climb higher than you would think and they can dig, so bury the base of the wire 30cm (12in) deep in the earth. The second option, and the most successful and convenient, is to run a strand of electrified wire along the top of a paling fence – powered by a battery. (You can buy simple and small electric fence kits at farm and country shops.) For the last ten years this method has worked for me during the day, and the chickens are shut in safely at night.

It's also necessary to protect henhouses from rats, which soon learn where to come to steal henfeed, and if they get away with it they keep coming back. They'll also pinch eggs. Baited rat traps can be set under angled paving slabs laid alongside walls and fences, or position poisoned traps in the same spot.

STARTING WITH CHICKENS

Most people start chicken-keeping by buying 'point-of-lay pullets', which begin laying eggs within a couple of weeks of being introduced to their new home. (Most hens can be reckoned to start laying at the age of 20 weeks.) 'Growers' are young birds which cost less to buy but need feeding for several weeks before they start laying.

Experienced poultry-keepers will sometimes buy young or even day-old chicks, which are far cheaper, but they need special facilities to keep them warm day and night, and they take a good deal of care and attention. The youngsters take several months to reach egg-laying age and some losses are inevitable on the way, so it's not always as cost-effective as it appears. It's also sometimes possible to buy fertile eggs which need to go under a broody hen or into an incubator to hatch, but this needs a bigger investment and more skill.

The cheapest and perhaps most satisfying way to start is to re-home retired battery hens. Several organisations save 'old' chickens from battery farms, when they'd otherwise be culled. A rescue chicken is normally 'retired' from commercial flock at one year old, but it will keep laying for another three years or more, often starting from within a few days of being re-homed. Because rescue chickens are not used to outdoor life, they need to be kept shut into the henhouse for a short while after their move, but once allowed out they quickly start wandering cautiously outside and soon begin to scratch around, flapping their wings, pecking greenery, and doing all the things that hens do in natural surroundings. They soon replace lost feathers and bald patches; some specialist animal feed firms supply special feeds for rescue hens, which provide extra calcium and minerals to help them make stronger bones, joints and feathers after life in battery cages where they get no exercise. It's a joy to watch them recover and take on a new lease of life. If you have to introduce new hens to an existing flock, pop them into the henhouse at night when the birds have gone to roost – it makes for a calmer form of integration.

CHICKENS IN THE KITCHEN GARDEN

Hens are very good at clearing up. They can be allowed to run around in an orchard or even – out of season – in a fruit cage. If you have a kitchen garden, you can let the hens out into the area when the crops are finished; they'll peck away at old cabbage leaves, weeds and weed seeds, soil pests and caterpillars, and they'll turn the ground over by scratching around, and manure it at the same time. Some keen veg gardeners deliberately position their chicken house in between two or four fenced veg plots in order to let the hens out into whichever patch is 'free' at the time. However, it's no good letting hens out into growing crops in the hope that they'll weed between rows or clear pests; they'll just eat your plants and scratch up your seedlings.

HOW MANY HENS DO YOU NEED?

If you're buying hens with egg production in mind, first work out exactly how many birds you'll really need. A hen in its prime, well fed and kept free from stress, will usually lay an egg every day, although productivity does decline in winter due to low light levels. Mine tend to lay daily between January and October, then go 'off lay' for about three months. Some hen-keepers cheat and leave a low-wattage electric light on in the henhouse for a few hours on winter nights to 'top up' the natural daylight to a total of 16 hours per day, which triggers the birds to keep laying year-round.

For most families, two or three hens will provide as many eggs as you can comfortably use up; if you keep more you'll be spending out needlessly on feed. But out in the country a lot of poultry-keepers sell their surplus eggs at the garden gate.

WHICH CHICKEN BREED?

Anyone intent on producing eggs reasonably seriously usually chooses one of the high-yielding, hybrid, commercial kinds, which lay far more eggs than pure breeds. But if you are keeping hens for home consumption and fun as much as for gain, choose one of the handsome unusual or rare breeds.

Wyandottes: *Available in various colours including white, lavender, black, buff and blue, but silver-laced and silver-pencilled are particularly showy.*

Leghorn: *The classic farmyard hen with a sleek shape, chestnut breast and dark grey back and tail.*

Maran: *Handsome chunky chickens barred dark grey / black and white, which lay deep brown eggs.*

Light Sussex: *Popular traditional breed of white hens with a black lacy collar round the neck, and also at the tip of the tail; lays white eggs.*

Rhode Island Red: *Popular, traditional breed of warm-brown hens laying brown eggs.*

Buff Orpingtons: *Big and fluffy with foxy-orange feathers. Often go broody, which may be an advantage if you want to raise your own chicks.*

Corals: *White speckled with cream, very friendly.*

Bantams: *These small breeds eat a bit less than full-sized chickens and lay slightly smaller eggs, but plenty of them. Some breeds are very good-looking, and some lay eggs with unusually coloured shells – such as green – which taste the same and have the same culinary uses as chickens' eggs. Bantams tend to 'go broody' a lot, and since they make excellent mothers, are often used to hatch the eggs and rear the young of other birds, especially exhibition chickens and ducks. The most popular bantam breed is the Silkie; these strange shaggy birds – usually white – have feathery feet and lay blue-green eggs. My favourites are Lavender Pekins, with blue-grey feathers and feathery feet.*

DO YOU NEED A COCKEREL OR NOT?

Hens will lay without a cockerel being present; the eggs will simply be infertile so they'll never hatch into chicks. Some chicken-keepers like to keep a cockerel as he looks big and showy with his large red comb and wattles and a long arched tail. If you're counting the costs, you might feel he is just an extra mouth to feed, but a cockerel keeps a close eye on 'his girls', giving audible warning and often going on the attack if there's a predator about, but in built-up areas, alas, some neighbours are not very keen on the sound of a cockerel crowing as he tends to be noisiest around the crack of dawn.

If you want to rear chicks then you'll have to keep a cockerel, so the hens will lay fertile eggs. The only slight drawback with having fertile eggs is that if you don't collect them daily, keep them in a cool fridge and use them fairly promptly, they'll often start to develop a red spot in the centre, which is an early chick embryo. Although an egg in this state is still okay to eat or use for cooking, a lot of people find it a tad off-putting.

POULTRY PROBLEMS

Hens need to be wormed to kill internal parasites; it's also possible to use a product to kill worm eggs on the ground in the hen run.

Hens also get mites; affected birds are irritable and don't lay well as they are under stress – it's a dead give-away if eggs have tiny spots of blood on them. Ideally use a mite-repellent product on perches or on the floor of runs before birds are affected; some products also contain disinfectants that protect against infections including E. coli, salmonella and listeria. You can also get mite powder to apply directly onto the birds. This is the reason I have 'plastic' hen houses – the mites are very difficult to get rid of in a wooden house with lots of crevices.

Various products to treat everyday ailments and for use as precautions, including natural chemical-free ones, are sold at pet shops, animal feed centres and agricultural stores and are also advertised in poultry-keeping and smallholding magazines, but always consult a vet in case of problems.

BROODY HENS

'Going broody' is natural for hens; it's what happens when a hen decides to sit on a clutch of eggs and hatch them instead of laying more. Broody hens look listless, go off their food and spend all their time sitting in a nest box – they can be aggressive with other hens who try to use the nest boxes, and may peck at humans who try to shift them to collect the eggs.

Broodiness happens most with bantams and pure breeds of chicken, least with commercial hybrids, and can happen even when hens aren't kept with a cockerel. If a hen turns broody, either pen her on her own for a week or so until she gets over it (fresh air and very little comfort is what she needs) or let her sit on a clutch of eggs and raise chicks. Either way, lift her twice a day to make sure she eats and drinks.

RAISING CHICKS FROM EGGS

A broody hen doesn't have to hatch her own eggs; indeed, if you don't keep a cockerel there's no point in trying as they won't be fertile – you can obtain fertile eggs of a different variety from a breeder, or even use a broody hen to hatch bantam, duck or turkey eggs, since bantams make particularly good mothers.

A broody hen won't be happy in the usual henhouse with other hens around. Move her and her clutch of eggs into her own nest box in a separate run, and leave her to sit on them until they hatch (it takes 21 days). Duck or turkey eggs take a few days longer to hatch, but most broodies will keep sitting for the extra time it takes. During the whole time a broody hen is sitting on eggs, you'll need to lift her carefully off them daily and take her to food and water, otherwise she may not bother to feed, and give her the chance to relieve herself – she won't do so while she's sitting on eggs. Then let her go back. Once the chicks have hatched, she'll look after them automatically. Within a day or so of hatching they'll be wandering round with her looking for food and water so you'll have to lay in a stock of chick crumbs. (This is very fine dried food that their tiny beaks can manage and which contain all the nutrients they need.) Good hygiene is vital, so make sure food and containers are cleaned daily, and clean out the pen they are kept in extra well and more often than usual.

CLIPPING WINGS

Despite their seemingly un-aerodynamic shape, chickens can fly – at least enough to flutter clumsily over a fence round their run – so most owners clip their wings to stop them getting airborne. It's easily done with a strong pair of gardening secateurs. Have an assistant to hold the chicken firmly but gently, and stretch out one wing. Snip through the large, long flight feathers at the tip of one wing, cutting them off at least a couple of inches from their base, so you are cutting through the 'quill' – this way, you won't draw blood and it won't hurt the bird. It's best just to clip one wing, since this unbalances the bird so it feels less inclined to try to fly – if it has a go it's very lopsided so it soon gives up. Since chickens moult regularly, you'll need to repeat the process a couple of times each year. Usually the first sign you get that it's time to clip wings again is when you spot hens trying to take off and fluttering a bit higher than usual, or you see a lot of cast-off feathers in their run, showing that they have started to moult.

DUCKS

Ducks are just as easy to keep as hens, but if you keep both don't keep them together – give them separate accommodation.

Ducks don't need perches or nest boxes, so their house can be a lot lower than a henhouse. A small hut will do, but a custom-made duck house is usually triangular in cross section, with a pop-hole fitted with a sliding door and a roof that lifts open for cleaning out and for collecting eggs. The house needs plenty of straw bedding on the floor – this is where they'll lay their eggs, so it needs to be changed regularly to keep it clean, and ducks make a heck of a lot of mess.

They also need a run, which needs to be bigger than a hen run. Ducks soon foul a small area of land so they need plenty of room; allow at least 1.4 square metres (15 square feet) per bird. Better still, make a second run adjacent to the first, so that one area of ground can be 'rested' for a few weeks while the grass recovers, before the birds are moved back. Alternatively, ducks can be allowed to roam freely in a farmyard or orchard during the day, but they must be shut up in a hut at night, and protected from foxes and rodents.

Ducks are happiest when they have access to a pond – even a small one is enough for them to bathe and splash about in. Make a small duck pond by digging out a dish-shaped hollow and lining it with concrete. A concrete pond is easy to keep clean – sweep out the water every week with a stiff broom and replace it with fresh. Whatever you do, don't try to introduce ducks to a decorative garden pond. Oh, they'll love it, but in no time at all they'll have eaten all the plants and the fish, and turned the surroundings into a sea of mud. They'll also foul the water and turn it murky and smelly. No, keep them to a pond of their own, which is inside their run and fenced off from the surrounding area so they can't get out into the garden or your veg patch. If there's no room for a pond, then give ducks a large tub that's sunk into a hole in the ground that they can splash about in. It's most important they can get their heads under water. Their eyes and beaks need to be rinsed frequently in clean water; if you're using a container make sure it's regularly cleaned out and refilled.

Ducks will find a lot of their own food if there's space to roam, but they will appreciate a bowl of pelleted food and one of fresh water. They need clean drinking water at all times, so provide them with a separate bowl (one that's too small for them to get into) and change it daily. Ducks can't drink from the same sort of water dispenser as chickens since their wide beaks prevent them dipping into the narrow trough area.

Ducks will find a lot of their own food if they have access to a large field or orchard in which to forage; they are especially good at clearing slugs and snails from land used for growing vegetables after the crops have been harvested (since they'll also eat plants) and if you can cope with their feet flattening the ground. But they do need something more solid as well; ducks do well on a homemade mixture of whole wheat, barley, crushed oats and flaked maize (special pellets are available). The food can be scattered on a clean bit of ground (which can be difficult to find in a duck run) or else tipped into a trough, which needs to be cleaned out regularly. Since their wide beaks mean they can shovel their food down quickly, they'll clear a meal quickly and keep eating until they can hardly walk, so give them as much food as they can eat within 20 minutes, and do this twice a day – morning and evening.

BREEDS OF DUCK

The type of duck you choose will depend on whether you want your birds for eggs, meat or ornament.

Muscovy ducks: *Large heavy-looking deep-grey/ black-and-white ducks with a reddish 'knob' on top of the beak, often kept as ornamental waterfowl on duck ponds. They are also known as Barbary ducks, which are favourites for meat; they fatten rapidly and are usually killed at 10 weeks old for the table. Muscovies make the best broody ducks.*

Aylesbury: *The classic 'table' ducks. These large, deep-chested white birds have orange beaks and also lay about 100 eggs a year, making them a useful dual-purpose breed.*

Indian Runners: *Very tall, striking, upright ducks, usually white or brown but also available in various colours, mostly kept as pets or for showing, though they do produce around 180 eggs per year.*

> **Khaki Campbells:** *Again of upright demeanour, dull, light brown ducks, the favourite egg-laying breed, and very productive, yielding 300 eggs per year. White Campbells are equally good. They rarely go broody, so if you want to raise more of your own it's best to put fertile Khaki Campbell eggs under a broody bantam.*

REARING DUCKS FROM EGGS

Domesticated ducks are very poor mothers, so it's better to give a clutch of fertile eggs to a bantam to hatch. You will need to splash the eggs with water daily to dampen them slightly, since a duck does this naturally but a bantam won't. Even though duck eggs take slightly longer than hens eggs to hatch (28 days instead of 21), a bantam foster-mother will keep sitting until they do, then she'll take on the job of looking after ducklings despite her obvious concern at their tendency to take an 'unhealthy' interest in water. Feed the ducklings with chick crumbs and make sure they always have access to clean drinking water, as well as a wide, shallow bowl of water in which to bathe and – if it's deep enough – swim around in.

GEESE

Geese are the easiest poultry of all to keep, for anyone with plenty of grassy space available. A small flock of geese is a good way to keep an area of rough grass cropped without the need for mowing, since they'll graze it short, and when grass is growing vigorously they can live on it without supplementary feeding, which keeps feed bills down. The only slight downside is that their droppings make a mess of the grass, especially if they are confined to a small area, so they need to be kept off your garden lawn.

Geese need a good-sized grassy area in which to wander by day, and ideally it should be fenced to protect them from foxes. They need a hut for shelter, with straw or wood shavings on the floor, and a pop-hole since they need to be shut in at night. Like ducks they don't need perches, though it's worth having a nest box area along one side, at ground level, in which they can lay their eggs, since this keeps them cleaner than leaving them on the ground. It's far quicker and easier to collect the eggs if the lid of the nest area opens from the outside, and there's no risk of a close encounter with a disgruntled goose in a confined space. A hut for geese needs a higher roof than a duck house, since geese are clearly much bigger, taller birds.

When there isn't enough grass to keep them well fed (usually in the winter and during dry summers), geese should be fed whole wheat and barley grains twice daily – morning and late afternoon – in a trough or thrown over a clean patch of ground.

They'll also enjoy fresh greens, so put out old cabbage, kale, broccoli and Brussels sprout plants to strip, and give them any lettuce plants that have run to seed, or let them into your veg patch in winter to clear the ground after the crops are finished. They are generally fairly problem free, though they should be treated regularly for internal parasites.

Geese appreciate access to a pond, which they can share with ducks, though they can be kept without one as long as they are given a deep trough or tub of clean water that's changed regularly; it's essential they can plunge their heads under water completely to rinse their eyes and beaks properly.

GOOSE EGGS

Geese lay the biggest eggs of any domestic poultry, weighing roughly half a pound apiece. A single one is equivalent to four large hen's eggs – enough for a whole omelette. Adult birds start laying in February or

March and continue until roughly midsummer, and over that time each bird will produce approximately 70 eggs. You can sometimes sell a few goose eggs at the gate, or to local farm shops, but they aren't well known to the general public so you'll probably end up using most of them yourself. But perhaps the best way to use surplus eggs is to allow a goose to hatch a clutch and rear the young for their meat.

RAISING GEESE FROM EGGS

Rearing geese from scratch is very simple as the mother goose does most of the work. Allow her to sit on a clutch of up to 14 eggs, ideally in a separate enclosure of her own where the other geese won't bother her. She'll need constant access to water, as she'll use some to splash the eggs with daily, or they may well not hatch – and you'll need to bring her food and water since she won't want to wander far. Keep her well fenced in because foxes find a sitting goose and her eggs a very appealing target; rats will also make a beeline for the eggs so take anti-rodent precautions. It's possible to hatch goose eggs under a broody hen, but you'll need to splash them with water daily and turn them – mark one side with a pencilled 'X' so you know which way they are meant to be, since they are too heavy for the hen to turn.

Goose eggs take 30 days to hatch. When the goslings emerge, they'll appreciate some shallow water to splash about in if they don't have a pond, and you'll need to feed them on chick crumbs. They'll soon start to eat grass and once they are doing well on their own you can stop supplementary feeding as long as there's plenty of grass. If you want to hurry them along to reach slaughter size fast, continue feeding them; give them whole wheat and whole barley, mixed in roughly equal quantities. Traditionally, goose was never eaten until Michaelmas (29 September) at the earliest, with most kept for Christmas. As a bonus, goose fat makes the best roast potatoes ever, and each bird produces a big bowlful.

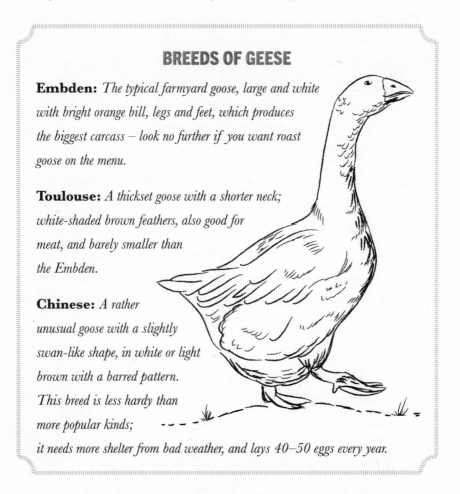

BREEDS OF GEESE

Embden: *The typical farmyard goose, large and white with bright orange bill, legs and feet, which produces the biggest carcass – look no further if you want roast goose on the menu.*

Toulouse: *A thickset goose with a shorter neck; white-shaded brown feathers, also good for meat, and barely smaller than the Embden.*

Chinese: *A rather unusual goose with a slightly swan-like shape, in white or light brown with a barred pattern. This breed is less hardy than more popular kinds; it needs more shelter from bad weather, and lays 40–50 eggs every year.*

TURKEYS

Of all poultry, turkeys are the trickiest to keep. They are susceptible to the cold and wet so they need a good-sized hut with deep bedding as they won't go outside much in bad weather, though it's a good idea to give them access to a large outside area (a grassy field or orchard is ideal – so when conditions allow it they can get out for some fresh air and exercise – they like to scratch about a bit).

Turkeys are also very prone to disease, so good hygiene is a must. Besides cleaning them out and replacing their bedding regularly, it's essential to keep feed and water containers scrupulously clean. Don't allow them to share living accommodation or outdoor grazing with other poultry because there's a risk they'll pick something up from their neighbours. Feed them on whole grain or special pellets for turkeys.

Though the females do lay eggs sometimes, turkeys are mainly kept for meat. Commercially, white hybrid turkeys are the usual choice since their flesh is light-coloured; they are fast to fatten and can reach 4kg (9lb) in 12 weeks or 7kg (15lb) in 16 weeks. But when you rear your own on a small scale you can go for a tastier alternative – the traditional Norfolk Black, which produces darker, richer meat, sells for a premium, especially if its kept free range and fed organically.

Breeding turkeys is the trickiest part of the exercise, so ideally when starting out you should buy young birds to rear. However, if you can get hold of some fertile turkey eggs, give them to a broody bantam – they take 28 days to hatch – and feed the young hatched birds on specially formulated turkey crumbs until they are big enough to start taking the usual whole grain or pellets.

GUINEA FOWL

Guinea fowl are second only to geese when it comes to easy upkeep. Like geese, guinea fowl are happiest when they are allowed to run around freely by day (in an area fenced against foxes and other predators) and they need to be shut into a suitably sized hut at night. Provide clean water and feed them twice daily on whole wheat grains with some kibbled maize or game bird pellets. If they're given a large area to roam in, they will find quite a bit of their own food while they are scratching around – they are very handy for clearing up a veg patch. The birds can be a bit noisy and rather nervy, and unless you keep their wings clipped they'll fly up into trees to perch or roost. A young bird is ready for the pot at 10 weeks old, weighing half a kilo to a kilo (1½–2lb).

If you want to raise your own from scratch, guinea fowl don't make good mothers so it's usual to give fertile eggs to a bantam to hatch. Eggs take 28 days to hatch, just as for ducks' eggs.

QUAIL

Domestic quail make an unusual alternative to other forms of poultry. They are ideal for keeping on a small scale, mainly for their eggs, though sometimes for their meat. Quail lay well; when kept indoors, birds start laying at 10–12 weeks old and commercial producers get 200–300 eggs per year from each hen. Even when kept outside they'll still be very productive. Four hen birds will give you more eggs than you need in spring and summer.

When kept for meat they mature quickly, and are ready for the pot at six weeks old, but the final carcass is so small – only 22g (½lb) – you really wonder if it's worth the effort of plucking, as it takes two birds to make a meal for one person. (When you rear your own, it might be worth treating them the same way a lot of country people treat wild pigeon: simply cut the breast off each side of the breastbone and discard the rest of the carcass, which has virtually no meat on it.)

My quail have a 'winter' home in what looks like a rabbit hutch with a wire-netting front and a side compartment filled with straw where they can go to lay their eggs. On cold nights I lower a double sheet of bubble wrap over the front since the birds are not quite as hardy as chickens. Some folk keep quail in this kind of 'rabbit hutch' all year round, but I like to move the birds to a wire-netting-covered outdoor run from spring to autumn – it has a wire netting floor, too (to keep out vermin) and sits on grass. Alternatively, it can be set on clean bark chippings or sand (which needs replacing regularly). Some logs or leafy branches to investigate and hide among will be appreciated. If they don't have a hen-type house to go into, give them a slightly screened off corner for shelter. (Don't use an open-topped run or your birds may fly away!)

Quail don't need perches or nest boxes and they lay their eggs on the floor – anywhere! – so they need collecting frequently.

Those kept for meat are usually housed in a shed or similar outbuilding as they'll grow faster, but ideally give them access to an open-air run during the day as they like to go outside, unless the weather is poor. They need cleaning out often. Like any poultry, quail need clean water at all times. Special ready-mixed quail feeds are available but can be difficult to find if local livestock feed suppliers don't have any other quail-keepers amongst their customers, in which case give them crumb-sized feeds formulated for turkeys or game birds – if you can't get these, use chick crumbs.

PIGS

HOW TO REAR WEANERS

You can rear young pigs in the open, given an ark for shelter, or in a concrete sty with a covered area and an outdoor run. They'll need plenty of straw bedding in their shelter – it needs topping up regularly – and they'll have fun rearranging it and sorting through in case there's anything interesting to eat that they've missed. Pigs are intelligent and appreciate something to do; some smallholders give them a football to play with. Pigs kept in the open will find a damp area to turn into a mud-patch to wallow in; they'll also like to have a big tree for shade, as pigs (especially pale pink hairless breeds) can get sunburnt on hot summer days. When they are kept in a sty, pigs will need cleaning out daily; they are naturally clean animals that will keep using the same corner as their loo. Between different batches of weaners, clean the living area thoroughly, disinfect it and rinse it well, and replace all the bedding entirely.

As for food, the old days when wartime smallholders collected food scraps from schools and householders to make into mash for fattening pigs are long gone – it's now illegal. There's just too much risk of diseases such as foot and mouth. (The 2001 outbreak was traced back to the use of untreated waste food.) You can, however, feed your pigs fruit and veg from your own holding, as long as you don't operate a catering business, and you can also feed surplus milk from your holding to pigs if you register with DEFRA. (But regulations change, so it's worth checking the current rules with your local Animal Health Divisional Office.)

When you only keep a few weaners, the easiest option is to use ready-made pelleted feed sold in bags; it can be bought in bulk and will keep for quite a long time if the bags are stored in a clean, dry, rodent-free place. Pellets are clean and easy to handle, and quick to feed. Give weaners two feeds each day, morning and late afternoon/early evening, in a trough, which must be cleaned regularly. As a rough guide to consumption, at eight weeks old each weaner will need 700g (1½lb) of feed a day, rising gradually to 1½kg (3lb) a day by the time they are ready for slaughter at 20 weeks old, when they'll be the perfect size for pork. (If you're using weaners from a rare breed such as Tamworths, they'll grow more slowly than modern commercial pigs, so expect them to take 26 weeks to reach slaughter size.) In cold weather, pigs use more energy keeping warm, so if you keep yours outside in winter, be prepared to increase their rations slightly to compensate. If you have surplus fruit and veg or milk, then they are best used as 'treats' to supplement their normal 'concentrated' feed; if you try to treat them as free food in place of part of their usual rations, they won't fatten so quickly.

BACON AND HAMS

If you intend rearing weaners to produce bacon and hams, they need to be kept longer than pork pigs so that they produce a larger carcass – bacon pigs are usually kept until they are about 32 weeks old. Naturally this means extra expense since they'll eat more and need more straw, not to mention labour for cleaning out, etc. Some smallholders prefer to keep old breeds of pigs that lay down far more fat than is acceptable for a modern porker, especially for bacon and ham production, since the flavour is in the fat. Traditionally, weaners for bacon and hams were bought in spring and fattened until shortly before Christmas.

WILD BOAR

The 'wild boar' meat sold in butchers is invariably a cross between real wild boar and Tamworth, which makes the pigs more docile and easy to manage. To keep real wild boar, which are regarded as dangerous wild animals, you need a licence, and have to keep them particularly well fenced in and display warning notices round the boundaries.

HOW TO BREED PIGS

A breeding sow will grow to a surprising size and get to know her keepers. Rare breeds in particular are great characters. Breeding sows, especially old and rare breeds which were bred for the job, are happy to live outdoors in a securely fenced grassy field, with an ark to shelter in. Several sows will happily share the same space if it's a reasonable size, with each sow having her own ark to retreat to and have her piglets in. They enjoy rooting around together, and they'll turn muddy patches into wallows, where they can take cooling mud baths (which protects against sunburn in strong sun). You can also move them around during the year; in an orchard they'll eat windfall apples, or can be turned out into a field that's grown feed crops for other livestock (such as kale or mangolds) or the veg patch at the end of the season. They'll do the land a power of good since they turn it over, eating roots and soil pests and manuring it naturally as they go.

But you can keep breeding sows in traditional-type sties, one in each. A sty needs to have an enclosed sleeping area plenty big enough for her to turn round easily in, with room for a litter of 14 piglets, and an outdoor run. To keep sties clean these are usually both floored with concrete, so deep straw bedding is necessary.

Whichever method you opt for, be prepared for the amount of water they'll need – an adult sow can drink up to 10 litres (17½ pints) a day, so it's worth investing in some drinkers of the type that refill themselves from a built-in storage unit, or if you're keeping breeding sows with litters, then use drinkers that are connected to a permanent plumbed-in water supply, which will save you carting an awful lot of buckets of water about. But check drinkers daily, since they can get blocked, and pigs will soon suffer if they go short.

Sows kept outside on grassy fields, in woods or in orchards will find some of their own food by digging about with their snouts, but they still need proper feeding. You can use barley meal moistened with water to make a mash, or specially prepared pelleted feed for pigs. In sties, they live almost entirely on concentrates.

A sow can produce two litters of piglets per year, and a young female pig, known as a gilt, can breed from the age of 6–8 months. To start the ball rolling you need a boar, but only a fairly large-scale pig breeder will go to the expense of keeping their own – most people hire or borrow one from a fellow pig-keeper. Boars are bigger than sows, and aren't always the best tempered of animals, so they need handling with extreme caution, especially when you don't know the individual animal well. After mating, the sow will produce her litter exactly three months, three weeks and three days later. Two weeks before the expected birth, clean out a special farrowing pen well and put in a particularly deep layer of clean straw, then move the sow into it. Shortly before giving birth the sow will make a 'nest' in it, which is a sure sign that farrowing will start shortly. Unlike a good many farm animals, sows will get on with it for themselves, especially when they are given a natural stress-free environment in which to do so. The farrowing pen should be fitted with a strong metal bar that keeps the sow out of part of it, and here the piglets can lie in straw under a 'creep lamp', which keeps them bathed in warmth. When the piglets are three days to a week old, the whole family can be moved back to their field and put into an ark with deep straw inside, provided the weather is warm enough.

Once she has piglets to feed, a sow will need more food herself – the rule of thumb in country families was to give her daily as many pounds of barley meal as she had piglets, plus an extra two pounds. She can be very defensive of her piglets, so keep dogs, small children and visitors safely on the other side of the fence. As the piglets grow older they'll continue to suckle but they'll start rooting around in the field and also take some of their mother's feed, until they are weaned at roughly 8–10 weeks, when they need feeding with concentrates of their own.

BREEDS OF PIG

Commercial pigs are usually hybrids, specially bred to fatten fast on the minimum of feed, but although they take longer to reach slaughter size, rare breeds are more fun to keep.

Tamworth: *A handsome medium-sized pig covered in reddish-brown hair, and rather wild-boar-like in shape. A popular breed with smallholders.*

Saddleback: *A very traditional-looking pig, black with a pale pink band round the middle and pale pink front legs.*

Large Black: *All-black pig with lop-ears, valued for producing particularly tasty meat.*

Gloucester Old Spot: *Another favourite smallholder's pig that's also popular as a 'paying pet'; it is large, rather block-shaped and heavily marked with black spots and blobs of varying sizes on a pale pink background.*

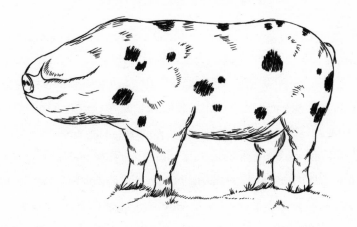

GOATS

....

HOW TO KEEP A GOAT

Goats are great characters and easy to keep. They aren't keen on being kept on their own and will go to great efforts to get out or cause mischief; however, if you don't want to keep a second goat they are quite happy to have a pony, donkey or other large livestock as a companion. (Though if you want continuity of supply, it's a good idea to keep two nannies together so that one is producing milk while the other one is pregnant.)

You'll need a hut large enough for the animal or animals to move around in freely, as they'll need to be shut in at night and during spells of bad weather. The hut needs to be high enough so the animals have plenty of headroom, as they'll sometimes stand up on their back legs with their front feet against the wall. If the hut has a window, use clear polycarbonate instead of glass so there's no risk of breakage. Put a layer of deep bedding on the floor; straw is best but wood shavings are a good substitute – and clean the hut out frequently. Ideally the hut is best situated inside a large, open pen, with the door left open during the day so the goats can return to it if they need to shelter from the weather. The pen can be grassed if it's big enough, otherwise cover the ground with straw and put a few large branches inside for goats to browse on – they'll enjoy munching the twigs and chewing the bark, so replace them every so often. They'll also enjoy having a whole bale of straw to jump onto, and if you cut the strings they'll break it open and push it around in case there's anything good to eat inside. A bucket of clean water to drink is essential at all times.

If you have a securely fenced grassy paddock, goats can be turned out in it to roam loose with other livestock (including poultry). Give them a field shelter they can go into if the weather turns inclement, but put them back inside a proper hut at night so they can be shut in.

Because goats are browsers rather than grazers, they particularly enjoy being turned out into a rough area full of weeds and brushwood – they eat far more semi-woody and weedy wild food than grass. But don't imagine you can use goats to clear wasteland for you; contrary to popular belief they are very selective feeders and will merely take what they fancy and leave everything else. They will, however, strip the bark from young trees, eat whole saplings and nibble at hedges, so it's no good introducing them to a newly planted 'conservation area', and it's risky keeping them in an orchard unless it's an old established one with very large trees, since goats will eat any twigs within reach. If you don't have a paddock or an enclosed pen to keep them in, goats can be tethered from a collar round the neck to a short metal 'post' with an 'auger' at the base that is screwed into the ground; in this way the animals can be moved from one area to another to ensure grazing is evenly used and to make use of small unfenced areas that otherwise couldn't be grazed. But don't just leave them out and forget about them; you'll need to take them a bucket of water and bring them in if the weather turns bad – and always at night.

Besides what they gather for themselves by browsing, goats need to be fed on hay, which is best secured in a hay net and fixed to the top of a fence post or a ring in the side of their hut, or else placed in a wooden hayrack fixed very slightly above a goat's head height inside their hut, so they have to reach up. If you feed them loose hay on the ground, or put it where they can pull it down, they simply trample it into the dirt, whereupon they won't eat it. Pregnant and milking goats also need extra rations, so give them a mixture of rolled oats and flaked maize, divided into two feeds, morning and evening. Resist the temptation of giving milking goats old brassica plants from your veg patch to browse on as they can make the milk taste slightly 'cabbagey'. But since the animals can't always get the full spectrum of minerals they need from their regular feedstuffs, it's vital to provide a mineral salt-lick that the animals have access to all the time. This is best placed inside the hut where it won't be dissolved by rain, fixed securely to the wall of the building at roughly a goat's head height.

The best way to start goat-keeping is to buy a pregnant nanny; once she's had her kid she'll start to produce more milk than the kid needs, so let the two continue living together until the kid is weaned and simply take the nanny aside to milk her twice daily, morning and evening. If she's used to being handled she should behave quite well, but secure her with a halter to a ring in the wall, and as 'bribery' it pays to give her a bucket of concentrated feed to distract her. You can milk a goat while she's standing on the floor if you don't mind crouching down, but people with several goats construct a solid 'table' on which the animal stands, so the owner can milk from a more comfortable position, standing upright.

HOW TO MILK A GOAT

Goats' milk is slightly different in character to cows'. The cream is distributed evenly through the milk itself, which means it won't rise to the top, so you can't make goats' milk into butter. But it is more easily digestible than cows' milk, and so often it is recommended for children who suffer from eczema or for anyone allergic to, or intolerant of, cows' milk.

Milk twice a day, morning and evening, at as near as possible the same time each day. This way the goat will come to expect the attention, and the

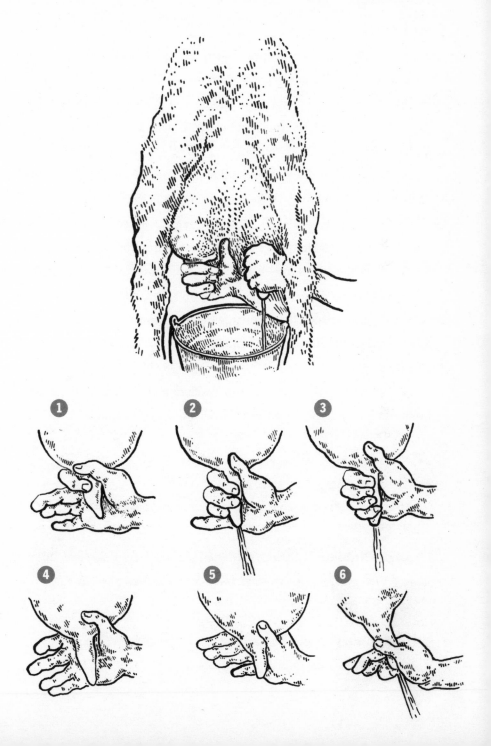

meal that goes with it, and – especially if you are gentle – she'll cooperate. Some goat keepers find it helps to talk quietly to the animal as they work.

Take a clean bucket, ideally stainless steel, which you've sterilised by scalding the inside well with boiling water. Ensure your hands are perfectly clean; wash them thoroughly with soap and hot water immediately before milking.

Sit the bucket under the goat's udder. Ensure she is quiet or she'll very likely kick the bucket over or step into it and spoil the milk.

Gently grip a teat in each hand, holding it with your thumbs uppermost. Use each hand in turn. Use the thumb against the side of your index finger to nip the top of the teat closed, then slowly and gently close the remaining fingers in turn to squeeze the milk from the teat. Then release your grip so more milk flows down, while you repeat the process with the other hand on the other teat. Continue until no more milk is let down. Er…it's a knack!

Straight after milking, transfer the milk to a clean, sterilised container or glass bottles and put it in the fridge so it cools down quickly.

BREEDS OF GOAT

Meat, milk or fleece? You can have any of the three depending on the breed of goat you choose.

Anglo-Nubian: *A favourite milking breed as it's a high yielder with rich milk that's good for cheese-making. A very distinctive-looking goat with lop ears and a Roman nose.*

Toggenburg: *Brown goats with white markings and a rather pretty deer-like face with a white stripe down each side.*

Angora: *A dual-purpose goat that looks like a faintly aristocratic, curly-coated sheep with horns. It gives useful amounts of milk and has a valuable fleece with very soft, fine, high-quality wool, better known as mohair. The animals can be sheared twice each year to maximise returns.*

Boer: *Relatively new to Great Britain, a rather chunky goat originally from South Africa with a barrel-shaped body, bred for its meat which is naturally low in cholesterol. It is starting to find a ready market as kid, for roasting, and it's also popular with ethnic communities who enjoy curried goat. Roasted kid tastes a lot like lamb.*

COWS

A cow is a very different proposition from a goat; it costs more to buy, it needs a bigger field shelter or a proper stall inside a well-built outbuilding, and a larger supply of straw for bedding. It also takes more land to support a cow since it eats a large amount of grass – allow at least an acre, but ideally two and a half. But a cow also needs a lot of extra feed. It eats a bale of hay per day in winter, when it's not out to grass (you'll need on average a ton of hay per cow each winter), and if you don't have enough grass you'll need to feed some hay all year round. A cow also needs feeding with concentrates in the form of sugar beet pulp and rolled oats or barley, or proprietary cattle cake, which needs to be calculated on the basis of how much milk it is giving – if you don't feed enough, the milk yield declines.

To keep costs down many owners grow an area of winter kale or mangels to supplement concentrates, though a cow can also be given potatoes if you have a surplus from the veg patch, and she'll also enjoy outer leaves from brassica plants when you've picked your cabbages, sprouts, cauliflowers and broccoli. You'll also need to provide a mineral salt-lick to avoid nutritional deficiencies which can cause all sorts of health problems. Ideally this needs to be kept under cover, somewhere the cow can get at it whenever she wants. Another essential requirement is plenty of water – a cow drinks getting on for 90 litres (20 gallons) every day when it is producing milk, so you need a proper trough connected to a mains water supply.

Once she's calved, a cow will produce milk for up to ten months, and she needs milking twice a day. (You can get away with doing it once if you leave the calf with the cow, since the calf will take what you don't for the rest of the day.) If it's for your own use, you can milk the cow out in the field, though it's easiest to put a halter on and bring her into a stall or tie her up to a metal ring in the side of a building, so she has a wall along one side of her, to stop her moving about too much. Since hand-milking takes time, it's most comfortable for the milker if they sit on a small stool. Use a scrupulously clean stainless steel bucket that's been scalded with boiling water to make sure it's perfectly hygienic, and give the cow a bucket of concentrated feed to keep her occupied while you do the deed. It's also a good idea to follow the same routine each time you milk, as it relaxes the cow. Cows are quite sensitive and develop a bond with their regular handler, so to keep the animal calm and stop her fidgeting, fretting or kicking, experienced milkers behave confidently, handle the cow without tickling, and talk quietly to the animal during the process. If she is upset she's likely to kick the bucket over, step in it, or refuse to let you near her. Good stockmen have a 'way' with livestock that comes from behaving quietly and treating them kindly.

Naturally, in order to produce milk a cow has to have a calf, so rather than dispose of this in order to concentrate on maximum milk yields, smallholders will often raise the calf themselves – a heifer can be sold later as a house cow or to join a dairy herd, but a bull calf can be reared for beef.

When choosing a breed to farm, check out the conditions in which that particular breed does best, since some were originally developed for lowland pastures with mild climates, and others for hardier surroundings in hills – they don't thrive in the wrong set of conditions.

HOW TO MILK A COW

Wash the udder gently using a cloth and warm soapy water. Sit on a stool and press the top of your head into the cow's flank – this establishes contact, acts like her calf, and gives you advance warning of any bad behaviour. Milk a cow like you would a goat (see page 190); the four teats (or 'quarters') need to be completely emptied. A cow produces up to 18 litres (4 gallons) of milk a day; roughly one large bucketful morning and evening. Chill the fresh milk immediately.

REARING STORE CATTLE FOR MEAT

Instead of keeping a dairy cow and raising their own calves from scratch, a lot of people with some spare grazing land will instead buy a few 'store cattle' (the proper term for half-grown young bullocks) to fatten for meat, in much the same way as rearing your own pork from weaners. Turn them out in a well-fenced pasture with a stream or a water trough that can be kept filled (ideally connected to a mains water supply so it's self-filling), though a lot of small-scale farmers rent saltmarsh fields for this job as they are cheaper than top-class pasture – and 'saltmarsh beef', as it's known, is especially sought after in food-lovers' circles. Buy store cattle in spring and by the autumn you can turn them into cash or put them in the freezer.

GOOD DUAL-PURPOSE HOUSE-COWS FOR SMALLHOLDERS

The popular milk breeds, Guernsey and Jersey, aren't known as great beef producers, so most smallholders choose a dual-purpose breed that gives them the best of both worlds – a reasonable milk yield plus a good saleable meat carcass.

Dexter: *An unusually small, almost miniature black cow, with short, upright horns. Needs less input and produces less milk than larger breeds, so popular with smallholders. Can be a tad feisty.*

Gloucester: *A very old rare breed with short, forward-curving horns, in black or brown with white markings and a white stripe down the back, white tail and white belly. This dual-purpose breed is now being used for conservation grazing.*

Dairy Shorthorn: *The top choice for smallholders and small family farms shortly after the war, when besides rearing the bull calves for meat, the old dairy cows would also be eaten – after lengthy stewing – which made them earn their keep several times over. Now a rare breed; these brown and white cows with short horns are good for keeping outside.*

Red Poll: *A rare breed that lives happily outside with just a field shelter, and on a home-grown diet of roots, cereals and hay with oats or barley. A good-looking cow with a rich, red-brown coat, with the big advantage of being naturally hornless. Originally from East Anglia, it was a dual-purpose breed, but nowadays is mainly kept for meat.*

Jersey: *A lovely-looking smallish cow with big, soulful eyes and a pale golden-tan colour, with a normally very docile temperament. Jerseys produce the richest, creamiest milk of all – even more so than Guernseys – but they're from a mild climate and need housing indoors in winter and ideally at night in summer too. Butchers don't like the carcasses of the bull calves, so they don't sell well, but they do produce good meat – you'll just need to raise them for home consumption.*

SHEEP

HOW TO KEEP SHEEP

Sheep are cheap to keep as they live outdoors, mainly on grass, with hay in the winter when the grass isn't growing, and a little concentrated feed to improve their condition just before the start of the breeding season. They also need a regular supply of water, and access to a mineral salt-lick at all times. This is essential to their welfare since a deficiency of copper (a mineral they particularly need that's usually lacking in the grass on their pasture) causes pregnant ewes to abort and eventually even adults may die as a result.

Sheep don't need a field shelter, since they'll huddle behind a hedge to escape bad wintry weather or for shade from the sun in summer, but at lambing time you will need to provide a temporary structure that you bring them into, so you can supervise the proceedings and intervene if need be. A lot of larger-scale sheep farmers will bring their ewes into a large permanent barn to lamb in cubicles divided up by straw bales or hurdles – this is particularly worthwhile because they rely on producing lambs very early in the year when the conditions outdoors are still harsh, since early lamb makes the best prices. On a small scale it's far easier to arrange things so your flock lambs a bit later in the season when the weather is better and there's plenty of young grass for the new growing lambs to eat. And if you choose a very hardy hill breed, they can often be left to get on with lambing all by themselves, out in the field – though to avoid losing lambs that could easily have been saved, it's still worth going out regularly to keep an eye on things.

However, sheep aren't quite as trouble-free as they might look. You will need to move them to fresh pasture regularly over the summer so they can't re-infect themselves with internal parasites, as well as to 'rest' the grass and give it a chance to re-grow. If you only have access to one field, this means dividing the area into strips with temporary fencing and allowing the sheep to graze only one strip at a time.

Sheep have quite a few problems that have to be treated or averted, too, so owners need to hone-up on shepherding skills such as foot trimming (to avoid foot rot which makes sheep lame), drenching (administering liquid medicines via a tube to kill internal parasites), shearing (to stop them getting too hot in summer and also to produce a woolly fleece for sale), dipping (done after shearing, to kill external pests living in and on the skin) and dagging (to remove dirty wool round the backside so that flies' eggs don't hatch out into maggots that burrow into the sheep).

You also need to borrow a ram every year to start the breeding cycle again. If your flock is big enough to justify it, then buy your own – but you will need to sell him or swap him every year or two so that he isn't fathering offspring from his own daughters, which often results in weak, defective or sub-standard lambs.

THE LAMBING YEAR

AUTUMN

Get ewes and the ram ready for the breeding season early in the autumn by feeding them concentrates (cereals or sheep nuts) for a few weeks to boost their condition. Check their feet at the same time, since sheep feel less like mating if they are lame or their feet hurt due to overgrown 'hooves' or infection between the two 'toes'.

The gestation period for sheep is 146 days, so time the introduction of the ram so that the first lambs will be born to coincide with decent spring weather and the first flush of good grass growth in your area. Commercial sheep farmers put a harness on the ram with a coloured marker on his chest, which will dab a blob of colour onto each ewe he mounts, so the farmer knows which should be pregnant and which won't be. Don't assume all your lambs will be born 146 days after introducing the ram, since the ewes only come into season intermittently; lambing continues over several weeks once it has started.

WINTER

Sheep will continue grazing, but since the grass isn't growing and the quality is fairly poor during the winter, it needs to be supplemented; anticipate each ewe needing roughly 230kg (500lb) of hay. Ewes will only need concentrates such as cereals or sheep nuts if the winter is particularly harsh, and they shouldn't be too fat at lambing time or the births can be difficult, which creates a lot of extra work and extra expense if the vet has to be called in.

SPRING

Construct a temporary shelter in the sheep field made from hurdles and straw bales, so ewes can be brought inside for the last day before lambing is due, in case they need assistance. A roof of corrugated iron or clear plastic sheet makes conditions more comfortable for the lambing assistant, though the sheep don't need it. And if there's no electricity available for lighting you'll need a powerful torch, since sheep invariably choose to lamb between early evening and on through the night till early morning. The signs to look for, when a birth is imminent, is a ewe that lies down, 'star-gazes' (raises her head with nose pointed upwards) and groans and strains. Most ewes will lamb perfectly well on their own; at a normal birth the nose faces towards the tail end of the sheep and the two front legs appear first, with the head in between. After a good push, the whole lamb emerges; all you need do is make sure its nose and mouth are clear of mucus so it can breathe straight away, then the mother will clean it up.

After an hour or so it should be strong enough to stand, so come back and check that it's started suckling – if not, it needs a helping hand to find the right place. There may be one or even two more lambs still to come, so watch out for further signs of labour. Sometimes you will need to intervene; if a ewe seems to be struggling for some time or seems distressed it may be that the lamb is the wrong way round, its forefeet are tucked back instead of pointing forwards, or multiple lambs may be tangled together. In this case the shepherd needs to reach inside and sort the problem out, or assist the lamb with a gentle pull on the forelegs. If for any reason a ewe rejects a newborn lamb, the shepherd needs to persuade another sheep to foster it – usually a ewe that's only had one lamb of its own – or else rear it in a warm indoor pen themselves. (Traditionally sheep farmers left this job to their wives, who often used the warm farmhouse kitchen to rear orphan lambs in front of the Aga.)

New lambs and their mums are usually kept in their shelter for a few days to make sure all is well (especially if the weather is a bit rough at the time or it's been a difficult birth) before turning them back out into the field with the other sheep. The lambs are fed by their mother for a time and start nibbling grass before grazing full-time. While they are still very young, male lambs being reared for meat rather than kept as breeding stock are castrated using proprietary rubber rings. It's also usual for sheep (at least commercial flocks) to have their tails docked using a similar method, since the tail stores fat, which means the animal doesn't reach slaughter size so fast.

SUMMER

Dag the sheep to remove messy or excrement-laden bits of wool that might spoil a fleece, then before the weather gets too hot, shear and shortly afterwards dip or otherwise treat them against pests in the wool or skin. For reasons of cleanliness and convenience, it's also worth dagging sheep with mucky backsides before you introduce the ram in autumn, or in spring shortly before the start of lambing season.

'CASTING' A SHEEP

One of the essential shepherding skills is knowing how to hold a sheep securely so you can trim its feet or administer medicine as a 'drench', and it's the first step towards keeping it still for shearing. It needs practice.

First catch your sheep; do so with as little stress as possible. Keep her calm and handle her gently. Hold her by the wool of the throat, and with a hand on the rump gently push her down so she's lying on the ground. Then roll her round on her rear to up-end her so she's left sitting on her bottom, with her back against your legs with your feet about a foot apart so you can grip her gently with your knees. This holds her firmly so she's less likely to wriggle or get away.

SHEARING

Sheep need to be shorn every summer, otherwise the animals become far too hot, and also at great risk from blowflies which lay their eggs in dirty fleece – the maggots that hatch out burrow into the sheep causing infections and great distress. It's often said that some of the more ancient rare breeds of sheep shed their own wool naturally without needing to be shorn, but that's not advisable. Unlike more modern breeds, they tend to cast their old wool off in large clumps which get pulled off their body when it snags on brambles or barbed wire, but as a general rule responsible owners prefer to shear these too. The only sheep that don't need to be sheared are lambs under a year old.

Shearing is usually done in May, June or July, depending on which part of the country you live in, but it's the state of the coat, not the calendar, which determines the timing. Wait until the old coat starts to lift away naturally on top of the new coat that's starting to grow through underneath. You don't have to do the shearing yourself; you can hire in a team of itinerant sheep shearers, 'gangs' of whom often come over from Australia to find work when their own shearing season is over. Several neighbouring small-sheep-owners will often group together to share their services for the day. If you are close to an agricultural college, you might be able to arrange for a lecturer to demonstrate the skill using your sheep on your premises, or for final-year students to do the job under supervision.

If you decide to do it yourself, have a training session with an expert or at the very least an experienced sheep-owner who does their own shearing. You'll need hand-operated sheep shears which are worked with one hand, leaving the other free to control the sheep, or electric clippers which are rather like a large chunky electric razor, which clearly have to be close to a power source. It's easiest to shear sheep in a large outbuilding, after rounding all the sheep up and corralling them in a temporary holding pen.

To go about shearing, remove an individual sheep from the holding pen, take her to a place where there's plenty of elbow-room and 'cast' her, so she is in a sitting position against your legs, then kneel down so both knees are on the ground, with the sheep belly-up over your knees and its head under your non-shearing arm. This way you can control her so she can't move, and if you are firm rather than hesitant she'll realise it's not worth fighting. Again, it takes practice!

First, clip away the wool from the stomach, which is usually dirty and tangled, full of burrs and weed seeds etc., and discard it. Then turn the sheep slightly so one side is uppermost. Clip the side of the sheep from the newly cleaned belly outwards, up the sides towards the spine, including the front and back leg, going right up the side of the neck. Then turn the sheep so the other side is uppermost, and repeat the process as before, but this time working down the side from the spine. The entire fleece will 'peel away' as you work.

An experienced shearer can strip a whole fleece in a few minutes without nicking the sheep, but a beginner can't always avoid the odd tiny cut, and if so, dab wounds with Stockholm tar applied straight from the tin with a twig. This stops the bleeding and cleans and disinfects the cut, preventing it becoming infected.

SHEEPDOGS

Sheep need a lot of rounding up, whether it's to move them to a fresh strip of grazing or to a different field, or to bring them in for shearing, medication or foot-trimming, and it's sometimes necessary to separate a particular sheep from the flock. If you've only got a few sheep you can do it yourself with the help of an assistant, but most owners of larger flocks find a good sheepdog invaluable, since it saves a heck of a lot of running around.

Sheepdogs are almost always Border Collies, though in other parts of the world other breeds are also used, especially if they also have to round up cattle. Most Border Collies from working parents will instinctively have the urge to round up sheep, so they are relatively easy to train to lie down, move forwards, or go to their right or left. Since instructions from their handler have to carry across large wide-open spaces in all weathers, the commands are given by voice (which is used more at closer quarters) or as a series of whistles, using a special whistle that's kept inside the mouth to make a conspicuously different sound for each manoeuvre. (It takes a bit of practice to use an in-mouth sheepdog whistle so as to produce the specific sounds that the dog understands, so new sheepdog handlers need to practise in private to avoid confusing their dog.) Not all sheepdog handlers use exactly the same commands for each manoeuvre, but they are usually fairly similar.

'Walk on' (two short blasts on the whistle) tells the dog to walk quietly up to the sheep, so as not to frighten them away. 'Come here' (phwee phwee phweet) calls the dog to its handler. 'Come by' (phweet pheeoh) tells the dog to move off to its left and circle the sheep in a clockwise direction, 'away' (phwee phwoo) tells it to move off to its right and circle the sheep in an anti-clockwise direction. 'Lie down' (one long blast of the whistle) means stop still and lie down, and it's often used just to tell the dog to slow down – the dog knows which from the tone of voice and if the command is repeated. 'Go back' (phoo hee hoo) is used to send a dog back to find sheep that are standing behind it, and 'get out' (phweet pheeoo phweet phweet) is used to send the dog further away from the sheep to avoid panicking them. 'Take time' (four short staccato blasts) slows the dog down when it's running too fast, and 'that'll do' (also four short staccato blasts) means the dog must stop whatever it's doing and come straight back to its handler. But when a flock of sheep is being driven by the dog cross-country, the command 'that'll do' is also used to keep the dog between the handler and the sheep, so the flock moves ahead of the shepherd. It all takes a deal of practice for both dog and handler, but the end result can be magical to watch.

Sheepdog trials are a traditional country pursuit that's since proved hugely popular with audiences on TV. For these competitions, the best dogs are trained to obey a larger and more complicated range of commands than a basic working dog and then put through their paces. Each team of dog and handler is given a small flock of sheep that have to be herded into a small open-fronted pen, which is then closed by the shepherd at the end of the exercise, all is done against the clock.

Due to the border collie's inbred willingness to do as it's told, dogs that prove inadequate with sheep often find a new lease of life as well-behaved family pets that easily learn tricks. They also excel at obedience trials, retrieving dumbbells, running obstacle courses, etc., which are also popular features at country fairs and agricultural shows.

SHEEP MEAT

Lamb comes from young sheep under a year old; the very best lamb is spring lamb, slaughtered at about three months old, when weighing roughly 3 kilos (75 pounds) and sold before about June; lambs need to be born as early as possible in spring (actually late winter). The cuts are quite small but the meat is very tender.

Hogget is older than lamb but younger than mutton, usually around 12–18 months old. Being older it's a tad tougher and needs a bit more cooking, but it has more flavour, and the cuts are larger, which is better for bigger families.

Mutton is coming back into fashion, with good reason. It is meat taken from older sheep, technically two years or older, but often from ewes that have produced several lambs or which have proved barren. Mutton needs a lot longer and slower cooking than lamb, but enthusiasts find the meat much more tasty – and the cuts are larger.

DIRTY WOOL

Dirty wool that you've gathered when 'dagging', or the wool from the belly of the sheep removed before you start shearing, is called 'shoddy'. It has no commercial value, but years ago it was once highly prized by gardeners as a soil conditioner, so it's worth putting on to your compost heap or digging straight into the bottom of a trench in your veg patch. It holds moisture and breaks down slowly, releasing nitrogen and trace elements into the soil, and any manure it contains is a bonus. But only save dirty wool before dipping, not afterwards, to avoid introducing unwanted chemicals.

BREEDS OF SHEEP

Some types of sheep are best for meat, others for wool – it's rare to find one that is good for both purposes. Some breeds have been developed for rich lowland pastures and others are adapted to life at higher altitudes with harsher weather and rougher grazing, so choose one that suits the area in which you plan to keep them.

Soay: *A very ancient breed of small brown sheep originally only found on the island of Soay in the St Kilda group in Scotland. Both sexes have horns. Soay sheep are popular as pets and 'lawnmowers'. Lambs are slow to mature;*

it takes a year before they are ready to send off for slaughter, and even so produce a very small carcass. They are a dab hand at escaping, so make sure fencing is secure!

Jacob: *Good-looking, small, brown-and-buff patterned sheep; both sexes have curving, backswept horns. The wool is popular for using, undyed, in crafts such as spinning and weaving, and the sheep are a great favourite as pets and 'lawnmowers'.*

Merino: *Widely kept in Australia, this breed produces the finest-quality wool used for weaving into cloth for suits and overcoats. A large, impressive-looking sheep.*

Suffolk: *Solid sheep with black faces, kept for meat – the wool is poor quality. Needs lowland grazing.*

LLAMAS AND ALPACAS

Llamas and their smaller relatives, alpacas, belong to the camel family and, since they originate from the harsh mountainous regions of South America, they are very hardy. They don't need lots of expensive feed, elaborate housing or special care. Since llamas and alpacas are relatively new to UK livestock keepers, there's a good demand for them, both as 'paying pets' and for breeding stock, but this means animals are expensive to buy. Breeders advertise in smallholders' magazines, and many offer training for potential new owners.

Llamas, being large, can be worked; they are sometimes used for llama-trekking, where the animals carry light loads (waterproof clothing, rugs, picnics, etc.) and accompany walkers who lead them on halters. However, both llamas and alpacas are also kept for their fleece. Like sheep, they need to be sheared annually. The fleece from llamas has limited uses as the fibre is rather coarse. Alpaca fleeces, though, are high quality – soft and silky – and much in demand for making yarn used for fabrics by the tailoring business, for making posh overcoats and suchlike. But neither animal is easy to shear, it's not something an amateur can easily get to grips with – a professional can do the job much faster, and without causing the animal too much distress. If the animals are being kept as pets rather than for fleeces, instead of shearing, owners will sometimes keep the animals' coats groomed to remove loose strands and avoid loose wool becoming matted and tangled as it's shed naturally, or they'll cut the wool on the backs, flanks and rump to about an inch long with strong scissors each spring.

Both llamas and alpacas are happy to live outside all year round since they eat grasses and wildflowers living in the turf, and they'll also browse on trees and shrubs. Their paddock needs very secure fencing at least 1.2 metres (4 feet) high (ideally 1½ metres/5 feet for llamas) to keep them in. (Avoid barbed wire; 10 centimetre/4 inch square woven wire is best, with a strand of electric fencing along the top if necessary.) They don't need a huge area; you can happily keep two llamas or four alpacas in a half-acre paddock – they are herd animals and prefer to be kept in small groups rather than singly – but you'll need to pick up the poop daily when they are kept in a relatively small area of pasture. They'll appreciate a large tree for shade, though it's not essential, but they will need a three-sided field shelter for protection from bad weather, and this should have straw bedding on the ground – it also makes a good place to feed the animals. Though they live on grass for most of the year, in winter, and any time the grass isn't growing well, they need hay as well. Concentrated feeds are available for llamas and alpacas, but normally only used for expectant females. The animals also need access to clean, fresh water at all times.

Since they occasionally need individual attention, it's advisable to have a small catch-pen in one corner of the field where animals can be enclosed. Llamas and alpacas don't like being handled; their camel-like nature means they tend to spit and kick if annoyed, so it's usually necessary to restrain them with ropes. Adult animals need to have their teeth ground down, otherwise they can become so overgrown that they can't eat; they need to be wormed, and they also need to have their horny toenails cut regularly because soft fields don't keep them worn down the way rocky hillsides do in the wild.

If you're keeping them in a small way, as pets, it's worth pointing out that they aren't the easiest animals to find 'sitters' for when you're away on holiday. Serious breeders usually have helpers or live-in family members who can take over.

BEES

Bees look as if they take care of themselves, but it actually requires a fair bit of knowledge and equipment to be a beekeeper. It's all best obtained through a local beekeepers' club, where you can also get training and advice, and find a supplier of bees and equipment.

The first essential is a hive, which consists of a series of stacked chambers inside a weatherproof outer shell. Between two of the chambers a queen excluder is fitted; this is a thin slatted layer that acts like a 'filter' to keep the egg-laying chamber (where new bees are produced) separate from the honey chambers or 'supers' where worker bees store the honey. Without the 'filter', bees would mix cells containing bee larvae in the same combs as honey, which doesn't make for a pleasant end-product. Each super is like an open-ended box that contains a number of frames which slot into it a small distance apart; it's inside these frames that the workers make the hexagonal wax 'cells' that form the honeycomb in which they store honey, which is produced as food for the bee larvae. At the very top of the hive is a roof, which lifts off for access, and at the bottom the base of the hive has a 'landing strip' projecting from the front, just below an opening where bees go in and out of the hive.

You can't just plonk a hive anywhere there happens to be room. A beehive needs a sunny, sheltered space, ideally with a hedge or fence along the back and a wide, open area in front, on the sunny side. (Some beekeepers also rent their hives out to local fruit farmers or veg producers to pollinate crops, and this involves transporting the hives and the bees inside to a new location for the summer.)

The bees to occupy the hive are bought as a surplus swarm from another beekeeper in summer. To work with bees without being stung you'll need a complete set of protective clothing including head-gear and veil. You'll also need a smoker, which burns bits of old dry cloth or hay to generate smoke, and some basic beekeeping tools.

Any time you need to open the hive, wear full protective gear and check there are no gaps where bees could get in. Have your hive tools on hand and your smoker lit and working, so you can minimise the time you'll need to have the hive open. Make sure there's no-one else in the surrounding area while you do this.

Waft plenty of smoke round the hive; the bees sense danger to the hive and gorge themselves on honey, which makes them rather 'dozy'; they'll then be less aggressive and less likely to sting. Prise the lid off with the hive tool and puff several generous squirts of smoke inside. Then do whatever you need to: remove supers to add the queen excluder, or put new supers on top, or remove supers filled with honey if you're harvesting. Waft a few more puffs of smoke over the interior every few minutes, especially if there seem to be more bees about than before, or you feel they are getting more assertive. After closing the hive, keep your protective gear on until you are reasonably well clear of the area, then leave the hive alone for a day or two afterwards so the bees can settle down again.

THE BEEKEEPER'S YEAR

The queen bee is one of the few inhabitants of the hive that survives the winter; she is larger than the other bees and quite distinctive-looking. In early spring she starts laying eggs in the brood chamber of the hive.

As spring flowers appear, the numbers of worker (female) bees starts to build up rapidly. The hive needs to be opened; put a queen excluder above the brood chamber to keep the queen 'downstairs' so all the bee larvae are contained in their own special area of the hive, and above this place one super, filled with frames. Use new frames each season, since bees won't re-use old or dirty ones. To give the bees a base to work onto, beekeepers slot a thin flat sheet of hexagonal patterned wax into each frame as a foundation to get them started. The frames are slotted into the super so they don't quite touch, and the exact size of the gap between adjacent frames is crucial, or the bees won't fill them properly – a special tool is used as a spacing guide.

Since bees tend to 'glue' shut any gaps in their hive with wax, you need to use a special hive tool for prising the lid off without damaging it. (Bees tend to abandon a damaged hive.) By the time the big flush of early summer flowers is out, bees will probably have filled the frames in the first super, so open the hive and add another super full of vacant frames, prepared as before, on top of the one that's already been filled.

As summer progresses, more supers may need to be added to cope with the volume of honey the bees are generating. There's no point in putting all the supers into a hive at once, because the bees won't fill them properly – they'll just dot cells of honey around in partly empty combs. An experienced beekeeper knows when another super is needed without opening the hive to check, basing his judgement on the density of bees flying around the hives, the weather, and the number of flowers in bloom at the time. It's all part of the skill and the knowledge. Fields of oilseed rape in the immediate area are a big draw to bees, which will temporarily desert garden flowers while rape is in bloom.

Around midsummer the workers 'bring on' a few bee larvae especially so they turn into queens instead of more workers. When a new queen bee finally emerges from the hive, she'll be followed by a large number of workers that go with her, forming a swarm. This flies off in a 'cloud' and settles somewhere nearby, perhaps in the branch of a tree, with the workers gathering tightly round the new queen, who by now will have met up with a few drones (male bees), one of whom will have mated with her. Collecting swarms is a useful way for beekeepers to increase their number of hives for free. Handling a swarm of bees, transporting them safely and introducing them to a vacant hive back home is a skill that needs to be learnt from an experienced beekeeper. Someone who's kept bees for years can usually tell when a swarm is likely to emerge by the restless behaviour of the workers, so they'll follow its path and be ready to 'take' the swarm as soon as it settles.

By late summer the hive is carrying a full load of honey, ready for collecting. This is when wasps may attack the hive to steal the crop; beekeepers keep a watch for wasps' nests in their catchment area and try to destroy them before this happens.

To collect the honey, open the hive, and insert a special board between the brood chamber at the bottom and the honey-bearing supers at the top; this lets worker bees come out of the honey chamber but it doesn't let them get back in, so 24 hours later, with luck, there should be very few bees inside the part of the hive you are interested in. Bees won't take kindly to having their honey stolen, so remove the supers quickly and take them somewhere the bees can't follow to extract the honey.

As autumn proceeds, the number of worker bees falls as fewer nectar-rich flowers are in bloom. Some beekeepers leave a few frames of honey inside the hive to feed the queen and the few worker bees that remain during the autumn and winter. Others take all the honey and feed the hive with a solution of sugar or syrup instead. If you choose to feed artificially, don't do so during the day; do it in the evening when bees have returned to the hive for the night, since they'll then be naturally quiet and sleepy and there's less risk of getting stung.

SINGLE FLOWER HONEY

Most honey is made from nectar and pollen from a mixture of different kinds of flowers, but when there's one particularly prominent flower in bloom in the area, the bees will make honey largely from that one type. The predominance of one species gives the honey a characteristic flavour. (Some beekeepers will move hives of bees out to moors for the heather or to pastures for the clover, deliberately to produce single-flower honey.) As soon as that particular flower has finished blooming, the beekeeper will then collect the honey from the hive, before any more can be added from other sources, so he can sell it as heather honey or clover honey. The hive is then restocked with new frames, so the bees can start again. Wildflower honey is another favourite, from hives kept out in the countryside close to a wide range of natural species.

BEE PLANTS

Medieval cottagers relied on a hive of bees down the garden to supply the honey that was their only form of sweetening, since sugar was imported and only affordable to wealthy homes. To ensure a plentiful supply of nectar and pollen for the bees to work on, cottagers made sure their gardens supplied plenty of suitable flowers during the main bee foraging season – spring till autumn. Today it's still a good practice for beekeepers. Good bee plants include lavender, sedums, Michaelmas daisies, buddleia (butterfly bush), also old-fashioned annuals such as calendula marigolds, poppies and sunflowers, and flowering herbs – particularly borage, rosemary, marjoram, and Greek oregano (wild marjoram).

HOW TO EXTRACT HONEY FROM A HONEYCOMB

Unless you use all the honey you collect as unprocessed honeycomb, you'll need special equip-ment for separating honey from the comb – this is usually done using a mechanical centrifuge. You'll also need strainers to remove any 'bits' from the liquid honey, and a supply of clean, sterile, glass honey jars with your labels on them.

Remove the wax cappings from each frame of honeycomb by running a long knife across it, using the wooden edges of the frame as the guide, then place it into the centrifugal extractor which flings the honey out of the cells, so you can collect it all. Small-scale beekeepers often manage without, simply by removing the cappings and standing the frame on edge so the honey runs slowly out – but this leaves quite a bit of honey still inside. On a commercial scale, honey is heated to make it runnier so it comes out of the honeycomb faster and more efficiently, and to ensure a larger haul of honey, but enthusiasts think that cold-extracted honey is of a higher quality as it's entirely unprocessed.

BEESWAX

When you keep bees, the process of extracting honey from the frames in which it's stored by the bees in the familiar 'cells' leaves you with a quantity of beeswax. Wash any remaining honey off the beeswax with warm water, then allow it to dry as much as possible before melting it – heating it will drive off any remaining water as steam. If you don't have any immediate use for melted wax, pour it into moulds to make small solid bars to store until you are ready to use it. Some can be used in making face cleansers, lotions, hand creams and other toiletries, also candles and furniture polish.

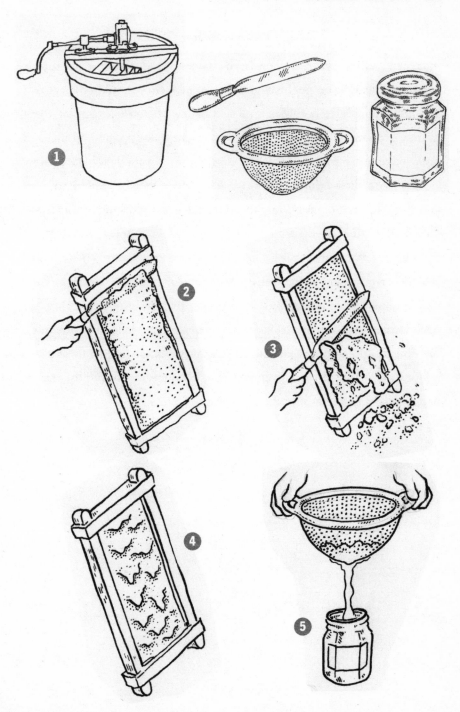

VARROA MITE

In recent years bee colonies have started to decline or disappear completely, leaving empty hives at a time of year they should be very busy, and although it's likely that several factors are responsible, one of them is the varroa mite. This tiny insect can sometimes be spotted on infected bees, looking like minute specks of dust. Mites sap the bees' strength by feeding from their bodies, which weakens them so they can't work well and they die prematurely; this means hives don't work as efficiently as they should – fewer worker bees are raised, so less honey is stored. Mites build up inside the hive so bees are infected when they return to it, if they weren't already. Due to the threat posed by varroa mites, beekeepers are having to take strict precautions by checking their hives any time they are open for routine jobs, and using suitable treatments, especially in winter. Treatments and advice regarding varroa mites change frequently as more is found out about the problem, so for the latest advice consult the British Beekeepers' website or a local beekeeping group.

GROWING GRASS AND HAY

....

When you keep livestock, you need grass for grazing and also hay for winter feed. Good grassland doesn't just contain one species; it contains a mixture of grasses but also a sprinkling of wildflowers, which don't merely look good (though they do) but also contribute to the nutrition of livestock. If you're starting new grazing or hay meadows from scratch, agricultural suppliers can provide suitable seed mixtures. Grassland and hay meadows aren't just lawns on a large scale, though, they need to be managed properly to produce good-quality, productive crops.

PASTURE FOR GRAZING

Secure fencing is vital, and it needs to be suitable for the type of animal you plan to keep since some are great escapers. Don't allow livestock to have access to the whole area all at once; unless you have several fields in which you can rotate livestock, divide the grazing up into strips and turn the animals out into one patch at a time. (Electric fencing is often used, powered by a car-type battery, or the cheaper nylon ribbon fencing which consists of long white 'ribbons' hooked onto loops in the top of slender metal poles knocked into the ground. Both are easily moved.) This allows the remaining pasture to grow and recover from trampling, for manure to be broken down by soil insects such as dung beetles and absorbed back into the ground, and for any parasites to die off.

Pasture needs to be walked over regularly so that any undesirable weeds can be removed by hand. Ragwort is the chief offender as it's very poisonous to livestock. Don't just chop it down; pull it out and remove the remains from the field since dead ragwort is even more attractive to grazing animals to eat than live ragwort, and just as poisonous.

Some weeds are merely a nuisance; livestock will normally graze round a dense patch of thistles or nettles since there's normally nothing worth eating in the patch, so it just spreads and takes up space that could have been used by decent grass. Weeds like these can be controlled by cutting them down regularly with a mower or scythe, which is preferable to using weedkillers. Dock is another useless weed that spreads quickly and wastes space, but it needs to have the thick tap root dug out rather than being chopped down, ideally before it can shed seed, to stop the next generation taking hold.

But some wildflowers are well worth having as they contribute to the nutrition of the animals grazing on them. Yarrow, dandelion, wild chicory, white clover, burnet and ribwort are often present in existing pasture. If you're growing a new meadow from seed, it's worth obtaining a mixture that already contains a selection of suitable wild flowers and herbs, otherwise buy the seeds separately and add them to a standard agricultural grassland mixture before sowing. If you need to turn livestock outside in winter, it pays to include meadow fescue in your mixture, since it stands up better than many grasses to harsh winters.

Whilst a lot of smallholders graze a mixture of different types of livestock in the same field at the same time, it's far better to rotate them over a period of time in order to make the most of the available grazing. The first animals to introduce are those that can eat long grass – cattle and horses – and then turn out sheep and goats which trim the grass shorter. (The goats will eat a lot of weeds and light scrub that cows and horses won't touch.) Geese will eat even shorter grass than sheep, so they can be turned out last of all, and hens will also enjoy scratching around. This way of 'rotating' pasture is also good practice when it comes to keeping livestock parasites under control, since the parasites of one species of livestock can't live in a different host.

On a large scale, commercial farmers use a fair bit of fertiliser to keep grassland growing strongly to provide as much rich grazing as possible, but you can avoid doing so by not overstocking (i.e. not keeping too many animals on a given area of land), by rotating the livestock so pasture is rested in rotation, and by including clovers and trefoils in the sward. These useful plants have nitrogen-fixing nodules on their roots where beneficial bacteria 'trap' nitrogen from the air and release it into the soil, where it helps to feed the grasses growing round them entirely naturally and for free. My own organic wildflower meadow, while not producing a massive crop of hay, still manages to produce a useful annual yield without the need for artificial fertilisers.

BUYING HAY

For a lot of people without much land, buying hay is the only option. It's available from agricultural merchants and livestock feed suppliers. Quality varies quite a bit depending on the condition and also whether it contains thistles and other unwanted weeds. Good hay should smell sweet and not musty, and it's usually possible to see thistles or docks by their thick brown stalks, even without cutting a bale open. If you are having a quantity delivered to take advantage of bulk prices you'll need dry storage space undercover. A lot of small-livestock-keepers simply take their car to the yard and load a couple of bales in the back of a car or pick up a small trailer-load every week or so, and use it virtually straight away.

You may also see 'haylage' offered – this is hay that's been made in the usual way but baled up while it's still damp and trussed up in polythene to keep the air out so it doesn't go mouldy or rot. It's a convenient way to make hay in a wet summer and keeps quite well – it can even be stored in the open – as long as the plastic isn't opened.

Silage is grass that's been cut and baled in polythene while it's almost fresh, and it 'ferments' in store. Cattle enjoy silage but not all livestock will eat it. Neither haylage nor silage can be made without special bale-wrapping equipment, so are probably not practical for most small-holders to do themselves, though you can buy them to help with the winter food supplies.

HOW TO MAKE HAY

The same mixture of grass and wildflowers used for pasture also makes a good hay meadow. It's not essential to keep two separate fields for grazing and hay; if part of the field used for grazing is sectioned off with electric fencing till June or so, you can often cut a crop of hay from it before turning livestock back onto it later.

It's still worth dealing with weeds, even in a hayfield. The presence of dried docks, thistle and above all, ragwort, lowers the quality of the hay, and dead ragwort is still poisonous. When it's cut for hay, grass must not be lush and green. Wait until mid to late June when it's flowered and seed-heads have started to form, by which time the stalks will just be starting to dry out naturally. Choose a time when the weather forecast suggests you'll have a week or ten days of continuous fine dry weather. Cut the grass off a couple of inches above ground level, by hand using an old-fashioned scythe, or using a mechanical rotary scythe if you don't have an area big enough to justify a tractor-powered hay cutter.

Leave fresh-cut hay lying on the ground for a few days to dry before turning it. It's worth turning it (an operation known as 'tedding') several times so that the sun and wind can air it thoroughly, to prevent it going mouldy when it's baled and stored. On a small scale you can simply rake it around to turn it or use a pitchfork, but on a larger scale a tractor-mounted implement with two rotating circular rake-like tines is used. When the hay is well dried it's baled; to use the baling machine the hay first needs to be raked up into rows, so either use an old-fashioned wooden hay rake or use a tractor-mounted hay turner (by adjusting it, it'll also throw the hay into rows).

Since bales of hay quickly absorb moisture if they're left standing on damp ground, it's best to get them shifted under cover and stacked in a dry shed or barn as soon as possible, ideally on the same day the crop is baled. If possible, raise the bottom course of bales up on old wooden pallets so some air can circulate underneath, otherwise there's a risk of condensation forming so the bottom bales start rotting – this can happen even on concrete floors.

If you only have a small quantity of grass to cut for hay, or you don't have the facilities to bale it, it is possible to store loose hay – the old-fashioned haystack (which is rarely seen nowadays) was just that. It was made of loose hay piled up in a circle, with each new layer raked as it was piled up, so the stems all ran in the same direction; the top rose to a central peak and was then thatched to keep the rain out. It's rather a lost art, but today it's possible to keep loose hay under cover in a dry barn, but it's essential that it doesn't get damp, If it does, the hay turns musty so livestock either won't eat it or if they do, it doesn't do them any good.

SMALL-SCALE FARMING EQUIPMENT

There's only so much land you can work by hand; an area about the size of an allotment is usually plenty for most people. But a larger smallholding or croft will normally need some mechanical help – to pull a trailer and cultivate land at the very least. These days there are all sorts of miniature tractors available new or second hand. Another option is to buy an old (well, vintage, really) small second-hand tractor such as the little grey 'Fergie' (as the Ferguson TE20 is affectionately known), and the equipment, such as ploughs and cultivators, to go with them. Two-wheeled tractors, also known as rotavators, can also be used for turning over soil, and these, too, can be coupled to a small trailer. All this type of equipment is available from specialist dealers who take stands at shows and advertise in smallholders' magazines, and from private individuals in the small ads. When it comes to the more specialist equipment that you might only need once a year, or expensive kit that it isn't worth buying when it's going to sit around for most of the time, then most people either hire it temporarily or call in contractors to do jobs like baling hay.

CHAPTER 5

GO WILD IN THE COUNTRY

IDENTIFYING BIRDS

Roughly 280 species of birds are regularly seen in the British Isles; they include full-time residents and migrants who visit temporarily – either to breed in summer or to escape harsh winters in the places they do breed. Others 'pass through' very briefly on their migration routes, stopping over to rest or refuel before moving on again. Very occasionally, we'll also get rare foreign birds that have been blown way off course. These attract a lot of excitement from 'twitchers', who travel huge distances to get a brief sighting of a rarity that's new to them, so they can add another 'tick' to their spotter's list.

The art of identifying birds lies in practice, plus a spot of study. The best way to start is by learning the easy ones first – the birds that you regularly see in your garden and in the countryside round your home. The commoner species such as house sparrows (though rarer than they once were), starlings, blackbirds, wrens, blue tits and great tits can turn up almost anywhere in towns or countryside throughout the country, and you'll probably also see thrushes, kestrels and sparrowhawks. Once you are familiar with those, start looking further afield. Certain birds are found in particular types of habitat; some are only seen at the coast, or in mountains, woods or moorland country. (You won't, for instance, find a grouse on your bird table in leafy Surrey, though you may see a woodpecker on your peanut-feeder.) It's worth carrying a small pocket guide to the birds of Britain, for ready reference – keep it handy in the car, or your backpack when you're out walking. I wouldn't advise getting a great thick book that includes birds of Europe as it'll be packed full of species you'll never see in this country, which just makes it more difficult to identify what you will see. A small pair of binoculars is also a big help; choose the lightweight sort that will fit in a pocket or which you can hang round your neck on a long walk without throttling yourself; 7 x 26cm or 8 x 28cm is ideal.

When you see a bird you don't recognise, try to compare it to something you do know, as a rough guide to size (e.g blackbird-sized, sparrow-sized, pigeon-sized) and make a note of colour, markings or other distinguishing features as it all helps when you look it up. Behaviour can also be helpful; a medium-sized bird hovering over a roadside verge is almost certainly a kestrel. A good bird identification book will tell you the time of year, distribution and habitats for each species in its pages, which helps you eliminate a lot of possibilities and home in on the right one.

If you visit an RSPB reserve, look for the 'sightings board' that they keep at the visitor centre listing all the birds that have been seen recently on the reserve, so you know what you might expect to see during your visit. You'll often find volunteers on duty in hides or in the visitor centre who can point out birds of interest and help you to identify them, but all members are usually very helpful when you make it obvious that you're an interested beginner. You'll know there's a real rarity around if you see groups of enthusiasts dressed in khaki-green birdwatching gear, all bringing high-powered telescopes to bear on the same distant point; ask what they're looking at. (Serious twitchers subscribe to a pager service that alerts them to the location of rarities, which is how they manage to arrive at the scene of an interesting sighting in large numbers, and they're also in touch with fellow twitchers via mobile phones.)

A good way to develop your interest further is to go on a course or a bird-watching holiday. Some bird reserves hold special walks accompanied by experts to help newcomers identify birds that turn up on their patch, and several organisations, such as the Field Studies Council, and specialist bird holiday firms, run courses or organised excursions to places of bird-watching interest with experts in attendance.

BIRD RECOGNITION: THE BARE ESSENTIALS

SMALLER THAN A SPARROW

Wren: *A little brown bird with a slightly barred pattern and conspicuously cocked tail, found all year round in woods, parkland, gardens and hedgerows. Solitary and with a wonderfully elaborate song.*

Long-tailed tit: *A small, dumpy-bodied, pinky-brown, white and black bird with a tail three times the length of its body, found in family groups all year round in edges of woodlands, hedgerows and gardens. 3 Firecrest: along with the goldcrest, our smallest bird and relatively rare. Pale brown with a red and yellow 'stripe' on the top of its head. Often nips about in conifers.*

SPARROW-SIZED

House sparrow: *A cheeky bird with black-and-chestnut-dappled back and wings with grey under-parts, and a rather blunt head and dumpy body, usually found in flocks; present all year round, once common in built-up areas as well as in countryside, but now becoming unaccountably scarce in some areas. Very 'chatty' in groups at roosting time.*

Hedge sparrow (dunnock): *A streaky brown bird with grey head and neck and a more streamlined shape than the house sparrow. Usually found in flocks, common and widespread in gardens, hedgerows, parkland and countryside all year round.*

Bluetit: *A lively, active, rounded blue and yellow bird common in gardens, hedgerows and parks, often hanging upside down to feed on insects under leaves. Solitary or seen in small family groups in summer. Present all year round.*

Great tit: *A size larger than the bluetit, but just as common, with strong black and yellow markings with a greenish back, found in all the same places, all year round. Solitary, or in small family groups in summer. Resident all year.*

Pied wagtail: *Striking grey-and-white bird with black 'trim' and a black eye in a white face, which bobs its tail constantly. Fairly common in towns, gardens and countryside all year round. Usually solitary or found in pairs in summer, but in winter they can gather in fair-sized flocks to roost. Resident.*

Chaffinch: *The male has a conspicuous pinkish chest and underparts with blackish wings clearly marked with two white flashes, easily seen when perching and in flight. The female is duller brown but also with black-and-white-striped wings. Seen in gardens, hedgerows and parkland, mostly individually or in pairs, year-round.*

Greenfinch: *Yellowy-green birds with a yellowish streak down the front edge of each wing; the colours are brightest in spring. Commonly found in small flocks in gardens, hedgerows and parkland, all year round.*

Goldfinch: *Showy beige, black and gold bird with a red-and-white face, the black, red and gold colours showing up clearly both in flight and when perched. Sometimes seen in fair-sized flocks in countryside and wasteland, especially where thistles or teazel seedheads are present, as the birds feed on the seeds. Resident.*

Robin: *The most instantly recognisable of any resident bird, dumpy with an orange-red breast and rather upright stance, often bobbing slightly; very common in gardens, hedgerows and parkland.*

BLACKBIRD-SIZED

Blackbird: *Male is all-black with a bright yellow beak and yellow ring round the eye; female and juveniles are all-brown. Common in gardens, hedgerows and parkland, mostly solitary but in spring parents often seen feed youngsters on the ground. Resident.*

Starling: *Rather slender shape compared to the blackbird and slightly smaller, with glossy, iridescent black feathers regularly spotted with silvery white, especially in spring. Youngsters are the same shape and size but a dull grey-brown shade. Commonly seen in small flocks in the countryside, and in winter large flocks swoop and wheel towards dusk as they gather to roost communally in large trees or reedbeds. Resident, though some migrate.*

Song thrush: *Brown-backed bird with cream face, breast and underparts heavily speckled with brown, almost chevron-shaped 'dots'. Mostly solitary; less common than some years ago; in gardens, hedgerows and parkland. Resident.*

Redwing: *Very similar to song thrush but with bright orange-red 'armpits' and a distinct cream eye-stripe, seen in small flocks; a winter visitor to hedgerows, parkland and sometimes gardens in search of berries.*

Great spotted woodpecker: *A showy, piebald-effect black-and-white bird with bright red undertail; male also has a red cap on his head. Hammers its beak on dead branches in spring to warn off rivals. Seen perching on upright tree branches, pressing its tail flat against the branch for support; often visits peanut feeders, also seen in countryside trees and parklands. Resident.*

PIGEON-SIZED

Wood pigeon: *A very common plump, pinkish-grey bird with a white collar, faintly surprised facial expression and yellow eye, making loud five-note cooing calls when perched. Often seen in flocks in fields and tall trees in parkland and countryside, especially in winter. Individuals or small groups often visit gardens. Resident.*

Collared dove: *Very common, less plump and slightly smaller than the wood pigeon; all-over beige-grey with a black collar, eye and beak. Sometimes solitary or found in small groups in gardens, farmland trees and parkland. Cooing call similar to wood pigeon's, but only three coos per phrase instead of five. Resident.*

Jackdaw: *Dark grey-black body and greyish neck. Bright eye with a white iris. Common in gardens, woodland and clifftops and a great nester in chimneys. Resident.*

Sparrowhawk: *Common bird of prey which flies rapidly through gardens or trees in the countryside from a safe perching place to catch other small birds; never hovers like a kestrel. Male has blue-grey upperparts and pale, faintly barred underparts; female is larger with brown upperparts and paler underneath. Resident.*

Kestrel: *Common small bird of prey, with chestnut-brown upperparts patterned with darker bars or spots, and lighter underparts which are also spotted or streaked, usually seen hovering over roadside verges and fields hunting for mice and other small prey, or perched at the top of telegraph poles. Resident.*

Green woodpecker: *Striking, bright green bird with bright red cap and yellow rump, best seen on the ground probing for ants and other grubs, or perched in trees. In flight it flaps and glides alternately. The loud, harsh yelping call gives rise to a common country name – 'yaffle'. Resident.*

LARGER THAN A PIGEON

Magpie: *easily identified black, blue and white 'crow' with a very long tail which is approximately 1½ times the length of the body. Usually spotted on its own or in small groups, especially in summer when the young birds tend to stay together, in gardens, farmland, parkland and countryside. Resident.*

Carrion crow: *Strong-looking all-black bird with glossy feathers, a slightly down-curved beak and bare, black legs. Solitary or found in small groups, in gardens, farmland, parkland and wild countryside. Resident.*

Rook: *Crow-like and similar size, but more tatty-looking, with shaggy feathers, a bald face and straight, dagger-like beak. Legs have long, loose, shaggy feathers hanging down round them so it looks as if it is wearing short, baggy trousers. Nests in large groups at the tops of clumps of tall trees, and flies or feeds on the ground in flocks. Resident.*

Buzzard: *A large bird of prey, bigger than a rook or a crow; dirty brown colour from a distance, at closer range you can see a barred pattern under the wings with a black outline round all but the leading edges, and white area inside, which darkens and develops the barred pattern closer to the body. Tail is barred. Resident.*

WATERFOWL

Mallard: *The commonest duck on inland ponds, lakes and rivers, as well as coastal estuaries and inlets. The drake is mostly grey and brown with a bottle-green head, a white-outlined blue panel in each wing, with black tail and orange legs. Female is dappled brown all over with a white-outlined blue panel in each wing, and orange legs. Resident.*

Brent goose: *Small, mallard-sized goose, with black head, neck and breast with a white ring round the neck, grey bars on its belly, and a black and white tail. A winter visitor, seen in flocks feeding on muddy estuaries and* saltmarshes at low tide, and in nearby fields at high tide, along the south and east coasts. A white-bellied form is sometimes seen on the west coast.

Teal: *Our smallest duck, seen in largest numbers in winter though some present year-round. The drake is grey-brown with a chestnut-and-bottle-green head, bright green panel on each wing, and a conspicuous fawn, almost-triangular patch near the tail, most visible when the bird is swimming or standing. The female is similar to the female mallard, but slightly smaller and with a green, not blue, panel in each wing. Found in flocks in lakes, reservoirs, wetlands and along the coast at estuaries and saltmarshes; mostly seen in winter.*

Mute swan: *The common swan that is seen on lakes, rivers, and coastal estuaries and inlets. It is a large white bird with a long neck carried upright, a bright orange beak and a black 'bump' at the base of the beak, which is larger in the male. Mostly seen in pairs or small flocks. Resident.*

Curlew: *A large dappled-brown wading bird with long legs, a very long, down-curving beak, and a mournful 'cur-lee' cry, which is found in wetlands, moorlands, coastal estuaries and saltmarshes, and also boggy fields. It is usually seen solitary or in small flocks, but in winter it can be seen in quite large groups.*

Heron: *A large, upright grey bird with a long black and white neck and dagger-shaped head with black cap, a long yellow beak and a rather determined look. Found at the waterside round coastal estuaries and inlets, also inland lakes, rivers and ponds – it can make a nuisance of itself in domestic fishponds. It flies with its neck bent back and feet trailing, which creates a* *distinctive shape, and flaps its large wings rather slowly. Usually solitary, though it does breed in colonies, with the nests grouped at the tops of tall trees. Resident.*

Egret: *Unmistakable large, white, upright, heron-like bird, but a size or two smaller, usually seen wading in shallow water or poised on the banks, at coastal estuaries, inlets and saltmarshes, also inland rivers and lakes. Usually solitary, or you see several well spaced out along the same bit of bank. Resident except in long, cold winters.*

Oystercatcher: *A distinctive black-and-white bird with long, bright orange beak, an orange ring round the eye and bright pink legs, found in small flocks feeding by probing the mud along rocky or stony coastlines, estuaries and inlets. Resident.*

Turnstone: *A very 'busy' little short-legged bird with dappled brown upperparts and white underneath with orange legs and a short beak. Usually seen scurrying around in small flocks along rocky or stony coasts, actively turning over pebbles and bits of seaweed looking for food. Not as shy as most seabirds, allowing you quite a close look. Resident.*

IDENTIFYING BUTTERFLIES

Of the sixty or so butterflies that can usually be found in the British Isles, only roughly a dozen are very well known; they are the ones that fairly commonly turn up in gardens as well as countryside hedgerows and meadows. Butterflies are the good-looking, day-flying end of the lepidoptera clan, which also includes a far greater number of moths, which (with a few exceptions) are usually duller-coloured night-flying creatures. All British butterflies and moths are rapidly declining in numbers, largely due to loss of natural wild habitat, so it's worth making special trips to visit good butterfly territory in summer if you want to see a good selection. Good places include wildflower meadows and long grassy areas in parkland around stately homes, chalky hillsides, nature reserves or our few butterfly reserves. In your own garden it's well worthwhile doing anything you can to increase the availability of nectar-rich flowers and suitable caterpillar food plants to help halt the decline.

It's best to start by learning the easy butterflies first – the colourful ones that visit your garden and the countryside in your immediate area. Once you know those, anything new that turns up automatically stands out, and by looking it up in a book you can soon add to your knowledge. (Again, a small pocket guide that only lists the ones you are most likely to see is the best way to start.) Things to look for when identifying butterflies are colour, size and any obvious markings, but also take note of the habitat (fields, woods, roadside verges), the flowers they are feeding on, and time of year. Take your butterfly book with you on countryside outings. It also helps to take photos to compare with pictures in a book later; try to snap a butterfly that's keeping still with its wings held wide open, sunbathing or sipping nectar from a flower, so all the markings show up well. Store your photos in a special file on your computer; it's a good way to build up a collection without harming the wild population – unlike Victorian naturalists who used to catch butterflies, chloroform them and pin them down in glass cases. The best times for spotting butterflies are summer days when the weather is warm, still and sunny, though a few species aren't fussy. Caterpillars are more difficult to identify since a good many of them are a nondescript green, which acts as brilliant camouflage when they live in grass or foliage, but a few 'regulars' can be identified by a combination of coloration and markings, not to mention the host plant they are living on.

BUTTERFLY RECOGNITION: THE BASICS

Small tortoiseshell: *A very familiar, medium-sized orange-and-brown butterfly with a row of alternate brown and cream 'squares' along the front edge of its forewings, and a row of tiny blue half-moon shapes along the other edges of the wings, seen June/July and August/September in flowery countryside, allotments and gardens. Caterpillar: hairy black-and-yellow-striped, seen in groups on nettles, May/June and July/August.*

Peacock: *An easily identified dull red butterfly with brown-edged wings and a conspicuous 'false eye' (a buff patch with a dark circle in the centre) on each wing-tip. Caterpillar: spiky and black, June/July, seen on nettles.*

Painted lady: *A fairly large, soft orange-brown butterfly, strongly patterned with black spots with black-and-white-spotted triangles at the tips* *of the forewings; they are migrants, reaching us from the continent May / June to spend the summer here. Found in flowery countryside, allotments and gardens. Caterpillar: spiky, on nettles and thistles, August / September.*

Red admiral: *A familiar, medium-large butterfly mostly black with orange bands outlining the hind wings and several large white spots at the tips of the forewings; seen May to October feeding on all the popular bee plants in gardens, also teazel, clover and ivy, and drinks juice of rotting windfall apples. Caterpillar: solitary, spiky, black and white, seen on nettles or wild hops.*

Comma: *A very distinctive orange butterfly with scattered brown spots and ragged edges to the wings; white 'commas' on the undersides; seen July, and September / October feeding from flowers of brambles, hemp agrimony, knapweed and thistles in countryside hedgerows and wasteland. Caterpillar: solitary and buff-coloured, disguised as bird droppings, mainly found on wild hops, also sometimes nettles.*

Gatekeeper: *A smallish, orange butterfly with brown 'trimmings' and a double 'false eye' on the wings, mostly seen in the south of Britain in July and August. It often follows people through gates and gaps in footpaths (hence the name) in the countryside or along grassy meadows; the adult feeds on nectar of brambles and other hedgerow flowers. Caterpillar: dull greyish 'grubs' living on grasses most of the year.*

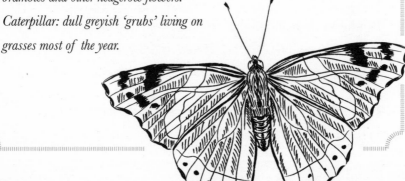

BLUE BUTTERFLIES

Holly blue: *A small blue butterfly, a deeper blue above and paler below the undersides, also faintly speckled with tiny black dots; females also have a darker navy / slate band round the edges of the forewings; seen March to October, fluttering around but rarely settling in hedgerows and gardens. Caterpillar: small, short, fat green caterpillars with hooked, dull reddish spikes; found on holly buds in spring and ivy buds in autumn, though they can also feed on buds of bramble, spindle and dogwood.*

YELLOW BUTTERFLIES

Brimstone: *A pale yellow butterfly with a small, dull orange spot in the centre of each of its four wings. Seen from February to November visiting wildflowers, especially primroses, for nectar, in countryside hedgerows. Caterpillar: all-green, exactly the same shade as the plant it is eating, which is either buckthorn (Rhamnus cathartica) or alder buckthorn (Frangula alnus) – both rather unexciting scrub shrubs, but worth growing as butterfly crèches.*

WHITE BUTTERFLIES

Orange tip: *The female looks suspiciously like a cabbage white; male is similar but with conspicuous orange tips to the forewings. Seen in May and June in countryside hedgerows, wasteland, allotments and gardens. Caterpillar: green, well camouflaged as they are the same shape and colour* as the seedpods of their food plants; found on lady's smock (Cardamine pratensis), garlic mustard (Alliaria petiolata) and run-to-seed brassica plants in kitchen gardens – the adult lays its eggs in the flowerheads.

Marbled white: *A large, showy, black-and-white butterfly which flies slowly and feeds with wings held open, especially on knapweed and scabious in July/August. Caterpillar: grassy-green, found on long grasses, especially fescues, over most of the year.*

Large white: *A very common large, white, butterfly with black tips to the forewings; the female also has two black spots on each forewing. Seen April to September in hedgerows, flowery countryside, wasteland, allotments and gardens where it is a notorious pest of brassica plants. Adults feed on the nectar of a wide range of wildflowers. Caterpillar: black-and-yellow striped, found in colonies on brassica plants and nasturtiums in gardens, and also on many wild members of the cabbage family.*

Small white: *Another very common butterfly, two-thirds the size of the large white, with dark tips of the forewings; males also have one black spot and females two. Seen March to September in the same places as the large white. Caterpillar: solitary, small and green, found on both wild and cultivated members of the brassica family.*

BROWN BUTTERFLIES

Meadow brown: *A large, dull brown butterfly with one 'false eye' on each front wing, seen in any weather from June to August in meadows.*

Caterpillar: solitary, striped in two shades of green, usually living on cocksfoot grass; can be found most of the year.

Ringlet: *A dark brown, medium-sized butterfly with white-ringed darker spots found in any grassy areas; flying in all weather from June to late August. Caterpillar: a dull beige 'grub' with a slightly darker central stripe, feeding on bramble; found most of the year.*

Large skipper: *A small, brownish butterfly with short wings that flits quickly from flower to flower in June and July. Caterpillar: grass-green, found on false brome grass and cocksfoot living inside a tube made by rolling the edges of a blade of grass and gluing them together.*

Speckled wood: *A fairly dark brown, medium-sized butterflies whose wings are edged with a row of small irregular-shaped buff patches, with one 'false eye' on each forewing and three on each hind wing. Adults found flitting about in shady places under trees and shrubs from late spring to late summer. Caterpillar; green, tubular and grass-like, found on several kinds of grass.*

IDENTIFYING WILDFLOWERS

The great thing about identifying wildflowers is that, unlike birds and butterflies, they stay still, so you can get a good long look at them, which makes it easy to compare what you see with pictures in field guides. Again, a pocket flower identification book is ideal to take with you when out walking, but it's handy to have a larger, more detailed book back home for further information. Again, whenever possible, take a photo to help with identification later or to add to the collection on your computer.

Things to look for when trying to identify flowers are the colour, shape and size of the flower, the height and shape of the plant (tall/upright, climber, or low/spreading), the habitat and time of year. It's also handy to have a good look at the shape of the foliage. Don't try to tackle the entire flora of Great Britain in one go; there are about 2,500 different species, a lot of which have only minor differences. Get to know the commonest flowers first, especially those that grow in your local area, and then look around for anything that's new to you. As with birds and butterflies, the showier flowers are always easiest. A good place to start when identifying something new to you is to see what its flowers look similar to – cow parsley-like, buttercup-like, daisy-like, dandelion-like – since that's a good clue as to the family to which it belongs.

WILDFLOWER RECOGNITION:
THE EASY-TO-SPOT, COMMONER ONES

WHITE FLOWERS

Large white waterlily (Nymphaea alba): *Large, flat, floating leaves present from late spring to autumn, and the biggest flowers of any British native plant, 15cm (6in) across, from June to August, opening only for a short time around midday. Grows in deep water in ponds, lakes, canals and slow-moving sections of rivers.*

Goosegrass, or cleavers (Galium aparine): *A familiar 'weed' with long, straggly stems growing to 1.7m (6ft) and bearing whorls of five narrow leaves, all having tiny hooks that enable the plants to scramble up into hedgerows, fences and other plants, creating dense mats. Towards the tips of the stems, tiny white flowers are followed by small round seedheads that come off on clothing.*

Yarrow (Achillea millefolium): *A familiar wildflower with feathery foliage and upright stems 15–60cm (6–24in) tall topped with flattish-topped sprays of white (sometimes pale pink) flowers all summer, which act as favourite mating grounds for several insects. Found on roadside verges and other, undisturbed grassy areas. Also occurs as a common weed in lawns, though regular mowing prevents it from flowering.*

Mayweed (Matricaria maritima): *Dome-shaped clumps 25–60cm (10–24in) high and much the same across of feathery foliage on green stems, topped by white daisies with yellow centres, flowering July to September.*

Looks a lot like garden chamomile, but lacks any scent. Grows round the edges of fields, on neglected allotments and wasteland.

White dead-nettle (Lamium album): *Short, clump-forming plants growing to 45cm (18in) tall with pairs of non-stinging nettle-like leaves and whorls of white hooded flowers clustered in the leaf axils from May to October. Commonly occurs as a weed in allotments and gardens, also on roadside verges, hedge bottoms and wasteland.*

Hogweed (Heracleum sphondylium): *A cow parsley-like plant, but more solid and chunky looking, usually 90cm–1.5m (3–5ft), flowering in all the same places as cow parsley – roadside verges, hedgerows and woodland edges – but several weeks after cow parsley flowers are over, from June to September. (Not to be confused with the rare giant hogweed, which is 2.5m (8ft) with enormous flowers and leaves, and thick stems; to be left well alone since the whole plant has irritant sap.)*

GREENISH FLOWERS

Cuckoo pint, lords and ladies (Arum maculatum):
A striking and unmistakable plant 15–30cm (6–12in) tall, with large, 15–20cm (6–8in) arrowhead-shaped leaves, sometimes heavily spotted with purplish black, and creamy or pale green hooded spathes 15–20cm (6–8in) tall, housing a brown spadix, in April and May. When the flowers are over, a cluster of orange berries forms at the end of the old stem. Grows in damp, shady places, usually woodland, hedge bottoms and ditches.

Stinging nettle (Urtica dioica): *A very well-known tall, clump-forming plant with upright stems to 1.5m (5ft) tall, bearing paired, jagged-edged leaves with powerful stings; from May to September short dangling stems of tiny greenish flowers grow towards the tops of the stems. Although generally disliked, the nettle is a valuable plant, being the well-defended home to five different kinds of butterfly caterpillar.*

Jack-by-the-hedge (Alliaria petiolata): *A common wildflower of semi-shady places round woods and along hedgerows; a narrow, upright plant 30cm–1.2m (1–4ft) tall, with frilly-edged, heart-shaped leaves growing alternately all the way up a single straight stem which is topped by a cluster of small white flowers from April to June.*

Dog's mercury (Mercurialis perennis): *Upright stems 30–45cm (12–18in) high, bearing paired leaves, topped with short, airy spikes of tiny green flowers that are barely noticeable, except that the plant grows in large, dense carpets so the flowers look like a faint 'haze'. Found in deep shade in woodland, flowering February to April.*

YELLOW FLOWERS

Marsh marigold, kingcup (Caltha palustris): *Like a giant buttercup, with large, golden, chalice-shaped flowers from March/April to July and glossy heart-shaped leaves, growing in mud and shallow water at the edges of ponds or streams, also in ditches and boggy areas that stay damp even in summer. 30–45cm (1–2ft) tall.*

Yellow water lily, brandy bottle (Nuphar lutea): *Large, flat, round floating leaves the size of dinner-plates. Present late spring to autumn; in summer bears yellow flowers resembling large, waxy buttercups which stand several inches out of the water, followed by green, flask-shaped seedpods, earning the plant its alternative common name. Grows in still water of ponds, lakes and canals.*

Hedge mustard (Sisymbrium officinale): *A strangely wiry-looking plant, with a shaggy rosette of leaves near the base of smaller ones on the lower stems, but mostly made up of a main, stiff upright stem supporting stiff side branches that stand out from it horizontally. The tips of the shoots bear tufts of tiny yellow flowers from May to September. Found on roadsides, along hedgerows and on wasteland and round the edges of fields, height 30–90cm (1–3ft).*

Fleabane (Pulicaria dysenterica): *A common wildflower that was used in medieval times as a strewing herb to repel insects, and also dried and burnt to repel fleas. It forms large colonies of upright stems, 30–60cm (1–2ft) high, with narrow, lance-shaped leaves arranged alternately along them, topped with loose clusters of yellow daisy flowers in late summer.*

Coltsfoot (Tussilago farfara): *A common wildflower with scalloped-edged leaves, white on the undersides with mauve-pink leafstalks and ribs growing straight out of the ground, as do the flower stems which are brownish-buff and very scaly-stemmed, topped by bright yellow 'daisies' in March and April. Spreads by underground stems to form large, dense colonies approximately 20cm (8in) high on cultivated ground, allotments and wasteland, especially on heavy and damp soil.*

Ragwort (Senecio jacobaea): *A common 'weed' of meadows, grassland and pasture, with tall upright stems and coarsely toothed leaves (which smell unpleasant if crushed) topped by loose sprays of yellow daisy flowers. Poisonous to livestock, but home to the stripy cinnabar moth caterpillars.*

Yellow flag (Iris pseudacorus): *A strong, clump-forming plant with long, spear-shaped leaves and tall stems up to 90cm (3ft) high, topped by yellow, three-petalled typically iris-shaped flowers in June and July. Grows in shallow water at the edges of ponds and lakes, also in marshy ground and ditches that stay wet even in summer.*

Meadowsweet (Filipendula ulmaria): *Straight, upright stems, 60cm (2ft) high, bear alternate compound leaves made up of five pairs of leaflets with a larger one at the tip, topped with sprays of aromatic flowers from June to August. Found in damp meadows, marshland and woodland edges.*

Rayless chamomile, pineapple weed (Chamomilla suaveolens): *Resembles mayweed, but with no petals on the daisy flowers, just greenish-yellow centres. The foliage smells strongly of something similar to pineapple. Plants are small and bushy rather than dome-shaped, 10–30cm*

(4–12in) tall and as wide, flowering June and July. Grows on wasteland, roadsides and field edges.

BLUE / PURPLE / LILAC FLOWERS

Tufted vetch (Vicia cracca): *A scrambling plant, 60cm–1.5m (2–5ft) high, with ladder-like leaves ending in a short curly tendril, bearing short stems topped by showy spikes of tiny, lavender-blue flowers from June to August. Grows along hedgerows and field edges.*

Sea holly (Eryngium maritimum): *A rather 'artificial'-looking seaside plant growing on pebbly or sandy shores, with prickly, silvery-green leaves and stems to 90cm (3ft) tall, topped with shaggy, metallic-silvery rosettes that surround a small cluster of bluish flowers, from July to August.*

Spear thistle (Cirsium vulgare): *Tall striking thistle with strong upright spiny stems growing to over 1m (3ft) high; bold, jagged foliage whose every jag is tipped with vicious spikes; the large, knobbly flowerheads have tufts of stiff, narrow, pale purple petals protruding from the tops of what look like very prickly, green 'pineapples' an inch or two high and almost as wide. Grows in grassland, roadside verges and meadows, and though less plentiful than many thistles such as creeping thistle, this is one of the most easily identified.*

Purple loosestrife (Lythrum salicaria): *Tall plants, 90cm–2m (3–6ft) tall, with leaves arranged in whorls of three along the upright main stems, topped by long, often quite showy spikes of mauve-pink flowers from June to August. Grows in damp areas, especially watersides and marshy places.*

Woody nightshade (Solanum dulcamara): *A bushy-looking wildflower with small, glossy leaves on semi-woody stems, bears clusters of purple, potato-like flowers with a yellow 'beak' on short stems towards the tips from June to September; followed by small oval berries that ripen from green through yellow to orange-red. Found scrambling into hedgerows or as a bushy plant on wasteland.*

RED / PINK / MAUVE FLOWERS

Lady's smock (Cardamine pratensis): *A petite plant, 15–38cm (6–15in) high, with a cluster of rather watercress-like leaves around the base and weak stems bearing ladder-like leaves, leading up to short heads of smallish, pale lilac-pink flowers in late spring and early summer. Grows in damp grassy places, such as meadows and waterside turf.*

Ragged robin (Lychnis flos-cuculi): *Airy stems with pairs of long, narrow leaves, 30–75cm (12– 30in) high, topped by loose sprays of shaggy pink flowers with branching, spidery petals in May and June. Grows in damp meadows, marshes and fens.*

Great willowherb (Epilobium hirsutum): *Very tall plants 1.2–2m (4–6ft) high, growing in large clumps often spreading to cover entire banks. The tall, upright stems are clad from top to bottom in evenly spaced pairs of narrow, lance-shaped leaves with very faintly toothed edges, and towards the top individual mauve-pink flowers grow from the leaf axils on short stalks in July and August; these are followed by thistledown-like seedheads. Grows in wet places, marshland, fens and riverbanks.*

Hemp agrimony (Eupatorium cannabinum): *Tall, striking plants 90cm–1.5m (3–5ft) high, with straight, upright stems bearing pairs of compound leaves that open out all round the stem like many tiers of frills. Stems are topped by roughly domed heads made up of many small, mauve-pink flowers in August and September, which are popular with several kinds of butterflies.*

Scarlet pimpernel (Anagallis arvensis): *A small, prostrate plant up to 30cm (12in) across with sprawling stems that radiate out from a central point, bearing pairs of small, heart-shaped leaves. Towards the tips of the short, slender stems are small five-petalled flowers in coral red from May to August. They close up at night and in bad weather, hence the common name of 'Poor Man's Weather Glass'. Grows on any cultivated ground such as allotments, wasteland and at the edges of fields.*

Butterbur (Petasites hybridus): *A solid, chunky-looking plant that spreads by underground stems, producing colonies of leaves and flowers that each grow on their own short stalks straight out of the ground. The rounded leaves have mauve-pink-tinged veins and leaf stalks, and strange flowers with short, thick, scaly, buff-coloured stalks topped by clusters of short, fluffy, pale pink florets, followed by white fluffy seedheads. The leaves, which are small and underdeveloped when the flowers appear in March to May, continue to expand during the summer and can end up very large indeed, up to 60cm (2ft) or more in diameter. Grows in damp areas, along roadside verges, ditches and streams.*

Common mallow (Malva sylvestris): *A large, bushy-looking plant with stiff, horizontal stems bearing typical mallow leaves and mauve-pink flowers with five slightly spidery petals that'll be familiar to anyone who* *grows cultivated mallows in the garden. 30cm–1.2m (1–4ft) high and the same across, flowering June to September. Grows on wasteland, roadsides and near seashores.*

Himalayan balsam or touch-me-not (Impatiens glandulifera): *A giant distant relative of busy lizzie, the plant is a dirty word with environmentalists since it's a foreign invader that spreads rapidly along inland waterways, smothering out our native flora. Tall, thick, succulent stems grow to 2.2m (7ft) high, with spear-shaped busy lizzie leaves, topped by airy sprays of pinkish-lilac, helmet-shaped flowers on thin, wiry stems, from July to October. The seedheads 'pop' explosively, sending showers of seeds some distance, which helps the plant spread.*

WILDFLOWERS BY HABITAT

Damp meadow, spring: *lady's smock*

Damp meadow, summer: *meadowsweet*

Hedgerow, summer: *honeysuckle, wild hop, bramble, dog rose, cleavers, bindweed*

Meadow, spring: *primrose, cowslip, lady's smock*

Meadow, summer: *ox-eye daisy, meadow and creeping buttercup, ragwort*

Pebbly coast: *sea holly, horned poppy, thrift, sea kale*

Pond and pondside: *yellow flag, bulrush, reed, great white waterlily, yellow waterlily, great willowherb, purple loosestrife, Himalayan balsam.*

Roadside verge, spring: *cow parsley*

Roadside verge, early summer: *hogweed*

Wasteland, neglected cultivated ground including allotments, strips round the edges of fields: *scarlet pimpernel, field poppy, field bindweed, groundsel, sow thistle*

Woodland, spring: *bluebell, wood sorrel, wood anemone, dog's mercury, violet, wild strawberry*

IDENTIFYING TREES

The main things to look for when trying to put names to countryside trees are leaves, bark and flowers, fruits, berries or nuts, depending on the season. It's also worth considering what sort of habitat you are in; certain trees are common in hedgerows, others in woods, while in parklands around stately homes you may encounter a mixture of native trees and large ornamental species that have been introduced from abroad. Normally you'll find several different kinds of trees growing in close proximity to each other, but forestry plantations and certain managed woods (especially ones that were once coppiced for sweet chestnut or hazel poles) may contain almost entirely the same species, as they are cultivated as a crop.

TREE RECOGNITION:
THE MOST FREQUENTLY SEEN SPECIES

Common alder (Alnus glutinosa): *Mostly seen on wet, damp or marshy ground and on banks of rivers and streams. Look for regularly spaced tiers of branches and a neat, almost conical shape, and clusters of tiny woody 'cones' which are the remains of female catkins. In spring, long, yellowy tails of male catkins can be seen on the same trees as round, greenish female catkins.*

Goat willow (pussy willow) (Salix caprea): *Common shrubby tree or larger, multi-stemmed tree of damp or marshy places, ditch-edges, and* banks of rivers or streams, with oval, grey-green leaves and rather straight stems; in early spring the silky grey male catkins (which later develop a 'fluff' of yellow anthers) are often picked as pussy willow.

Beech (Fagus sylvatica): *A classic large parkland tree which also grows in shady woodlands on chalk downland. Spreading and stately, with a thick trunk of smooth grey bark and semi-shiny, oval leaves marked with a strong herringbone pattern of ribs. Instead of dropping their leaves, mature trees retain them until late into the following spring (a characteristic known as 'marcescence').*

Sweet chestnut (Castanea sativa): *Another classic large parkland tree, with thick trunks of characteristic, deeply ribbed bark that spirals slightly up the trunk. Leaves are long, narrow, pointed at the tip and outlined with serrated edges, and bearing a very pronounced, regular herringbone pattern of ribs. In autumn large spiky cases house the nuts.*

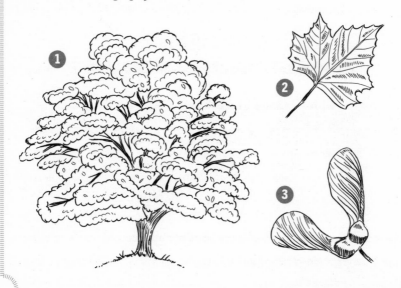

Sycamore (Acer pseudoplatanus): *Our largest member of the maple family, with rough-textured grey bark and fairly large, three-lobed leaves, dark green above and pale green below, often showing blackish 'tar spots' (caused by a common fungus disease). From late summer onwards, clusters of winged 'keys' can be seen hanging down from near the tips of branches, and in autumn these ripen to brown and spiral down to earth, giving rise to colonies of fast-growing saplings.*

Oak: *Perhaps the most traditional of British trees, with some very elderly examples to be found in Sherwood Forest and the New Forest. The oak is actually two different species. Both look very similar, growing to a good size with neatly and evenly fissured bark and the classic oak leaves and acorns, and both can occur anywhere in Britain. But English oak (Quercus robur) is the commoner in the south of England and has acorns with stalks, while Sessile oak (Quercus petraea) occurs mostly in northern Britain and has acorns without stalks, which grow straight from the twig. Some of the ancient oaks in Windsor Great Park are more than a thousand years old.*

Horse chestnut (Aesculus hippocastanum): *Another popular parkland tree that's also much planted as avenues leading up to grand country houses and along smart old residential streets in towns. Bark is scaly textured and reddish to ash-brown; leaves are unmistakable 'fans' of eight long, spatula-shaped leaflets arranged in a circle at the end of each stalk; flowers are fat 'candles' made up of many smallish white or deep pink florets arranged in short, squat, upward-facing spikes that are dotted all over the outer canopy of the tree in late spring/early summer. Shortly before the leaves turn brown and fall in autumn the prickly cases fall, splitting open to reveal the shiny conkers.*

Ash (Fraxinus excelsior): *An elegant tree with compound leaves made up of several small leaflets arranged in pairs along a stem, with one sticking out at the far end; buds at the tips of the stems are matt black (a good identification point, especially in winter). In spring, clusters of long, narrow green 'keys' can be seen near the tips of the stems. More common in countryside with limestone or chalk.*

Scots pine (Pinus sylvestris): *One of the original native species that colonised the country after the ice age, today most common in Scotland. Tall, straight, upright, reddish-brown trunk whose bark has a platelet-like pattern. Conical green cones, pointed at the tips, develop near the ends of the shoots and turn brown in their second year, but it's not until their third year that they mature, open and release their seeds. The long, slender needles grow in pairs, joined by a brownish scale at the top.*

HOW TO TELL THE AGE OF A TREE

If the tree has been cut down and you can see a cross-section of the trunk, count the growth rings. Trees 'lay down' one growth ring each year, and besides revealing the age, you can tell by the width of each ring how good the growing season has been – the annual growth ring is wider in a year in which there was plenty of rain and temperatures were mild.

You can estimate the approximate age of a large old tree by measuring its girth at 1.5 metres (5 feet) above the ground. This is only reasonably accurate for a deciduous tree with a full crown of branches and which is growing on its own. On average, a tree grows 2.5cm (1 inch) 'fatter' every year. So a tree measuring 3 metres (10 feet) round the trunk will be roughly 120 years old.

To tell the age of coniferous trees, count the whorls of branches from ground level all the way up the trunk; the number is approximately the age of the tree, since a conifer grows a new 'ring' of branches from the top of its trunk each season.

HOW TO TELL THE AGE OF A OF A HEDGEROW

In late Georgian times, landowners planted hedges to enclose their land, creating fields for livestock. A lot of these hedges are still with us; they were originally planted entirely with a single kind of hedging plant, often hawthorn, but since then wild trees have usually managed to selfseed into them, so you'll find the occasional hawthorn, oak, elder, hazel or other tree standing up above the hedge-line, and if the hedge hasn't been managed too tidily there may also be brambles, honeysuckle, wild hops and other scramblers.

Some hedges, however, are far older, and some in existence today still mark the boundaries of medieval fields. These tend to be made up of a very much larger mixture of wild trees, native shrubs and climbers, since they usually 'happened' completely naturally, without any original planting.

As a very rough guide to the age of any old countryside hedge, count the number of species of woody plants – trees, shrubs and climbers – that you can find in a 30 yard stretch of the hedgerow. It's generally assumed that each species equals a century, so a hedge with five different species in a 30 yard run could be five hundred years old. This technique is known as Hooper's Hedge Hypothesis, after the naturalist Dr Max Hooper who invented it.

TRACKING ANIMALS

Large animals are very easy to identify when you can get a good view of them, but since they are usually nervous of humans, the best clue you will often have of their presence is their tracks in mud, soft earth or snow. But tracks can tell you much more than which animal has been there; they show you which direction it was travelling in. The depth of the footprint plus any smudged skid marks also give a clue to how much of a hurry the animal was in – and a set of predator prints running through the first sometimes shows what might have been chasing it. Look out too for smaller prints of the same sort, suggesting a mother animal with young. Besides tracks, look for tufts of fur trapped on barbed wire fences – it's easy to spot the reddish fur of fox or the long, bristly hair of badger – and look out for characteristic droppings. When animals regularly use the same route, you may also see a distinct 'tunnel' through undergrowth where they push through the same place regularly, and at the waterside you can sometimes see 'slides' where ducks slither down a steep muddy bit of bank into the water. With practice you can become quite a good countryside detective.

FOX

A fox leaves paw prints similar to those of dogs and cats, with four toes round a larger 'pad'. Look for claw marks at the end of each 'toe print'– cats don't leave claw marks. Dogs and foxes both do: dogs have rounder and often larger paw prints, those of foxes are narrower. Fox tracks can be found almost anywhere in town or country and also (perhaps rather surprisingly) along the seashore. You may sometimes spot the remains of prey or perhaps just scraps of fur or feathers showing where a fox has had a successful hunt.

RABBITS AND HARES

These leave very distinctive paw prints consisting of a pair of long outer prints with two smaller ovalish prints between them, as the animal moves by hopping from both back feet to the smaller front feet which it 'runs' with, placing one down after the other. It's not easy to tell rabbit from hare prints; rabbits are usually smaller, and the animals occur in groups, while hares are mostly solitary, though in spring two or three will chase each other. But both animals are reasonably easy to see out in daylight. In a large rabbit colony you'll find piles of droppings in a conspicuous spot, used as territory markers, and you'll almost certainly see rabbit holes and tufts of soft grey fur caught on brambles.

DEER

Deer leave cloven hoof prints (i.e. a pair of roughly teardrop-shaped indentations per footprint with a gap up the middle). Deer hoof prints have pointed tips at the front and are slightly wider at the back. You can tell them from cloven-hoofed farm livestock because sheep, pigs and goats all have rounded tips to their prints, and those of cows are very much bigger and deeper. (When prints are left by livestock you can usually see the animals in the fields, or at least their characteristic droppings, though in places where livestock roam freely in the countryside, such as the New Forest, it can be harder to tell straightaway.)

RODENTS

Rodents leave tiny tracks close together in rows; look for a good set of prints and count the toes – rodents always have five toes on the back feet and four on the front feet. Rat tracks look like a staggered row of small starbursts; mouse tracks have occasional narrow lines between the footprints, since a mouse drags its tail along the ground. Squirrel tracks show pronounced claw marks at the ends of the toes.

BADGERS, WEASELS AND STOATS

All the members of this family, which includes mink and otters, have five toes on each foot, so look for some clear prints and count all the toes. Size is a bit of a clue.

BIRDS

Birds have three-pronged footprints, sometimes with a long toe print sticking out of the back as well. It's fascinating to observe the winding tracks of wading birds in soft mud left on seashores as the tide retreats, and you can sometimes see the bird responsible at the far end of a line of footprints, probing for marine worms and crustaceans. But in practice it's almost impossible to tell more than roughly the size of the bird concerned, and see if it has webbed feet (indicating ducks, geese and swans) or not (indicating a wader)

CHAPTER 6

COUNTRYSIDE SKILLS

'Townies' might be dab hands at shopping, but country folk have always known where to find the things they need for basic everyday existence for free, from the land. And even today, when you'd think there's no need, a lot of people are enjoying re-learning country skills and bringing the results to the dinner table.

FORAGING

Foraging for wild food goes right back to our hunter-gatherer roots, and the instinct is still present in modern man. Holidaymakers often indulge in a pleasant afternoon's crabbing from the quay or cockling on the beach, and nowadays wild greenery, hedgerow fruit and edible fungi are becoming of interest to fashionable chefs, TV cookery presenters and food lovers. There's lots to be found for free. You may already have a few wild salads and 'greens' growing as weeds in your own garden, and the seashore and hedgerows alongside country lanes can be very productive.

While there is a lot you could eat if forced to live off the land, the things I've listed are some of the best for eating – besides being easy to identify. But at the risk of sounding like your granny, it pays to pick wild foods with care. Avoid polluted or litter-strewn places, anywhere close to busy main roads due to traffic fumes, or anywhere that weedkillers or other chemicals may have been used, and do ask the landowners' permission before gathering any goodies from private land. Pick with due consideration for the countryside, so don't strip an area bare, and only take perfect material that you'll be able to use without waste, back home. It's also advisable to be very certain of your identification, especially when dealing with potentially tricky customers like fungi. Look out for foraging courses and, particularly, fungus-hunting walks organised by experts.

EDIBLE PLANTS RECOGNITION

SALADS

Hairy bittercress: *Commonly grows as a weed in patio containers, veg and flower gardens. The plants are small and rosette-shaped; the tiny leaves take a long time to pick but have a pleasant, watercress-like tang when used raw in salads.*

Jack-by-the-hedge: *Also known as hedge garlic, it has a light, leafy taste with a faint hint of garlic; the young leaves are good chopped in sauces or raw in salads in spring.*

Dandelion: *A tasty salad leaf full of minerals and vitamins, available from early spring. Pick a few of the youngest leaves from the centre of a rosette, or better still blanch the whole plant under an upturned bucket or large flowerpot for a week first, taking care to evict snails that gather underneath, then pick the young leaves when they are pale green to yellow in colour, which makes them less bitter. If you prefer to grow your own in rows in the veg garden, seeds of a French culinary dandelion are available from specialist seed firms.*

Miner's lettuce (Claytonia perfoliata): *An unusual but easily identifiable plant with circular leaves whose stems are joined to them in their centres, like tiny saucers on sticks, which is very tender and tasty in early spring. Sometimes cultivated as a winter salad; good for growing in tubs or window boxes.*

LEAFY VEG

Fat hen: *A common annual weed that quickly appears in gardens when rich, fertile ground has been turned over and left uncultivated. Pick healthy, intact young leaves, ideally before the plant starts to flower, and cook like spinach. Its perennial close relative, Good King Henry, was a popular vegetable in Elizabethan times, but was superseded by the introduction of spinach.*

Ground elder: *Introduced by the Romans as a culinary crop but now a nuisance weed to gardeners, so if you have an infestation you'll be pleased to know it can be put to good use. Harvest young leaves in summer and cook like spinach.*

Chickweed: *One of the first weeds to infest newly dug ground and is very prolific. The young shoot-tips make a good green vegetable, cooked quickly in melted butter. Don't be tempted to stew great handfuls pulled up when you're weeding; the older stems are tough, stringy and tasteless. Just snip off the best young bits. Sorrel is a wayside weed also cultivated as a fresh, zingy, lemon-flavoured herb and can be cooked like spinach or with lots of butter and made into sorrel sauce to eat with white fish. It also makes a wonderful soup.*

Stinging nettle: *Tips of young leaves picked (with rubber gloves) in spring are perhaps even better than spinach, chopped and cooked in butter. Don't bother with them in summer when they are tough and woody.*

Alexanders: *A relative of cow parsley, found along roadsides and in the bottom of hedgerows in spring, particularly along the south coast of England. It emerges from the ground in early spring and flowers several weeks earlier than cow parsley, with slightly thicker and more robust stems topped by pale* *yellow flowers. It was grown as a vegetable in medieval Britain, having been introduced by the Romans for culinary purposes. Use the small flower buds raw in salads, cook young leaves like spinach, and boil the stems like asparagus and eat them with lots of butter.*

Burdock: *A large, striking plant with a rosette of huge, rhubarb-like leaves; as kids we used to throw the prickly burrs at girls on our way home from school, so the hooks caught in their hair or cardies – happy days! The young leaf stems, cut in early summer and peeled, can be eaten raw rather like cucumber, sliced in salads, or steamed and eaten with butter in the same way as asparagus.*

ROOTS

Horseradish: *Often grows wild on rough waste ground, and is easily recognised by its large, loose rosette of long, slightly crinkly, green dock-like leaves. In the garden – even in wild areas – it can be quite invasive since the clumps spread vigorously so you are doing yourself a favour by digging it up to make horseradish sauce. Dig some roots – you don't have to dig up the whole plant – any time from early September to early December, peel, grate (be warned, it's worse than peeling onions) and mix with double cream, a little mayonnaise and some French mustard. It's far better than anything you can buy in a jar.*

Dandelion roots: *These were once dug up, scrubbed, and roasted lightly in the oven for a longish time till they were hard, then ground in a coffee grinder to make an economical and caffeine-free substitute for coffee. If you want to, do so when the roots are at their plumpest, in autumn (see page 108).*

NUTS

Beechnuts: *Commonly known as beech mast, these are small, three-sided nuts inside a husk with an outer covering rather like coconut fibre door-matting, in miniature. They ripen and fall in September and October and, though small, are quite tasty when peeled and eaten straight from your hand during a country walk, or taken home, warmed lightly in butter or olive oil and sprinkled sparingly with salt. Gather beech nuts up from the ground as soon as possible, before squirrels or other rodents find them. However, the trees produce empty husks for three out of four years, so the crop is unreliable.*

Sweet chestnuts: *Traditionally roasted in their shells over an open fire in winter, these are also favourite ingredients to use in stuffing for Christmas turkey. The plump nuts we buy in the shops mostly come from specially cultivated plantations in California and southern Europe, but you can sometimes gather home-grown chestnuts on a country walk around the end of October. (They are smaller than 'bought' chestnuts and some years the crop is very disappointing.) Pick up whole nuts, still inside their prickly casings, off the ground; the usual way to remove the nuts from the protective exterior is by stamping on them with a heavy boot. Roast them over the hot embers of a fire, or use a proper chestnut roaster which looks like a very long-handled, lidded skillet with holes in the lid – sit this over the fire until the first nuts explode, then the rest will be ready. They are easiest to shell while still hot.*

Hazelnuts: *Often grown on cultivated hazelnut bushes and filberts (a closely related variety), which are carefully pruned and cared for in nut orchards. Hedgerows containing hazel trees rarely yield much of a crop, but it's worth searching for green nuts towards the end of September to crack and eat fresh. Nut shells lying on the ground are invariably empty.*

FUNGI

Make absolutely certain you know what you are identifying here before you pick them, since many poisonous mushrooms and toadstools look similar to those that are edible. Correctly identified, you will find that wild fungi are delicious.

Chanterelle: *A very superior wild mushroom, popular with wild mushroom enthusiasts, found in late summer and autumn in colonies, mostly in beech woods. It is bright yellow and shaped rather like a funnel 2.5cm (1in) or so high and almost as wide, with long gills running up the stalk and branching up the outsides of the funnel. To check its identity, sniff for a faint scent of apricots. Good in omelettes or scrambled egg.*

Parasol mushroom: *This has a large, distinctive, wide-open, buff-coloured, umbrella-like caps up to 15cm (6in) across, with scaly surface and a faint boss in the centre; white gills underneath. Find it growing in grassland and roadside verges from late summer to late autumn. Individual mushrooms grow far apart in loose colonies. Pick younger specimens and avoid older ones whose gills or cap are turning brown. Superb flavour, best fried with bacon or added to casseroles.*

Shaggy inkcap: *Also known as lawyers wig because the young mushroom has a tall, narrow cap up to 15cm (6in) high with thin slivers of skin curling back all the way up it, like a judge's wig. It is best picked at this stage – don't wait till the cap starts to open out and the gills underneath go black and inky. Good lightly fried or used in mushroom sauces or soup. Don't drink alcohol with inkcaps, as the combination reacts with some people and makes their faces turn red.*

Field mushroom: *Looks just like the cultivated mushroom bought in greengrocers' shops, with a white cap that starts as a 'button' with pink or white gills inside and slowly opens out to a flattish cap with buff-coloured gills underneath. Mostly found on fields where horses are grazed, but sometimes on lawns – or even on vegetable gardens where spent mushroom compost has been used as a soil improver.*

Giant puffball: *An enormous, white, football-like fungus that can be found growing in fields, hedgerows or woods. Whilst not considered the absolute best for flavour by mushroom fanciers, it's very acceptable sliced and fried in bacon fat like a mushroom steak. Regrettably rather rare now. Only pick a young specimen that's still firm and pure white; leave an older, softer or darker one to 'puff' and send its spores out to make more giant puffballs.*

FRUIT

Wild strawberries: *Tiny fruits which often lack flavour, but are fun to munch on during a walk in the woods if you spot some in early summer. Cultivated wild strawberries, grown from seed, produce larger, tastier crops if grown in the garden.*

Blackberries: *These ripen in country hedgerows from mid-August and may continue until the first hard frost, though fruit produced late in the season isn't of very good quality. Locals usually know the best blackberry patches and go out walking prepared with bags or baskets, plus crooked sticks for pulling down high branches to get at the best fruit, which usually grows out of reach.*

Rosehips: *The ripe, flask-shaped fruits of dog-rose, were heavily picked during the last war, when country families gathered them to make rosehip syrup, which was taken, a spoonful each day, as a rich source of vitamin C since oranges weren't available. Make your own today to pour over ice cream; it's also very good drizzled on to a baked apple or rice pudding instead of honey or jam.*

HOW TO MAKE ROSEHIP SYRUP

Put 450 grams (1 pound) of clean whole rosehips through a mincer to break them into small bits, but don't liquidise them. Add the minced fruit to half a litre (1 pint) of boiling water and simmer very gently for a quarter of an hour, then strain through several thicknesses of clean cotton material – it's essential to get out all the seeds and the tiny hairs that are attached to them, which are highly irritant. (They were once used by small boys as itching powder!) Strain twice to be on the safe side, using a fresh piece of cloth for the second straining. When you have obtained all the juice (don't squeeze the fabric to try and get more out of the residue), measure the quantity and to each 300ml (½ pint) of juice, add 140 grams (5 ounces) of sugar and boil for five minutes, stirring until the sugar dissolves. The thick liquid can be kept in the fridge for up to a week in a screw-top jar.

SEASIDE HARVEST

It's not just on dry land that you can find food for free; some seashore plants are surprisingly good, and are traditionally gathered for use in island communities. But the seaside has more to offer to keen wild-harvesters.

SEA VEG

Gather sea veg from saltmarshes, rocks etc., where the water is clear and clean, and where there's a good tidal range to keep crops 'washed'. Keep well away from sewage outlets and avoid areas where there is litter and rubbish strewn along the shoreline, as there may be pollution or dangerous waste such as broken glass or worse hidden among the plants. And avoid overpicking, so that colonies can recover quickly and you don't destroy the looks of coastal beauty spots. Anticipate sea veg being quite sandy or gritty, so wash them very well in several changes of water before using them.

SEA VEG RECOGNITION

Sea beet: *These are 60–90cm (2–3ft) mounds of thick shiny leaves, growing on saltmarshes. Pick young, healthy-looking, intact triangular leaves that are roughly the same size as baby spinach leaves from the tops of the plants any time from late spring to the end of summer. Cook like spinach – steam or stir fry, and eat with plenty of butter.*

Samphire: *This bears strange thin, green, segmented cylindrical shoots, faintly asparagus-like but without the tips, sold by posh fishmongers in early summer, and in smart restaurants as an accompaniment to pricy fish dishes. But if you can find a site where it grows, in saltmarshes and mudflats on estuaries and parts of the coastline, you can pick your own. Traditionally its peak season is for the few weeks either side of the longest day, though you can cut it from late spring onwards. Pick the shoots when they are about 7.5cm (3in) long. Wash the shoots thoroughly and use short young stems raw in salads, or you can steam, boil in water or cook them in butter for a few minutes; don't add any seasoning, since their flavour is naturally salty.*

Laver: *This grows round rocky and stony shores all round the west coast of Britain and is traditionally used in Wales to make laver bread (which is basically a purée of the well-boiled seaweed mixed with oatmeal and fried for breakfast, eaten with bacon). The fronds are purplish-coloured, slender, and unevenly shaped; they need washing very well a s they trap lots of sand and tend to be gritty.*

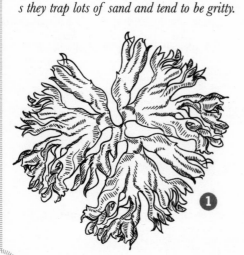

Dulse: *A robust seaweed that clings to stones quite well, down on the shore; the tough stems are chewed raw in the Hebrides in much the same way that we'd use chewing gum, or stewed for hours until tender.*

Carragheen (Irish moss): *An edible seaweed traditionally used for thickening jellies, blancmange and ice cream. The purplish-brown fronds can be found on rocky Atlantic shores of Britain; it's best collected in April and May, then washed well and either dried to use out of season or used fresh straight away. Simmer fresh carragheen slowly in three times its volume of water or milk until the seaweed dissolves completely, then add flavouring and use as usual to make fruit jelly or blancmange.*

Kelp: *A strong-growing, broad, thick, ribbon-like seaweed growing at and below the low water mark, also sometimes in quite dense beds in deeper water offshore. It can be sliced raw in salads, but is often dried and cut up to use later (on its own or with other dried seaweeds) as a sea vegetable; small crumbled pieces are good sprinkled into salads or cooked rice, to be eaten with shellfish or other seafood.*

Sea lettuce: *A delicate, soft, pale green seaweed which, in the sea, looks almost like floating green tissue-paper; it's found on most shores sticking to stones or rocks. This is the seaweed sold in health food shops and oriental stores as nori, the thin, dry, green sheets used for wrapping round a mixture of raw fish and sticky rice to make sushi. It's also good dried and crumbled to sprinkle over rice or into salads, or mixed with other dried seaweed as mixed sea vegetables.*

SHELLFISH

Shellfish are often considered to be out of season in high summer, but they don't become poisonous as people often believe. The myth probably began in the days before proper refrigeration was available, when seafood quickly went 'off' in warm weather, and eating dodgy mussels or winkles would have been the cause of many a gippy tummy.

But there's a good practical reason for not collecting shellfish during the summer holidays: it is the season when shellfish spawn, so they are best left alone to produce the next generation and maintain stocks. And from a gourmet's point of view, it's fair to say that shellfish are not such high quality as usual in the breeding season because they lose weight when they are busy producing eggs, so the shells aren't so well filled.

If you're going to collect your own shellfish, avoid parts of the coast close to sewage outfall pipes (often marked on large-scale local maps, or ask in fishing tackle shops as the people in there will know), and clean the shells well before cooking. Remove the 'beard' from mussels and reject any shellfish with broken shells. Leave those that are selected for eating sitting in a bucket of clean water for 12 hours or overnight before cooking so they can flush themselves through and get rid of a lot of grit and 'bits'. Change the water several times if lots of muck comes out, or if the water looks dirty.

When dealing with bivalves (mussels, cockles, oysters), reject any which don't close themselves after they've been in their bucket of water for a while, also any which stay tightly shut and don't put up a fight when you squeeze the shell between forefinger and thumb and try to slide the two halves slightly past each other, since they'll be dead and already starting to build up bacteria inside. After cooking, reject any that haven't opened as they can't be trusted either.

SHELLFISH RECOGNITION

Winkles: *Smallish, dark grey and very pointed 'snail shells' found on rocks and seaweedy sections of breakwater that are covered by water at high tide. To cook the cleaned winkles, plunge them into a large pan of boiling water and simmer for ten minutes. The shells don't contain very much meat, but half the fun of winkles is 'winkling' them out of their shells with a pin after removing the thin film that seals the hole at the entrance to the shell. The content is all edible.*

Cockles: *Familiar bivalves about 2.5cm (1in) across with pairs of pale, ribbed shells joined by a hinge at the back. They are found about halfway between the high and low water mark on wide sandy or muddy-sand shores and silty-looking saltmarshes round most of the UK. They tend to congregate in particularly favourable areas known as cockle beds, where it's easy to collect a good crop. Find them several inches under the surface; cocklers feel around for them with their feet or fingers, or use a strong garden rake. Leave small specimens behind to grow and take only the full-sized ones. After cleaning and sorting, plunge cockles into boiling water and remove as soon as they open fully, which only takes a few minutes.*

Mussels: *Very common all round the coast, but be very careful only to collect them from places with clean, unpolluted water and avoid collecting mussels in summer, especially when there's an algal 'bloom' in the water (local fishermen and tackle shops will know all about these), and be sure to give them several changes of water while they are undergoing the cleaning process. Collect them from rocks well down on the shoreline at low tide; they live in decent colonies so it's easy to gather enough for a meal. To cook, plunge them*

*into boiling water and boil for ten minutes, or follow your favourite moules
marinière recipe.*

Razor shells: *Scarcer shellfish, with long, narrow shells having square-ish
corners, found several inches under the surface of very clean sandy beaches,
along the low tide line. (Look up a tide table and hunt for them during the very
lowest tides of the year, and take care you leave enough time to get back up the
beach before you're cut off.) You may be able to tell a good razor shell site by
plentiful empty shells higher up the beach; locals usually keep quiet about good
sites. As you walk the sands, look out for a hole or slight disturbance, then dig
fast to grab the creature, which can move surprisingly fast. After cleaning the
shells well, drop them into boiling water for five to ten minutes, then extract the
meat and reheat in some oil in which you've fried finely chopped shallots and a
little fresh stem ginger.*

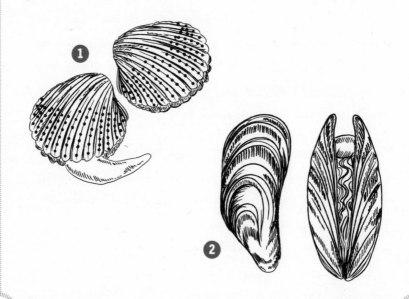

SHRIMPING

Shoals of tiny common or brown shrimps can often be found in the warm shallow water of bays and sandy beaches, and small numbers can also often be seen in rock pools at low tide. In their live state they are light grey or pale buff, but being almost transparent they are quite difficult to see. They rarely swim around by day, and instead usually walk along the bottom of the sea, so you need to watch for signs of movement and then you may spot them.

To catch shrimps you need an old-fashioned shrimping net, which has a catch net (the bigger the better) with a flat edge along the bottom and a curved top which is attached to a long handle. The way to use it most effectively is to wade out into the sea and push the net along in front of you so that the flat edge 'trawls' along the seabed, disturbing the sand as it goes and sending any shrimps up and into the net. Every few yards you should stop and see what you've caught. If you've been lucky, tip your shrimps into a bucket of seawater to keep them alive until you've caught enough, and use it to carry them home in.

Boil them straight away – there's no need to leave them in clean water first – a few minutes is all it takes. When they're cooked, pinch the heads and tails off with your fingernails; don't bother trying to peel them – unlike the larger prawns you simply eat shrimps shell-and-all. They are good eaten as they are with bread and butter, but if you want to make them into something more 'special' make potted shrimps. To do this, head-and-tail your cooked shrimps, mix them with melted butter flavoured with a pinch or two of mace, then decant them into pots and leave in the fridge over-night to solidify. Eat them with wafer-thin triangles of toast.

Prawns – the larger relative of shrimps – may sometimes be found on sandy southern and western shores and in rockpools round the British coastline. Catch them in the same way as shrimps and cook them the same way, but for slightly longer; they only turn the familiar pink when they're cooked. A pint of prawns makes a good 'finger' lunch, with brown crusty bread and a glass of white wine.

CRABBING

The brown crab is the familiar species in fishmongers' shops, with a wide, smooth, flat, pinkish-brown carapace and large, black-tipped claws. It lives mostly on rocky coasts, and is caught commercially using crab pots baited with fish-heads or bits of mackerel, lowered by line from small fishing boats, tethered to buoys, and hauled in daily to collect the catch. But crabs can also be found under jetties or small quaysides that accommodate only small hobby boats and light local traffic.

In some areas there's quite a strong custom for holidaymakers – and particularly their children – to go crabbing from these sorts of places, and occasionally you may find a crabbing competition – they are regular events in some Norfolk fishing villages. The crabs are caught using a piece of fish (usually heads or other uneatable bits) as bait, tied to a fishing line – hooks aren't required, and in any case aren't allowed in competitions. The crabber sits up on the quay, lowers the baited end of the line into the water and waits till they feel a 'bite', then the line is carefully hauled back in, hopefully with the crab still hanging on to the bait. Though a lot of the crabs caught in this way are too small to eat and they should be thrown back, you can sometimes catch one that's a good size.

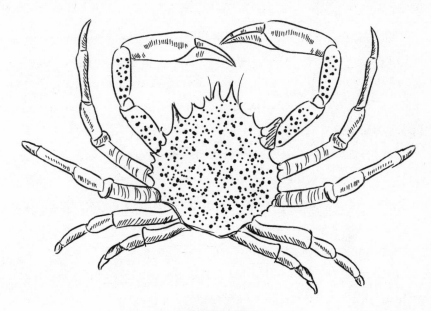

SPIDER CRABS

Well known to continental crab-lovers, spider crabs are now fairly commonly found off the south coast of England. They are easily identified: they have smallish, rather rounded bodies that are very spiny, with long, thin, spiny legs and narrow claws. They are good eating, but there's a lot less flesh in them than the traditional brown crab, and most of it is inside the body, there's hardly anything inside the claws. Still, the contents will make a hugely enjoyable sandwich, even if crab is considered to be the poor man's lobster!

SEA-FISHING

You can fish from the beach or from small boats off the coast without a fishing license (which you'd need for freshwater fishing, or for commercial sea fishing). Fishing from the beach is convenient since you can just wander down and get started straight away. You'll need a long (2.5–2.7m/8–9ft) fishing rod; the sort known as a spinning rod is fine, and a good, basic, beginners one along with line and reel, hooks and all the other bits and pieces that you need can be bought (often as a complete package deal for under £50) from any fishing tackle shop near the seaside – the staff will be happy to advise.

You'll need to buy live bait from the tackle shop (it doesn't keep long so buy it the day you want to use it) or dig your own lugworms or ragworms from the beach before making a start. (Look for small, slightly bubbling holes, and use a garden spade or fork to dig down quickly and catch the worm before it escapes.)

Local sea-fisherman and local tackle shops will know the best places to go beach-fishing, but the area either side of a breakwater is usually quite good. The best times are a couple of hours either side of low tide, and night-time is especially fruitful. The fish you are likely to catch will vary at different times of the year. The best way to find out what is likely to be around on your particular stretch of coast all year is to buy a set of tide tables that come complete with a fisherman's calendar and other information from a local tackle shop. Most beach fishermen fish from about April to October; there's not much around in winter, when the fish stay further offshore.

You'll catch a wider range of species and in larger quantities from a boat. In seaside areas you'll sometimes find adverts for fishing trips on boats at so-much per head, with fishing tackle and bait provided in the price, and these are a good way to have a go since the skipper will know all the best places to find decent catches. (If it's your first time, be forewarned – a boat anchored in 'good' fishing places experiences a lot of sideways rolling motion which can cause queasy stomachs.) If you own a small boat, you can take yourself out fishing. The sort of small boat you might keep for 'messing about in' on the sea is fine for waters inshore, but be wary of venturing too far, especially in fast ebb currents. The best places to fish are usually round wrecks or over seaweed beds. Keen sea fishermen will some-times invest in a proper little sea-fishing boat with a large area of clear deck, lockers for storing kit and a small cabin to shelter the helmsman. You can use a spinning rod (the same one you use for fishing from the beach) from a boat, or buy a special rod for the job, or simply use a fishing line with several hooks and a weight at the end.

MINIMUM SIZES

Although you can take away sea fish that you catch using a line, in order to conserve fish stocks there are minimum sizes laid down for each species by law – anything smaller has to be thrown back. (The limit is not always the same for fish caught from boats as from the shore.) Local fishing-supply shops can advise; a combined tide table and fisherman's guide usually gives this information. The Angling Trust is also a useful source of advice.

SEA FISH RECOGNITION

Sea bass: *A slim, silvery grey fish, one of the most popular for eating, and also often caught by people fishing from the shore round the south of England in summer. Easily recognised by its two dorsal fins, the one nearest the head is spiny and half circular in shape when extended, the one nearer the tail is a softer, almost elongated triangular fin. Look also for a dark patch over each gill cover.*

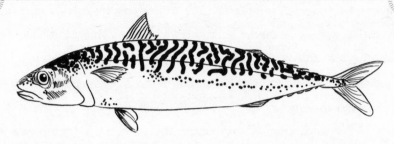

Mackerel: *Familiar long, lean fish with blue-green and black striped backs and silvery undersides, often caught from boats offshore during the summer. Fresh-caught fish don't keep long, so cook and eat them or freeze them straight away.*

Herring: *Long, narrow, grey-green fish with silvery scales; small herrings, which are more often found in coastal waters than adults, are also known as sprats (when very small) or (a few sizes larger) sardines or – especially in Cornwall – pilchards.*

Grey mullet: *Steely silver-grey fish with large scales and thick lips, common in estuaries, natural harbours and also marinas. They are rarely seen in fishmongers' shops but are a great favourite with sea fishermen, though reputed by some to have rather a muddy flavour due to their feeding habits.*

Pollack: *A slender fish with large eyes and a lower jaw that projects further than the upper one; found close inshore during the summer and often caught by sport fishermen. This is one of the fish we are being encouraged to eat instead of traditional favourites like cod and haddock as it's a more sustainable resource.*

Dab: *A common flatfish of coastal waters, with a light brown skin faintly patterned with indistinct darker brown blotches. Rarely seen in* *fishmongers', but good eating, and often caught by beginners on organised fishing boat excursions.*

Plaice: *A popular flat fish whose upper surface is brown dotted with bright orange spots.*

Cod: *The familiar large, mottled, light brown-to-greyish fish with three dorsal fins and a pronounced 'barb' projecting down from the lower jaw, can be caught from many British beaches in the autumn; larger fish are caught by boat further out.*

FRESHWATER FISHING

There's a huge difference between sea fishing and freshwater fishing. Freshwater fishing, or angling, is done for sport, and the fish have to be put back – the challenge is to use your skills to catch and land them. You need an annual fishing licence, which you can buy online or from a post office, and you can fish at streams, canals and rivers (depending on local bylaws), or at specially stocked and managed lakes or fisheries which are either privately owned or run by a club, where you'll need to buy a day ticket or become a member.

There's a lot of skill involved in knowing the right sort of rod, equipment and bait to get good results or to target particular species of fish, as well as the best part of the bank to stand on. Anglers will take a boxful of kit with them, including ground bait such as sweetcorn or special flavoured pellets, plus a folding seat, sandwiches and thermos of tea to set in for a long session, but it's very relaxing – enthusiasts often admit it's a great excuse for sitting around in the countryside.

Fisheries and angling societies sometimes organise special days for beginners, which is a good way to start if you don't have a 'fishing friend' to show you the ropes. You can go out for a few hours or a day on your own, and serious enthusiasts sometimes take part in matches, where the biggest weight of fish caught by the end of the day and stored in a keep net in the water, wins. (You'll sometimes see anglers taking part in a competition ranged out along the banks if you are out for a waterside walk; their concentration is immense.) Keen anglers often aim to catch the biggest-possible fish and keep note of their personal best for each species; they will often invest in special equipment for targeting particular types of fish – carp are a big current favourite. Keen anglers may even stay out overnight in all weathers, even in winter, sleeping in a bivvy tent and a down suit (which is like a fitted sleeping bag), using a 'bite alarm' to alert them that they've caught a fish.

Fly fishing (as opposed to 'coarse fishing', which uses a float and weighted line) takes place on stretches of carefully managed salmon rivers or trout streams while standing in the water wearing thigh-length waders. Instead of the usual sort of bait, fly fishermen use an artificial fly, and many different types are available to duplicate *real* flies that fish are taking from the water surface at different times of year and in different conditions. Part of the skill of fly fishing lies in knowing which particular sort of fly to use and when. (Many serious fly fishermen like to tie their own flies, which is an art in itself.) There's a great art to casting – sending the line out over the water to the right place to find a fish, and make the fly mimic the movements of a real live fly. The trick is all in the arm movement; it's a bit like cracking a whip in slow motion. This is an art where you really do need a few lessons; you'll then need to buy 'days' or take out a membership, or rent the fishing rights to a short stretch of water. It doesn't come cheap, and while you can take a limited number of fish, you have to put anything above your allotted quota back in the water.

MAKE YOUR OWN FISHING ROD

As small boys we made our fishing rods from a long, straight, slightly flexible pole (hazel is ideal, though many lads used bamboo canes), and some button thread pinched from Mum's sewing box (it's thicker and stronger than cotton thread), which was tied to the thin end of the pole. We'd use a bent pin tied to the cotton as a hook, and as bait we'd dig up a fat red worm from the compost heap. To be honest, I don't remember ever catching anything, but it was fun hoping! This is almost exactly the way early fishermen caught fish in the days before rods as we know them today. Early fishermen even braided horsehair to make fishing line. If you want to do-it-yourself now, use proper nylon fishing line and a barbed hook from a tackle shop, though a pole 'handle' and a worm bait will still do the job.

MAKING FISHING NETS

Traditionally fishing nets were made by fishermen themselves using hemp twine, during the winter when bad weather meant they couldn't take their boats out fishing. They'd also mend their own nets when they got torn or damaged, and very picturesque the process looked on the quayside.

Today nets are made from synthetic twine and bought factory-made, but fishermen still repair their own. To make or mend nets you need a flat piece of wood cut to the same width as you want the finished mesh to be, to act as a guide, and a netting needle – which looks like a shuttle with a bite out of one end – which the twine is wound on to. The twine is knotted together to make diamond mesh. (Square mesh is also used, but more difficult to make; both benefit from a practical demonstration, so try to watch a fisherman at work on the quay.)

To make the top line of the net, stretch a piece of lightweight rope taut between two uprights. Now, using the netting needle, tie the twine to the left-hand end of the rope with a clove hitch. Place your wooden spacer guide below this knot, loop the twine round the front, under and back up to the horizontal rope, using the spacer to show the correct width, then tie another clove hitch. Work from left to right along the rope until you have a row of half-meshes hanging evenly along the rope. To make the second row, go to the other side of the rope and work from there. Pass the needle and twine round the end of the last loop (now the first one of the next row), then pass it through the back of the loop above and tie a sheet bend. Work along the row, from left to right, tying a sheet bend in each loop. At the end of the row, go to the other side and continue until you've made your net.

Yes, you'll probably want to buy one now, but it's worth pointing out that these days you aren't allowed to use nets for fishing – even at sea – without a commercial fishing licence.

BOATBUILDING

At one time there were boatyards all round the coast making different types of wooden boat to cater for particular jobs and various types of coastline. You can sometimes still see Thames barges and Norfolk wherries – both large, rather flat-bottomed boats with huge areas of sail, which were once used for local deliveries of goods such as coal, before the days of rail. Nobbys were fast sailing boats used for trawling fishing nets, especially for prawns, and then getting the catch back to harbour quickly so that it stayed fresh before the days of refrigeration made it possible to keep a catch on ice.

There are two basic types of construction used for wooden boats. Clinker-built boats look as if they are made from lots of narrow planks that overlap slightly along the edges. It's a technique that's thought to have been used first by the Vikings. It was mostly used for fairly small boats, such as rowing boats, sailing dinghies and tenders to larger boats. Carvel construction uses planks that are fitted together flush; such boats are stronger, but more time-consuming and difficult to make since each plank has to be carefully chosen so that it makes a perfect fit against its neighbour. The technique is mostly used for larger boats.

TRADITIONAL BOATBUILDING

Traditional boatbuilding is a rare craft these days since wooden boats take much time and considerable skill to construct, and they also need regular and expensive maintenance afterwards. A few old traditional sailing boats have been restored by enthusiasts or converted for leisure use, but nowadays new boats are mostly made of glass fibre or steel.

For inland use, it was traditional to use coracles in some parts of the country, especially in Wales. A coracle was originally made by stretching an animal hide over a semi-circular basketwork framework made from flexible willow stems, with a woven willow floor something like a hurdle, and a plank fitted across the centre to sit on. The boat was propelled using a single paddle – there's quite an art in making a round boat go forwards instead of spinning round and round. The coracle was deliberately made lightweight so that the occupant could pick it up and carry it when need be; the plank seat had a carrying handle attached, so the craft could be slung over the boatman's back.

Today coracles are still made in much the same way, but using tarred or bituminised canvas or similar materials, and even if they aren't used in earnest, a lot of coracles are bought by people who appreciate the craftsmanship involved, parking them alongside their garden pond for decoration. I had one myself, though ten years on, it has now disintegrated! It's still possible to go on a course to learn how to build a traditional coracle, at the Green Wood Centre near Ironbridge in Shropshire.

OUTDOOR SURVIVAL SKILLS

When you're out in the countryside, on foot, bike, horse or in the car, and even on camping holidays, it's useful to know a few basic skills – and it's far more vital if you're making long-distance trips.

MAP-READING

Put aside the GPS for once: a good current road atlas is ideal for car trips where you're keeping to A or B roads and covering long distances. But when you're walking, horse-riding or cycling, using little back lanes and public rights of way, then a much larger-scale map covering a smaller area is far more useful. (It's also easier to carry as it can be folded open at the right part and put in a rainproof plastic map carrier, for quick reference in any weather.) The standard Ordnance Survey (OS) Landranger Series 1:50,000 scale (2cm to a kilometre/1¼ inches to the mile) is useful when you're touring by car, but large-scale maps made especially for walkers – the OS Explorer Maps 1:25,000 scale (4cm to the kilometre, 2½ inches to the mile) show all sorts of landscape features that help you to keep tabs on exactly where you are, even when you go off-road. It's far easier to follow your progress along public footpaths and other rights of way when every landmark and turn in the track is shown in detail. Even if you don't go in for serious hiking, it's worth having one or two maps of this sort that cover the immediate area round your house or somewhere you're staying on holiday, as they show up a wealth of landscape features and places of interest that may be fun to investigate.

To really make full use of any map, it's worth spending time learning the symbols shown on the legend – the 'key', which you'll find running up one side of the map. From this you can see at a glance which part of the terrain is covered by coniferous woods, mixed woodland or parkland, and you can tell the steepness of gradients in the land by how closely spaced the contour lines are. You can see the location of electricity pylons, church steeples and radio or TV masts, identify ancient burial mounds (tumuli), find public houses, a post office, camp or caravan sites, parking places, public loos or tourist information centres – any of which may be handy on a day out in the countryside.

When you know the scale of the map, you can also tell very easily how far it is between two points, just by measuring the distance on the map. As a rough and ready guide, if your thumb measures 6cm (2½in) long, you can quickly hold it against the Explorer map to measure distance – each thumbs-length being a mile (1.6km), so you can tell in advance how long a walk will be, or how much further you have to go when you'realready out.

When you need to identify a precise place on the land, this is easily done by giving a map reference, also known as a grid reference. (Local branches of the Ramblers, for instance, supply a map reference for car parks where members are to meet to go for a walk, but it's also handy if you want to pass on details of a location to friends.) A map reference is made up of two letters and two sets of three numbers, e.g. TQ 235 678. The two letters are to enable you to quickly find the square in which the point lies – you'll find the letters printed in the corners of large squares on the OS map. The first three numbers are the eastings – the horizontal lines running across the map; the first two numbers of the group of three are printed in the margin up each side of the map. The second group of three numbers are the northings, the vertical lines running up and down the map; the first two numbers of the group of three refer to the numbers printed along the top and bottom margins of the map. Find the right horizontal line and the right vertical line, then follow them to the point where they cross, and you'll be very close to the spot you are looking for. The third figure in each group of three helps you home in on the exact spot, if you haven't already found it, as it indicates tenths of the distance between grid lines. (SO 235 will be found halfway between the 23 and the 24 lines.) It's worth thoroughly familiarising yourself with maps and how to use them properly if you intend doing any serious outdoor activity such as fell-walking, where getting lost can cause real problems.

READING A COMPASS

If you're going walking, learn how to use a compass. Besides making sure you are heading in the right direction, a compass can help to pinpoint where you are since you can tell the direction of conspicuous landmarks.

To use a compass, hold it steady, well away from any ferrous metal (e.g. iron) or anything else that's magnetic, and place it on top of a wooden fence post or similar flat surface, making sure it is as level as possible. The needle will point to magnetic north. Rotate the compass slowly until the north marked on the face lines up exactly with the needle. It's then easy to see which direction a feature such as a railway line road or path runs (perhaps east–west) which is helpful for pinpointing it on a map. You can also take a bearing on a distant landmark such as a tower, which tells you the direction it is from where you are now. If you can find a second very visible landmark, well away from the first, and take a bearing on that, you can pinpoint your position on the map fairly accurately by plotting the point where the two bearings cross. Some superior compasses have a sight that you can rotate over the face to enable you to take more accurate bearings. But for most general walking, all you really need is a small, light-weight compass that you can carry in your pocket.

MAKING A CAMP FIRE

A camp fire is really just a wild barbecue you make from scratch; its main use is for cooking food or heating water to make tea, but it's handy for keeping you warm for drying wet clothes or even signalling for help in emergencies.

The main concern, any time you think about lighting a fire in the countryside, is to ensure it can't spread, so first clear the site of anything inflammable – dead leaves, dry grass etc. It often helps to make a circle of large stones or to excavate a shallow, saucer-shaped depression, since the raised sides give the flames a bit of shelter. This makes the fire easier to light as well as keeping it contained. Have a pile of loose sand or soil nearby that you can use for dousing stray flames if needed.

While one person prepares the site for the fire, send someone else off to collect suitable materials to burn. You'll need a fair stack of dry wood; look for dead branches on the ground under trees – don't break off living branches because besides damaging the trees, living wood won't burn well as it's full of sap. Have firewood in a mixture of thicknesses; thinner branches are good to get the fire going, but you need thicker bits once it's going well, as they'll burn longer. You'll also need a selection of small, very dry material to light the fire with. Dry fir cones, dry pine needles, dry twigs, dead gorse and dry leaves are good, bone-dry lichen or even moss can be good if they are the loose, fluffy sort. If you are using paper to start the fire, fold it lengthwise several times and then roll it onto a coil; this burns longer and slower than a flat piece of paper.

Make a small 'nest' of kindling, light the paper spill with a lighter or matches, and touch it to the dry material. As the fire 'catches', lay twigs into the centre of the blaze, making a pattern like the spokes of a wheel, and slowly add larger branches as the centre becomes hot. When the fire is going well, push a long, stout stick into the ground to one side of the fire, clear of the flames, positioning it at an angle so that the top of the stick is above the flames. Cut a notch near the top of the stick and hang your billy can from it. Alternatively, wait for the fire to die down to embers and balance a flat mess-tin on hot stones round the edge of the fire.

MAKING FIRE WITHOUT MATCHES

Various techniques are used by survival experts, but they are trickier than they look and can take time to perfect – you need a bit of practice at home first, when you aren't freezing cold, wet and hungry or desperate for a hot drink. The best method is to carry a small tin containing a flint and a metal bar for creating a spark, and some dry tinder (which can be wood shavings, hay-like dry grass stems or similar) to ignite. Strike the flint and metal together to make a spark an inch or two above a small, fist-sized 'nest' of your highly inflammable bone-dry tinder; when the tinder starts to smoulder, pick it up and hold it in your cupped hands whilst blowing across it very gently. When a small flame erupts, put it down on the ground in your prepared fireplace and start adding small twigs.

USEFUL RULES OF THUMB

If you stand with your back to the wind, the area of low pressure will be on your left – if clouds are moving towards you from the left, expect the weather to worsen. If the clouds are coming from your right, the weather can be expected to improve. If the clouds are passing straight towards or away from you then expect the weather to stay much the same for a while.

HOW TO STAY SAFE IN A THUNDERSTORM

People are very rarely struck by lightning but it does happen occasionally, and being outside in a storm can be quite frightening, especially if you are stranded in the open with no shelter.

Keep well clear of tall, and especially metal objects, since they are the likeliest places for lightning to strike. Golf courses are surprisingly danger-ous since they are wide open, and golfers carrying bags of metal clubs are likely to prove the tallest conductors in the area. Tall trees may also sometimes be struck, so don't shelter underneath – you are better behind a hedge, on the side that's sheltered from the wind, or down a natural depres-sion in the land. If there's no better alternative, lay flat on the ground so you're as level as possible with your surroundings.

Rubber boots or rubber-soled walking boots or shoes provide some insulation, but perhaps the safest place to be in a thunderstorm is in a car, since the tyres stop the charge reaching earth. Church steeples are usually protected by lightning conductors which prevents them coming to harm, and you should be safe inside any kind of building or field shelter.

Head for the pub is my advice.